HUMAN FACTORS IN REMOTE SHIP OPERATIONS

Human Factors in Remote Ship Operations examines the psychological, ergonomic and cognitive challenges faced by remote ship operators as maritime navigation shifts from traditional crew experience to technology-driven remote monitoring and control.

Readers will learn strategies to enhance human performance in remote maritime environments through case studies, best practices and design guidelines. The book delivers valuable insights into designing effective remote operations centres, enhancing situational awareness, addressing sensory input challenges and implementing appropriate training methodologies – all essential for ensuring safety and operational excellence in autonomous shipping.

This comprehensive guide is written for maritime professionals, instructors, researchers and policymakers involved in the technological evolution of the maritime industry. It serves as a resource for maritime education and training institutions developing programmes for remote-control operators, as well as for professionals seeking to understand the human factors critical to the successful implementation of maritime autonomous surface ships (MASS).

Tae Eun Kim is a professor of maritime safety management at UiT The Arctic University of Norway.

Are Kristoffer Sydnes is a professor of societal security and the study programme leader for the master's in societal safety at UiT The Arctic University of Norway.

Bjørn-Morten Batalden is the head of the Department of Technology and Safety and an associate professor in nautical science at UiT The Arctic University of Norway.

Lokukaluge Prasad Perera is professor of maritime technology at UiT The Arctic University of Norway.

HUMAN FACTORS IN REMOTE SHIP OPERATIONS

Edited by Tae Eun Kim, Are Kristoffer Sydnes, Bjørn-Morten Batalden and Lokukaluge Prasad Perera

Routledge
Taylor & Francis Group
LONDON AND NEW YORK

Designed cover image: ©Getty Images Credit: Suphanat Khumsap

First published 2026
by Routledge
4 Park Square, Milton Park, Abingdon, Oxon OX14 4RN

and by Routledge
605 Third Avenue, New York, NY 10158

Routledge is an imprint of the Taylor & Francis Group, an informa business

British Library Cataloguing-in-Publication Data
A catalogue record for this book is available from the British Library

ISBN: 978-1-032-95861-3 (hbk)
ISBN: 978-1-032-95860-6 (pbk)
ISBN: 978-1-003-58688-3 (ebk)

DOI: 10.4324/9781003586883

Typeset in Sabon
by Apex CoVantage, LLC

CONTENTS

CONTRIBUTORS

Arbresh Ujkani, Fraunhofer Center for Maritime Logistics and Services (CML), Hamburg, Germany

Are Kristoffer Sydnes, University of Tromsø (UiT) – The Arctic University of Norway, Tromsø, Norway

Bijan Johansen, The Oslo School of Architecture and Design, Oslo, Norway

Borgar Kløve Sandnes, The Oslo School of Architecture and Design, Oslo, Norway

Chia-Hsun Chang, Liverpool John Moores University, Liverpool, UK

Christos Kontovas, Liverpool John Moores University, Liverpool, UK

Dimitrios Paraskevadakis, Liverpool John Moores University, Liverpool, UK

Engy Awad, Fisheries and Marine Institute of Memorial University of Newfoundland. St. John's, Canada

Erik Veitch, Faculty of Architecture and Design, NTNU, Trondheim, Norway

Etienne Gernez, The Oslo School of Architecture and Design, Oslo, Norway

Hanne Lockertsen, The Oslo School of Architecture and Design, Oslo, Norway

Jon Erling Fauske, The Oslo School of Architecture and Design, Oslo, Norway

Kjetil Nordby, The Oslo School of Architecture and Design, Oslo, Norway

Koen van de Merwe, Group Research and Development, DNV, Høvik, Norway

Lokukaluge Prasad Perera, SINTEF Digital, SINTEF AS, Oslo, Norway

Mehdi Belabyad, Liverpool John Moores University, Liverpool, UK

Muhammad Adnan, Department of Technology and Safety, UiT The Arctic University of Norway, Tromsø, Norway

Pascal Hohnrath, Fraunhofer Center for Maritime Logistics and Services (CML), Hamburg, Germany

Robert Grundmann, Fraunhofer Center for Maritime Logistics and Services (CML), Hamburg, Germany

Robyn Pyne, Liverpool John Moores University, Liverpool, UK

Sofie Irene Nygard Branstad, University of Tromsø (UiT) – The Arctic University of Norway, Tromsø, Norway

Steven C. Mallam, Fisheries and Marine Institute of Memorial University of Newfoundland. St. John's, Canada, The Oslo School of Architecture and Design, Oslo, Norway

Sunniva Lislevand Wildhagen, The Oslo School of Architecture and Design, Oslo, Norway

Tae Eun Kim, University of Tromsø (UiT) – The Arctic University of Norway, Tromsø, Norway

Zaili Yang, Liverpool John Moores University, Liverpool, UK

PREFACE

It is our pleasure to welcome you to this volume, human factors in remote ship operations. Over the past decade, the maritime industry has experienced a transformation driven by advances in automation, digitisation and remote-control technologies. Remote operation centres (ROCs), autonomous and semi-autonomous ships, AI-assisted navigation and data-driven decision-making systems are no longer experimental concepts – they are increasingly embedded in real-world operations across commercial, defence and research fleets.

However, while technological maturity progresses, the human element remains critical. Even in highly automated systems, human operators, designers, regulators and engineers shape and are shaped by the technologies in use. The performance, safety and resilience of remote maritime operations depend not only on technical reliability but also on how humans interact with, adapt to and manage these complex systems.

Many questions remain, and they are human ones:

- How can navigators stay alert when the sea is only pixels?
- How do navigators and engineers trust a vessel they cannot touch?
- How does a designer show intent on a screen of icons?
- How can we ensure the safety of crewed vessels when operating alongside autonomous ships at sea?

This book is motivated by the need to systematically examine the human dimensions. It seeks to support a deeper understanding of how remote operations impact situational awareness, workload, decision-making, trust, training and team coordination. It also explores broader systemic concerns, including the implications of regulatory frameworks, organisational practices and socio-technical integration in the shift towards remote and autonomous operations.

Contributions in this volume are grounded in interdisciplinary research and practice. Chapters have strong interaction across multiple research fields such as human factors engineering, cognitive systems, marine operations, ergonomics, safety science, human-machine interaction and maritime regulations. The work presented includes theoretical reviews, experimental studies, case analyses and applied design recommendations.

This collection opens with a chapter focused on patent-based analysis of remote-control technologies, which trace how innovations have evolved to support autonomous ship operations. As these operations become more dependent on digital infrastructure, cybersecurity emerges as a critical concern not only in autonomous maritime operations but across all transportation sectors. Chapter 2 highlights the cybersecurity risks and the current research status related to securing maritime autonomous surface ships, drones and vehicles, showing how interconnected vulnerabilities can threaten system reliability.

With this technological groundwork laid, attention turns to how we see, evaluate and improve human performance in these advanced environments. Chapter 3 follows with a discussion of the role of human oversight in ship autonomy, asking how and to what extent humans should remain in the loop as vessels become more self-governing. Human interaction with autonomous systems brings many cognitive challenges, and this is explored in a dedicated Chapter 4 that examines the demands placed on remote operators navigating high-tech environments. To support such operations at scale, the ROC architecture is introduced in Chapter 5, which outlines the structural and technological requirements for managing fleets of remote ships.

Human performance within the remote-control centre remains critical, and their performance measurement is important to recognise the room for improvement. Therefore, in Chapter 6, systematic measurement methods that evaluate human performance are presented and analysed. The final chapter turns to the future workforce and addresses the training and research infrastructure needed to prepare operators for remote-control roles in this evolving industry.

Together, these chapters give a picture of the technological, human and institutional changes shaping remote maritime autonomy. Overall, this book is intended for researchers, practitioners and regulators involved in maritime technology, operations and regulation. We hope it will also serve as a reference for remote-control operators, educators, system designers and future professionals who are navigating the growing complexity of human roles in remote and intelligent marine systems.

We would like to extend our sincere thanks to all chapter contributors for their high-quality work and dedication to this topic. Your expertise, whether drawn from research, simulation, operations or field expertise, has made this volume both timely and relevant for readers. We gratefully acknowledge the reviewers for their expert feedback on each chapter, as well as the partners who supported the development of this project. Furthermore, we would like to acknowledge the funding support from the Research Council of Norway (Project No. 343256) under the forskerprosjekt for unge talenter REFRAME project (*https://site.uit.no/reframe/*).

As the maritime sector continues its transition towards hybrid, remote and autonomous operations, it is important that human factors remain a core part of this conversation. We hope this book is a step towards building the knowledge base and collaborative momentum needed to ensure that future maritime systems are not only technologically advanced but also safe, usable and resilient.

1

EVOLUTION OF REMOTE-CONTROL TECHNOLOGIES FOR MARITIME AUTONOMY

A Patent-Based Analysis

Mehdi Belabyad, Robyn Pyne, Dimitrios Paraskevadakis, Chia-Hsun Chang, Zaili Yang and Christos Kontovas

1 Introduction

Remote-control technologies in shipping have evolved, moving from theoretical frameworks to practical implementations. The industry has witnessed a surge in innovation, particularly in propulsion systems, power management and vessel control algorithms (Ivanova et al., 2021). Yet, despite this momentum, there is a lack of comprehensive understanding of how these technologies interconnect and which areas are likely to see accelerated development in the coming decade.

While existing literature has examined individual technological components like navigation interfaces (Burmeister et al., 2020) and remote perception methods (Clunie et al., 2021), less attention has been paid to mapping the entire technology ecosystem. Maritime remote control consists of numerous interlocking systems spanning navigation, perception, communication and safety functions – all of which must work in harmony to enable effective shore-based operations.

Patents offer a window into technological evolution, capturing formalised "*deeds to intellectual property*" that give innovation pathways (Campbell, 1983). As the World Intellectual Property Organisation (WIPO) notes, roughly 70–90% of technological information in patent documents is not published elsewhere (Asche, 2017), making patent analysis an important approach for understanding emerging technologies.

Despite the growing body of literature on individual maritime technologies (e.g. Burmeister et al., 2020; Clunie et al., 2021), there remains a significant gap in understanding how these technologies interconnect as an integrated ecosystem and which specific areas will drive future innovation.

DOI: 10.4324/9781003586883-1

Additionally, while patent analysis has been extensively applied in other sectors (de Oliveira et al., 2024; Cho et al., 2021; Qiu and Wang, 2022), its application to maritime remote-control technologies is limited and does not allow mapping of technology relationships or forecasting of development trajectories. Furthermore, recent advances in patent-based technology mapping have shown promise for understanding maritime autonomous systems broadly (Belabyad et al., 2025b), yet comprehensive analysis specifically focused on remote-control technologies remains absent.

This chapter addresses three core questions: *(1) What are the key technology clusters in maritime remote-control systems? (2) How do these technologies interconnect and influence each other within the innovation ecosystem?* and *(3) What is their relative maturity and potential future trajectory?* By answering these questions, this chapter contributes to the body of knowledge. First, a systematic categorisation of maritime remote-control technologies is provided using BERTopic modelling. Second, the network analysis quantifies technological relationships through centrality metrics, identifying critical bridging technologies that facilitate cross-domain integration. Third, technology maturity is assessed and forecasted using Bass diffusion modelling, providing clear trajectories for the technology landscape for various stakeholders, including shipowners, shipbuilding companies, maritime education and training centres, seafarers and maritime professionals and academics.

The chapter is structured as follows: Section 2 reviews current trends in maritime autonomy and relevant literature on technology diffusion and patent analysis. Section 3 provides the methodological framework. Section 4 presents the findings on technology clusters, their interconnections and development trajectories. Finally, Section 5 discusses the implications, concluding with limitations and future research directions.

2 Literature Review

2.1 Current Trends in Maritime Autonomy and Remote-Control Systems

The maritime industry is heading towards enhanced remote-control capabilities and increased vessel autonomy, transforming traditional approaches to ship management and navigation. Early studies by Rødseth and Nordahl (2017) and Porathe et al. (2018) discussed the emergence of advanced remote operation technologies within a multi-tiered ecosystem including interconnected sensing, telecommunication and decision-support frameworks. Recent industry standardisation efforts by Det Norske Veritas (DNV) (DNV-CG-0264) and assessments by the European Maritime Safety Agency (EMSA, 2024) conceptualise maritime remote control along a continuum including varying degrees of off-ship control and monitoring functionalities.

Ivanova et al. (2021) documented a surge in innovations, particularly in propulsion, power management and ship control algorithms. Their review indicated that communication technologies, which are important for remote operations, saw patent filings double between 2018 and 2019, driven by the demand for connectivity in distributed systems. At the same time, the integration of artificial intelligence (AI) and the internet of things (IoT) aligns with the "Industry 4.0" paradigm, enabling real-time data exchange and decision-making (Razmjooei et al., 2023).

A key example of these advancements is the remote navigation interfaces, which have developed significantly, going from simple command transmission systems to complex control platforms that support sophisticated decision-making in maritime settings (Burmeister et al., 2020). This parallels the rise of advanced remote perception methods, which combine sensor data from radar, LiDAR, optical and infrared technologies to establish comprehensive situational awareness frameworks for operators at a distance (Clunie et al., 2021). As a result, operators at shore-based facilities can now achieve environmental awareness that matches or surpasses that of traditional onboard navigation.

Moreover, maritime remote-control communication infrastructures are now enabling high-bandwidth, low-latency data transmission essential for real-time vessel monitoring and intervention from shore-based facilities (Höyhtyä et al., 2017). This progression has facilitated the development of remote operations centres (ROCs), which function as centralised hubs for monitoring vessel performance and environmental conditions across distributed maritime assets (Porathe et al., 2014; Ramos et al., 2019).

Furthermore, remote decision support systems using AI and machine learning algorithms have enabled more sophisticated functions such as remote collision avoidance, route optimisation and anomaly detection (Zhang et al., 2023). These computational frameworks provide predictive capabilities that go beyond simple reactivity to environmental conditions, allowing anticipatory decision-making in complex operational scenarios even when vessel control is distributed between onboard systems and shore-based operators.

These remote-control systems demonstrate significant operational differentiation across navigation functions, engineering systems, safety protocols and commercial operations, reflecting the multi-domain nature of maritime activities that must be addressed in remote operation contexts (Ringbom, 2019).

2.2 Technology Diffusion: A Theoretical Background

Understanding how innovations get adopted is key to predicting where remote-control technologies are heading next. Technology diffusion is a concept that explains the process through which new tools and innovations catch on with users. It shows a path from first adopters to widespread use (Stokey,

2020). This back-and-forth between innovation and adoption is not new; just like radar completely changed maritime shipping decades ago, today's autonomous systems are following similar paths to becoming integrated in the maritime sector (Clott and Hartman, 2022; Yusup, 2024).

Different theoretical models help us understand how technology diffusion works. The Bass model, which is a fundamental one in this area, suggests that technology adoption follows an S-curve – starting slow, then escalating quickly and eventually saturating (Bass, 1969). Research shows that the speed of adoption is significantly influenced by network effects and economic conditions, highlighting how innovation and diffusion strategies depend on each other (Wang et al., 2007; Yu, 2011). For instance, deploying autonomous vessels depends on having the right ecosystem in place, including regulations, technological infrastructure and a culture that's open to innovation (Clott and Hartman, 2022).

More recent work in diffusion research points out how important social networks are in adoption behaviours (Rao and Kishore, 2010). In maritime autonomy specifically, the interconnected nature of shipping, with collaborations, knowledge sharing and joint projects, plays a key role in driving broader acceptance. Organisations rarely operate in isolation; they rely on collective expertise and shared practices to navigate technological shifts. External factors such as policies and financial incentives also shape this diffusion process, either accelerating or slowing the adoption of new technologies (Yang et al., 2023; Wang et al., 2024).

2.3 Technology Mapping and Forecasting Using Patent Analysis

Patents are basically formalised "deeds to intellectual property" that capture evolutionary technological trajectories, offering standardised documentation of innovation pathways shaped by scientific frameworks, market pressures and the interactions between technologies (Campbell, 1983; Nelson and Winter, 1982). Their value for analysis comes from the exclusive information they contain, with roughly 70–90% of technological information in patent documents not published anywhere else, making them a unique resource for forecasting technology trends (WIPO, n.d.; Asche, 2017).

The International Patent Classification (IPC) system provides a hierarchical taxonomy with eight sections and around 80,000 subdivisions, offering precise positioning and mapping of technological trajectories (Gomez and Moens, 2014). This standardisation enables analytical approaches that go beyond traditional bibliometric analyses. Current methodologies demonstrate how advanced text mining techniques, combined with network analysis, can visualise technological relationships and emerging patterns (Aristodemou and Tietze, 2018).

Patent analysis methodologies have demonstrated particular efficacy in various sectors. For example, de Oliveira et al. (2024) applied network analysis on sustainable aviation fuel patents in order to track biofuel technologies. Cho et al. (2021) used cross-citation analysis and main path analysis, which revealed technological evolution patterns in autonomous driving systems. In the robotics domain, Qiu and Wang (2022) used topic modelling (via the latent Dirichlet allocation (LDA) algorithm) and citation network modelling to discover the development trajectory of robotics technologies.

While patent analysis is being widely applied for technological mapping and forecasting across numerous sectors, its application in maritime research, particularly in autonomous shipping technologies, remains surprisingly constrained in both scope and analytical sophistication. Recent studies demonstrate accelerating patent activity in autonomous maritime technologies, with over 70% of applications submitted after 2018, indicating rapid technological advancement (Karetnikov et al., 2020). The patent landscape in maritime autonomy exhibits unique characteristics of technological clustering, primarily around vessel control systems, navigational intelligence and operational safety mechanisms. Ivanova et al. (2021) identified three primary patent clusters comprising 14 subgroups (246 patents) in core autonomous technologies, 12 subgroups (164 patents) in supporting systems and four subgroups (26 patents) in specialised applications, demonstrating the hierarchical nature of technological development in this field. Recent analyses of maritime propulsion technologies through patent data observed significant technological convergence, particularly in green fuel technologies, with only four distinct sub-technologies accounting for 34.6% of patents and 38.3% of citations (Sun et al., 2024). Liu et al. (2024) and Lin et al. (2024) employed LDA topic modelling to analyse patent data, with the former identifying emerging technologies in intelligent control systems and ship equipment intelligence, while the latter revealed a pattern of technological fragmentation and integration across 14 distinct topics. More recently, Belabyad et al. (2025b) demonstrated the effectiveness of integrated patent analytics for maritime autonomous systems, identifying 20 technological domains and highlighting the critical role of sensor integration technologies, while illustrating technology maturity patterns across different maritime domains.

3 Methodology

Figure 1.1 provides the overall analytical framework that integrates bibliometric analysis (step 1), BERTopic modelling (step 2), network analysis (step 3) and technology forecasting (step 4) to analyse the technology landscape. It progresses from descriptive analytics to predictive modelling.

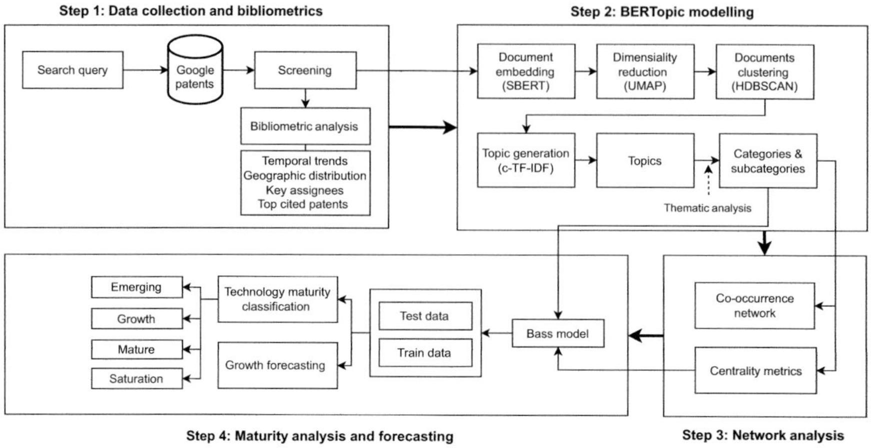

FIGURE 1.1 Research framework

3.1 Step 1: Data Collection and Bibliometric Analysis

Patent data is collected using Google Patents via BigQuery, focusing on remote-control technologies in maritime autonomy. For clarity, within this chapter, these technologies are defined based on previous work by DNV (DNV-CG-0264) and EMSA (2024) as

> Systems that enable vessel functions to be operated, monitored and controlled from a distance, without requiring personnel to be physically present at the location of operation, facilitating On-board control and/or Off-ship control.

These systems serve the following core functions:

- Navigation functions (e.g. route planning, collision avoidance, manoeuvring)
- Engineering functions (e.g. propulsion, power management, machinery control)
- Safety functions (e.g. fire detection, watertight integrity, emergency communications)
- Operations functions (e.g. cargo operations, commercial activities)

Based on this definition, a comprehensive search query is developed:

> *(("remote control" OR "remote operation" OR "remote supervision" OR "remote monitoring" OR telecontrol OR "off-ship control" OR*

"remote operations center" OR "remote operations centre" OR ROC OR "remote workstation")

AND

("maritime" OR "marine" OR "nautical" OR "naval" OR ship OR vessel* OR boat* OR "watercraft" OR "water craft" OR "sea-going" OR seagoing OR "ocean-going" OR "oceangoing" OR "waterway" OR "offshore" OR "coastal")*

AND

("propulsion" OR "navigation" OR "steering" OR "maneuvering" OR "collision avoidance" OR "object detection" OR "situational awareness" OR "monitoring system" OR "control system" OR automat OR autonomy* OR "decision support" OR "supervised autonomy" OR "connectivity" OR "communication link" OR "data link" OR "connectivity link" OR "fallback state")*

AND

(IPC:(B63B OR B63H OR B63J OR B63K OR G05D1 OR G08C OR H04B7 OR G06Q50/30))

NOT

("toy" OR "model" OR "hobby" OR "fish" OR "fishing" OR "recreational" OR "sport").

Please note that in the query, words are included in the search when the 'AND' operator is used, alternatives are considered with 'OR', and words are excluded using the 'NOT' operator. The wildcard symbol (*) expands the search to include words that begin with the same letters.

The first official traces of autonomous shipping date back to 2015 when the United Kingdom, International Association of Institutes of Navigation (IAIN) and the Institute of Marine Engineering, Science and Technology (IMarEST) submitted a document entitled "IMO Regulatory Framework and its Application to Maritime Autonomous Systems" to the IMO Maritime Safety Committee (Stępień, 2024). The 2010–2024 timeframe is selected to cover the pre-regulatory innovation works up to the most recent available yearly data.

Patents were collected using filing dates rather than publication dates, as filing dates more accurately reflect when inventions were created and legally protected. They also help avoid the lag introduced by publication delays, which usually take around 18 months on average.

The initial search resulted in 3,341 patents, which were refined to 1,875 after removing duplicates and irrelevant patents. Duplicates were identified and removed manually by comparing patent titles and publication numbers to ensure no patent was counted multiple times. Moreover, irrelevant patents were excluded based on predetermined criteria: patents focusing primarily on offshore oil and gas technologies without maritime vessel applications, aquaculture and fish-farming technologies that lacked remote-control elements for vessel operations, and recreational or toy vessel technologies that did not address commercial maritime applications.

A bibliometric analysis was conducted, focusing on four critical elements: time distribution, assignees, regional distribution and most frequently cited patents.

3.2 Step 2: Topic-Modelling Using BERTopic

The topic-modelling technique BERTopic was chosen for this analysis due to several key advantages over traditional methods like LDA or non-negative matrix factorization (NMF): (1) it leverages contextual BERT embeddings that capture semantic relationships more accurately than LDA's bag-of-words approach, (2) it automatically determines the optimal number of topics without requiring manual parameter tuning, (3) it can identify outlier documents that don't fit into main topics, which LDA cannot handle effectively and (4) it generates more coherent and interpretable topic clusters through its combination of uniform manifold approximation and projection (UMAP) dimensionality reduction and hierarchical density-based spatial clustering of applications with noise (HDBSCAN) clustering (Egger and Yu, 2022).

BERTopic integrates bidirectional encoder representations from transformers (BERT) embeddings with class-based term frequency–inverse document frequency (TF-IDF) to generate more coherent topic clusters. The algorithm operates by first embedding textual data using sentence-BERT (SBERT), reducing dimensionality via UMAP and subsequently clustering similar documents through HDBSCAN (Grootendorst, 2022). BERTopic can automatically determine the optimal number of topics without manual preset parameters and identify outlier documents that do not fit neatly into main topics.

BERTopic operates through three stages (see step 2 in Figure 1.1). First, document embeddings are generated using SBERT, transforming each document d_i into an n-dimensional vector $\vec{v_l} \in \mathbb{R}^n$ where semantic similarity between documents is preserved as cosine similarity in the embedding space:

Equation 1

$$\text{sim}\left(d_i, d_j\right) = \frac{\vec{v_i}, \vec{v_j}}{\left|\vec{v_i}\right|\left|\vec{v_j}\right|} q$$

Second, dimensionality reduction via UMAP transforms these high-dimensional embeddings into a lower-dimensional manifold $\mathbb{R}^m$ where $m \ll n$(typically $m = 5$) preserving both local and global structure through:

Equation 2

$$\min \sum_{i,j} p_{i,j} \log\left(\frac{p_{ij}}{q_{ij}}\right)$$

where $p_{i,j}$ are high-dimensional similarities and q_{ij} low-dimensional similarities.

Finally, HDBSCAN performs density-based clustering by identifying regions of high density separated by regions of low density, generating clusters without requiring a pre-specified number of topics.

Each cluster c_k is then characterised using class-based TF-IDF:

Equation 3

$$c - TF - IDF_{t,c} = \frac{f_{t,c} / w_c}{\sum_i f_{t,c} / w_c}$$

where $f_{t,c}$ is the frequency of term t in class c, and w_c is the number of words in class c.

For our implementation, we combined patent titles and abstracts since these contain the highest density of relevant technical information, and such a technique is usually used in previous patent-based analysis studies (Qiu and Wang, 2022; Ghaffari et al., 2024). One advantage of using BERTopic is that there is no need for preprocessing as with traditional topic-modelling approaches. The contextual embeddings capture semantic relationships between words regardless of their form, and even stopwords can carry meaningful information in context. We only performed minimal cleaning to handle special characters and formatting inconsistencies in the patent text. When applying BERTopic to our dataset, we experimented with different UMAP and HDBSCAN parameters to balance topic granularity and coherence.

3.3 Network Analysis

Based on the topic modelling results, a co-occurrence network is constructed to visualise and analyse relationships between technology subcategories. In the network representation, each node corresponds to a technology subcategory identified through topic modelling in step 2. Node size is proportional to patent count, and edge weights represent the co-occurrence frequency of technology pairs within the same patents, highlighting convergence between the technologies.

Applying citation network analysis (CNA) (McLaren and Bruner, 2022), node importance and network structure are quantified by calculating three key centrality metrics: degree centrality (measuring how many direct connections a technology has, which indicates its breadth of integration across the ecosystem), betweenness centrality (measuring how often a technology serves as a bridge between other technologies, showing which technologies are essential for connecting different technology clusters), and eigenvector centrality (measuring connections to other highly connected technologies, which help identify technologies that are embedded within the most influential parts of the network and therefore likely to drive future development) (Wasserman and Faust, 1994; Li et al., 2020).

3.4 Maturity Analysis and Forecasting

In technology evolution modelling, the literature uses a foundational assumption that technology adoption typically follows an S-curve pattern, where diffusion begins slowly during the innovation phase, accelerates during widespread adoption, and then plateaus as the market saturates (Foster, 1986; Christensen, 1992), forming a sigmoidal curve. This pattern has been observed and validated across numerous technology domains (Andersen, 1999; Chen et al., 2012; Miwornunyuie et al., 2024).

Among various S-curve growth models available for technology forecasting, the Bass diffusion model, introduced by Bass (1969), was selected. This model was considered an effective approach for forecasting technology diffusion patterns in different sectors (Meade and Islam, 2006; Daim and Suntharasaj, 2009; Wang and Sun, 2021). It's suitable for patent analysis as it assumes that technology adoption is governed by innovators (coefficient p: early adopters who decide independently to adopt the innovation, uninfluenced by others) and imitators (coefficient q: those influenced by previous adopters; social influence), who both characterise technology diffusion.

Mathematically, the core of the Bass model is expressed by the differential equation:

Equation 4

$$\frac{dN(t)}{dt} = \left(p + q\frac{N(t)}{m}\right)(m - N(t))$$

where $N(t)$ represents the cumulative number of adopters at time t, p is the innovation coefficient, describing the rate of adoption due to external effects (e.g. regulatory policies, first-mover incentives), q is the imitation coefficient, capturing the adoption caused by social or network effects (e.g. firms adopting based on competitor actions), and m is the total market potential, representing the upper limit of adoption.

In its implementation, network centrality metrics calculated in step 3 were used to parameterise the Bass model. Following the theoretical works of Muller and Peres (2019) and Burt (1999), betweenness centrality was used to parameterise the innovation coefficient (p), while eigenvector centrality was used to parameterise the imitation coefficient (q):

- High betweenness centrality suggests that a technology (or firm) introduces novel connections and serves as a conduit for knowledge flow, much like innovators in the Bass model who adopt independently of earlier adopters.
- Technologies with high eigenvector centrality are embedded within a dense network of influential adopters, meaning their adoption is likely influenced by previous adopters, similar to the imitation effect (q) in the Bass model.

A train-test-forecast methodology was employed to validate the proposed approach. The model was first fitted to data from 2010 to 2019 using non-linear least squares optimisation. Validation was conducted on test data from 2020 to 2024 by calculating out-of-sample prediction accuracy using the mean absolute percentage error (MAPE). For future projections, forecasts were extended to 2033 (a 10-year horizon) and 95% confidence intervals were generated using Monte Carlo simulation with 1,000 iterations.

Technologies are then mapped using both the q and p to construct a two-dimensional diffusion characteristic matrix, positioning each technology based on its primary adoption mechanism: high p (innovation-driven), high q (imitation-driven) or a combination of both.

Finally, to assess technology maturity, progress percentage is calculated as the ratio of current cumulative patents to the estimated market potential (current patent cumulative count divided by m). Based on this metric, technologies were classified into four maturity stages (following Andersen's (1999) seminal study on S-curves):

- Emerging ($P < 25\%$): Technologies in early adoption
- Growth ($25\% < P < 60\%$): Technologies in the acceleration phase
- Maturity ($60\% < P < 80\%$): Technologies approaching saturation
- Saturation ($P > 80\%$): Technologies with limited growth potential

4 Results and Analysis

4.1 Bibliometric Analysis

As shown in Figure 1.2, the number of patent filings started increasing gradually from 2010, reaching its peak in 2022 at 253 patents, after which it declined rapidly up to 2024. This can potentially be attributed to changing R&D priorities in the sector following global economic uncertainties. In

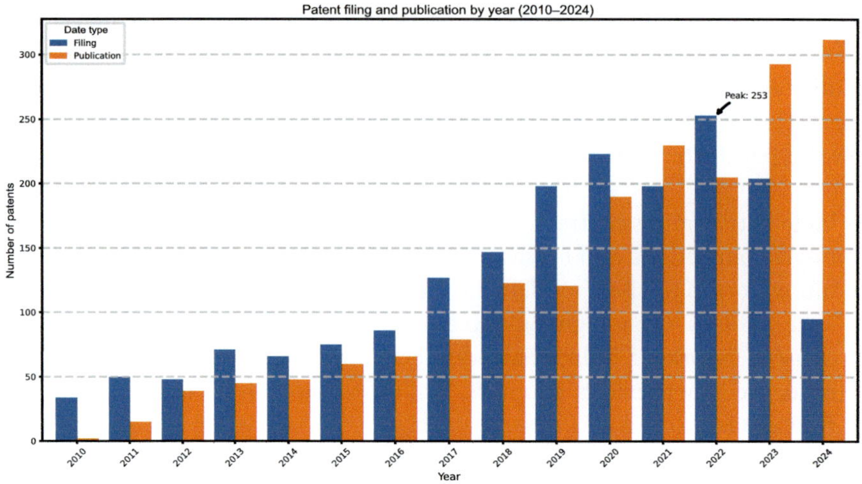

FIGURE 1.2 Distribution of patents by years (filing versus publication years)

contrast, patent publications experienced continued growth from 2010 to 2024, except for 2023, when they decreased slightly. This pattern reflects the typical 18-month lag between filing and publication in the patent system. Up to 2021, the number of patents filed was higher than those published, except for 2021. From 2023 onwards, the number of patents published is significantly higher than the number filed, highlighting the processing of the backlog of applications from the peak innovation years.

In terms of assignees (Figure 1.3), Furuno Electric (a Japanese electronics company) is leading with 74 patents, followed by Brunswick Corporation (an American international marine manufacturer) with 49 patents, and Yamaha Motor (another Japanese manufacturer) with 39 patents. Looking at the assignees figure, we observe that this ecosystem is diverse, comprising marine and navigation technology organisations (e.g. Furuno Electric, Brunswick), automotive and motor manufacturer (e.g. Yamaha Motor, Honda Motor), shipbuilders (e.g. Daewoo), shipping organisations (e.g. Nippon Yusen), technology and IT solutions (e.g. Fujitsu Limited), and universities and research institutions (e.g. Wuhan University of Technology, Dalina Maritime University). Interestingly, six universities are competing within the top 15 assignees, indicating the significant role of academic research in this area.

Concerning the regional distribution of patents (Figure 1.4), 51% of patents are registered in China, followed by 17.5% in Korea and 10.9% in the United States. These three countries comprise almost 80% of all patents. A fraction of patents is registered with the World Intellectual Property Organisation (WIPO) and the European Patent Office (EPO), which manage patent applications in the international and European context respectively.

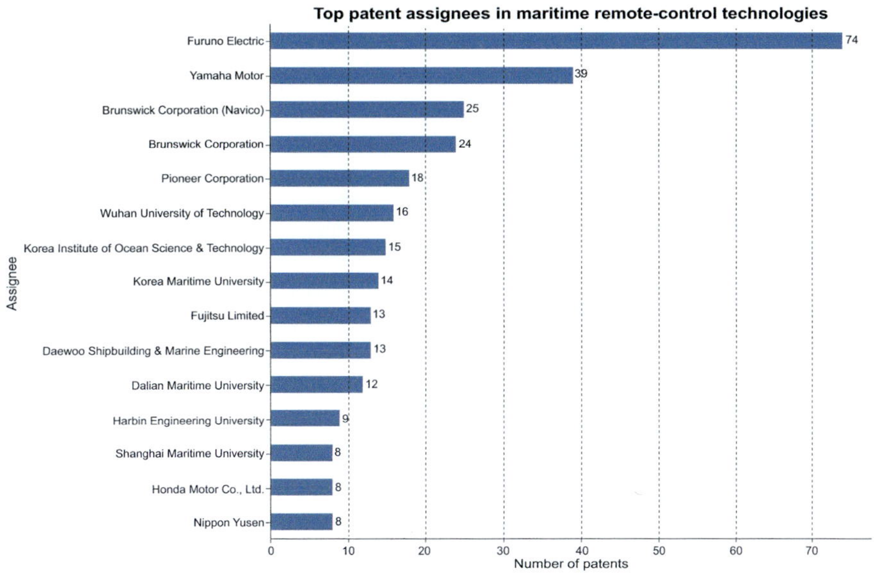

FIGURE 1.3 Top assignees in maritime remote-control-related technologies

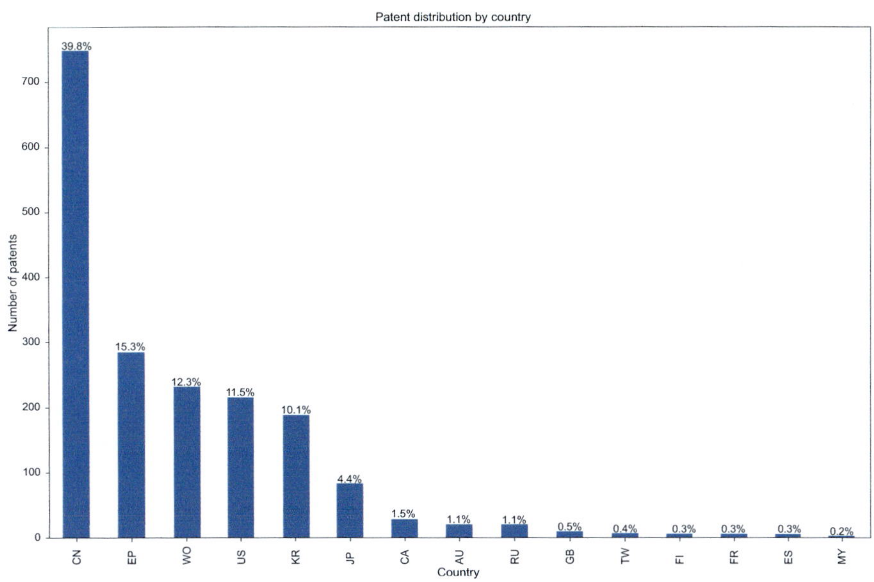

FIGURE 1.4 Patent distribution by country

Table 1.1 presents the most cited patents in the dataset. It shows that foundational control systems, collision avoidance and autonomous navigation technologies are influential in the innovation network.

TABLE 1.1 Top cited patents

Patent number	*Patent title*	*Overview*	*Cited*
US-6273771-B1	"Control system for a marine vessel"	A marine vessel control system that uses a communication bus to manage multiple devices.	19 times
KR-101937439-B1	"Alternative route generation and rudder angle control support system for collision avoidance of autonomous ship and other ships"	A system that generates alternative navigation routes and controls the rudder for collision avoidance.	12 times
KR-101941896-B1	"System for controlling auto sailing of vessel"	An autonomous navigation control system that stabilises a vessel in emergencies	11 times

4.2 Topic Modelling Using BERTopic

Using BERTpoic, 30 topics were generated and further categorised into eight main categories. The sunburst diagram (Figure 1.5) shows these categories and sub-categories with their sizes according to the number of patents.

BERTopic generated keyword distributions for each identified topic, grouping semantically similar patents into coherent clusters. These keyword clusters were then qualitatively and thematically analysed to infer the underlying technological domains. For example, clusters containing terms such as "camera", "vision", "image", "video", "visual" and "recognition" were classified under the "camera & visual systems" subcategory within the broader "perception & detection" category.

"Remote Control Systems" is the largest category, with subcategories including "Remote Navigation Interfaces" (which dominated this space), followed by "Command & Control Infrastructure", "Wireless Control Systems", "Remote Propulsion Control" and "Teleoperation Networks". A representative patent in this category is US-12214854-B2, "Vessel azimuth control apparatus and azimuth control method", which enables precise remote control of vessel direction through an intuitive interface that compensates for environmental factors. This dominance suggests that foundational control infrastructure remains the primary innovation focus, indicating continued investment in making remote operations more reliable and intuitive.

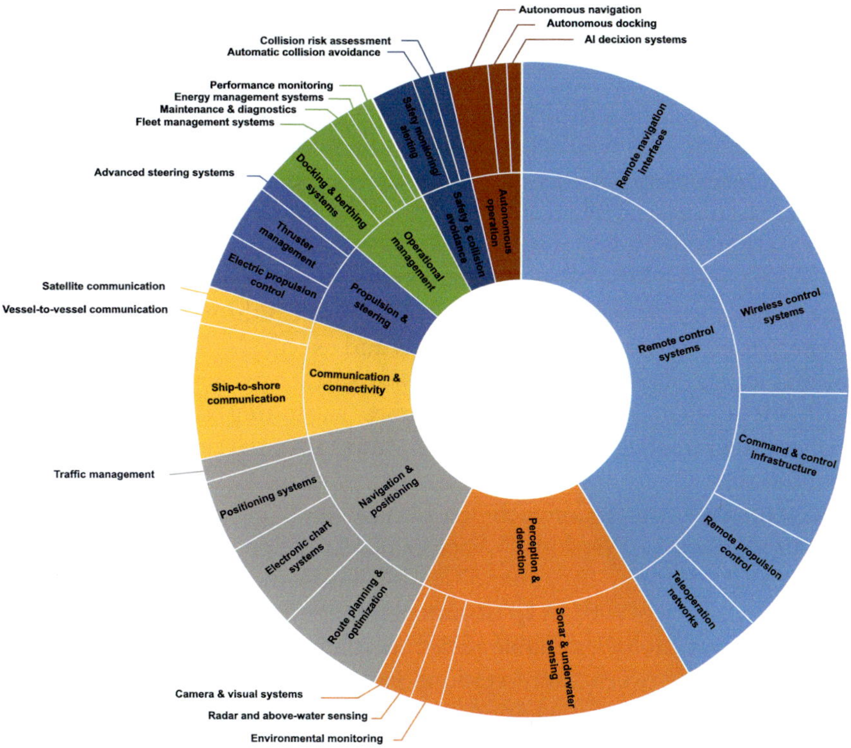

FIGURE 1.5 Technologies categories and subcategories

"Perception & Detection Technologies" formed another major cluster, with "Sonar & Underwater Sensing", followed by "Camera & Visual Systems", "Radar & Above-Water Sensing", "Multi-Sensor Integration" and "Environmental Monitoring". These technologies essentially form the "eyes and ears" of remote and autonomous maritime systems. US-2025036144-A1, "Underwater vehicles for vessel characterisation", exemplifies this category with its innovative approach to using autonomous underwater vehicles to gather data about vessel hulls and underwater structures. This cluster indicates that achieving comprehensive situational awareness remains a fundamental requirement for significant technological development in remote-control technologies.

"Navigation & Positioning Technologies" includes "Route Planning & Optimisation", "Electronic Chart Systems", "Positioning Systems" and "Dynamic Navigation and Traffic Nanagement". These are technologies that establish where vessels are and where they should go. EP-4506663-A1, "Systems and methods for generating routes for watercraft", demonstrates advanced algorithms that optimise vessel routes based on multiple factors, including weather, traffic, fuel efficiency and safety parameters. The centrality of route optimisation within this category suggests that this area serves as a critical foundation for effective maritime operations.

"Safety & Collision Avoidance Systems" are composed of "Safety Monitoring & Alerting", "Collision Detection Systems", "Collision Risk Assessment", "Automatic Collision Avoidance" and "Emergency Response Systems". The relatively smaller patent counts in this category may be surprising given safety's importance in the sector, but many safety functions are likely integrated within other systems. KR-102617981-B1, "Collision avoidance system for autonomous ships", represents breakthrough technology that can autonomously identify collision risks and execute avoidance manoeuvres without human intervention. The relatively smaller patent counts in this category are notable given safety's importance, suggesting that safety functions may be integrated within other systems rather than developed as standalone technologies.

"Communication & Connectivity Technologies" included "Ship-To-Shore Communications", "Vessel-to-Vessel Communications", "Satellite Communications", "Maritime Broadband" and "Communication Security & Resilience". WO-2018149901-A1, "Route planning of a vessel", illustrates how connectivity technologies enable real-time route adjustments based on information shared between shore stations and vessels, highlighting the critical nature of reliable communication links. This suggests the enabling role of connectivity in maritime remote operations, facilitating real-time information exchange and coordination.

"Propulsion & Steering Technologies" covered "Electric Propulsion Control", "Advanced Steering Systems", "Thruster Management" and "Propulsion Efficiency Systems". EP-3978352-B1, "Marine propulsion control system and method with collision avoidance override", shows the integration of safety protocols with propulsion systems, allowing automated override of propulsion commands when collision risks are detected. This cluster focuses on electric propulsion control and efficiency systems, suggesting a shift towards more environmentally sustainable and precisely controllable propulsion technologies.

"Operational Management Systems" encompassed "Energy Management Systems", "Docking & Berthing Systems", "Fleet Management Systems", "Performance Monitoring" and "Maintenance & Diagnostic Systems". These handle specialised aspects of maritime operations. EP-3898405-C0, "System for docking a submarine vessel to a docking port", presents sophisticated technology that enables precise automated alignment and connection procedures for underwater vessels, demonstrating the complexity of operational management systems. This suggests that shore-based operational models are becoming increasingly sophisticated and specialised.

Finally, "**Autonomous Operation Technologies**" included "Autonomous Navigation", "AI Decision Systems", "Autonomous Perception", "autonomous docking" and "Human-Autonomous Interaction". WO-2021242413-A3, "Adaptable control for autonomous maritime vehicles", showcases an advanced framework that balances autonomous decision-making with human supervision, allowing the dynamic shifting of control authority based on situational complexity and risk assessment. The emphasis on balancing autonomous capabilities with human supervision indicates that hybrid human-machine operations represent the current focus of autonomous maritime development.

4.3 Network Analysis

The network analysis examines how different technology clusters connect and influence each other. Looking at the co-occurrence network visualisation (Figure 1.6), there is a dense cluster centring around "Safety & Collision Avoidance Systems" in the top portion of the network, showing tight integration between sensing technologies and safety systems. A second major cluster forms around "Navigation & Positioning Technologies", connected to autonomous operation capabilities. "Remote-Control Systems" and "Communication & Connectivity" technologies form a third significant grouping, with multiple connections to other clusters.

In terms of centrality (as shown in Table 1.2), "Route Planning & Optimisation" has the highest degree centrality (0.162), meaning it has the most direct connections to other technologies. This reflects its key role in connecting various requirements (navigational and operational). Its high betweenness centrality (0.090) further confirms that it serves as a bridge between different technologies.

"Safety Monitoring & Alerting" shows the highest eigenvector centrality (0.389), suggesting a strong connection to other influential technologies. This indicates that safety systems must integrate with numerous other vessel systems to operate effectively. Similarly, "Collision Detection Systems" and "Collision Risk Assessment" (both with an eigenvector centrality of 0.266) form part of this critical safety cluster.

"Command & Control Infrastructure" exhibits high betweenness centrality (0.254) despite having fewer connections, indicating its role in bridging different technologies. "Remote Navigation Interfaces" has the highest patent count (285) but relatively low centrality metrics, suggesting it is a specialised area that has seen substantial development but with limited integration across the innovation landscape.

Furthermore, several technologies show zero connections in the network, including "Emergency Response Systems", "Automatic Collision Avoidance"

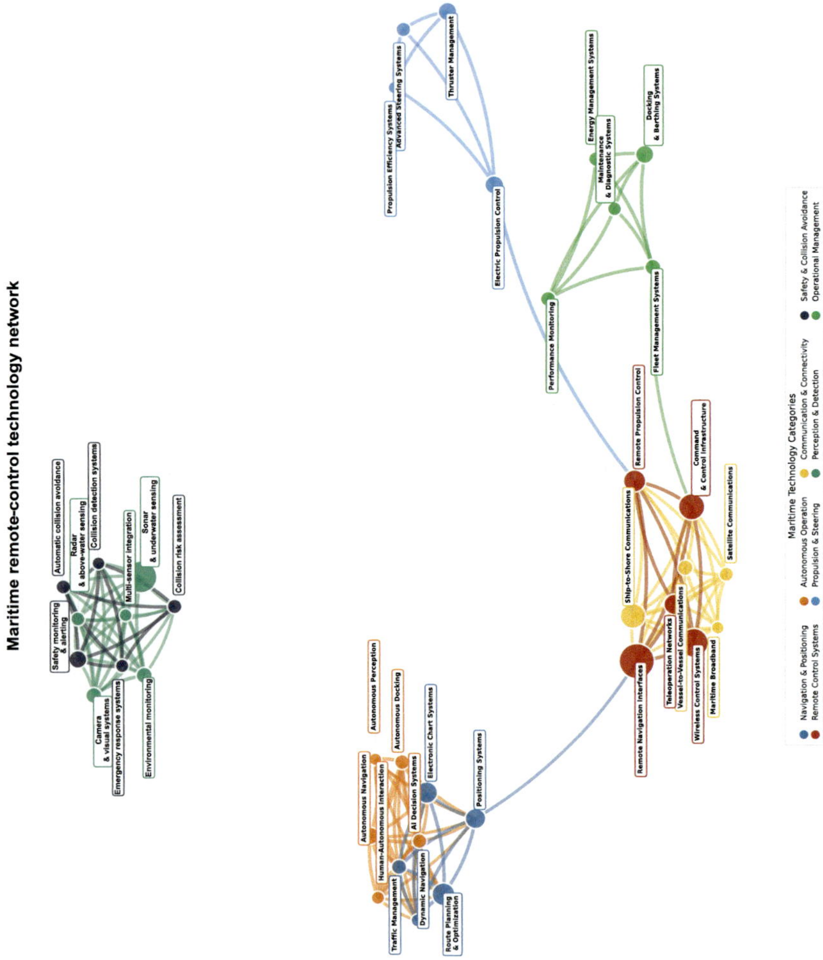

FIGURE 1.6 Network visualisation: co-occurrence relationships between maritime remote-control technology subcategories (node size = patent count, edge thickness = co-occurrence frequency, colours = technology categories)

TABLE 1.2 Key technologies based on centrality metrics

Technology subcategory	*Category*	*Patent count*	*Degree centrality*	*Betweenness centrality*	*Eigenvector centrality*
Route Planning & Optimisation	Navigation & Positioning	96	0.162	0.090	0.380
Safety Monitoring & Alerting	Safety & Collision Avoidance	41	0.135	0.058	0.389
Command & Control Infrastructure	Remote-Control Systems	142	0.054	0.254	0.260
Wireless Control Systems	Remote-Control Systems	178	0.054	0.000	0.105
Electric Propulsion Control	Propulsion & Steering	51	0.108	0.032	0.161
Sonar & Underwater Sensing	Perception & Detection	232	0.054	0.029	0.105
Remote Navigation Interfaces	Remote-Control Systems	285	0.027	0.000	0.078
Autonomous Navigation	Autonomous Operation	37	0.081	0.004	0.196
Ship-to-Shore Communications	Communication & Connectivity	124	0.027	0.000	0.027
Autonomous Docking	Autonomous Operation	17	0.135	0.075	0.329

and "Human-Autonomous Interaction" and therefore are not presented in the table shown. This suggests these areas are either emerging innovations or are being developed in isolation from the main innovation streams.

Overall, we have a network organised around several key technology hubs. Navigation and safety technologies form the most connected clusters, while newer autonomous technologies show less integration. We can infer that the industry, in this area, is transitioning as established remote-control technologies are well-developed but not fully integrated with emerging autonomous capabilities.

4.4 Maturity Analysis and Forecasting

The maturity analysis directly addresses our third and final research question regarding the relative maturity and future trajectory of maritime remote-control technologies, as outlined in Section 1. The Bass diffusion modelling results provide clear evidence that this technological domain remains in active development rather than approaching standardisation.

Given the large number of technology subcategories identified in this analysis, this Section focuses primarily on the main categories for forecast visualisation while incorporating subcategories for maturity assessment.

The citation-based Bass model was fitted to training data (2010–2019) and then tested against actual patent data for the period 2020–2024. This validation approach resulted in MAPE values ranging from 2.98 to 13.11, confirming the model's predictive accuracy. The model was compared with linear and exponential forecasting approaches, and the citation-based Bass model consistently outperformed these alternatives.

The S-curve forecasts are shown in Figure 1.7.

- **"Remote-Control Systems"** (five subcategories, 42.4% of potential, growth stage): This largest category shows strong continued growth potential, with forecasts suggesting cumulative patent counts could reach 1,640 by 2033 from the current 765 patents. The steep slope of the forecast curve indicates accelerating innovation in this area.
- **"Navigation & Positioning"** (four subcategories, 18.6% of potential, growth stage): Currently at 265 patents, this category shows substantial room for growth, with projections reaching approximately 520 patents by 2033. The moderately steep S-curve suggests steady rather than explosive growth.
- **"Perception & Detection"** (four subcategories, 26.3% of potential, growth stage): With 296 current patents, this category shows considerable growth potential, projected to reach approximately 710 patents by 2033.
- **"Autonomous Operation"** (three subcategories, 21.6% of potential, growth stage): Despite relatively few current patents (74), this category shows steep projected growth, potentially reaching 185 patents by 2033. The steepness of the forecast curve suggests this emerging area may see accelerated development.
- **"Communication & Connectivity"** (three subcategories, 18.7% of potential, growth stage): Currently at 159 patents, projections suggest growth to approximately 365 patents by 2033. The moderate slope suggests steady development.
- **"Propulsion & Steering"** (three subcategories, 36.3% of potential, growth stage): With 118 current patents, this category shows moderate growth potential to approximately 245 patents by 2033. The flatter slope suggests these mature technologies may see more incremental innovation.
- **"Safety & Collision Avoidance"** (three subcategories, 23.9% of potential, growth stage): With 81 patents currently, this category could reach approximately 215 patents by 2033. The steepening forecast curve suggests increasing attention to safety as autonomous systems develop.
- **"Operational Management"** (four subcategories, 6.6% of potential, emerging stage): This is the only category in the emerging stage with just 113 patents and substantial growth potential to approximately 300 patents by 2033. The J-shaped forecast curve suggests this area may be approaching an acceleration point.

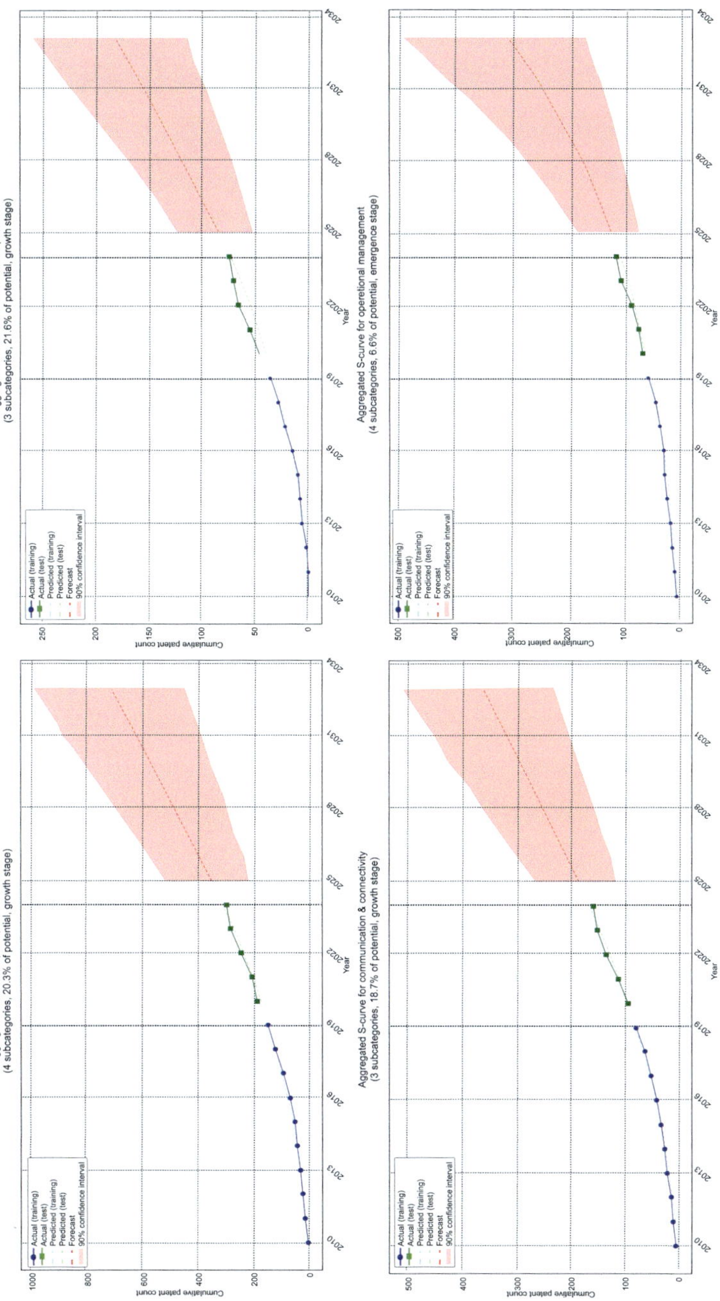

FIGURE 1.7 S-curve fitting and forecast

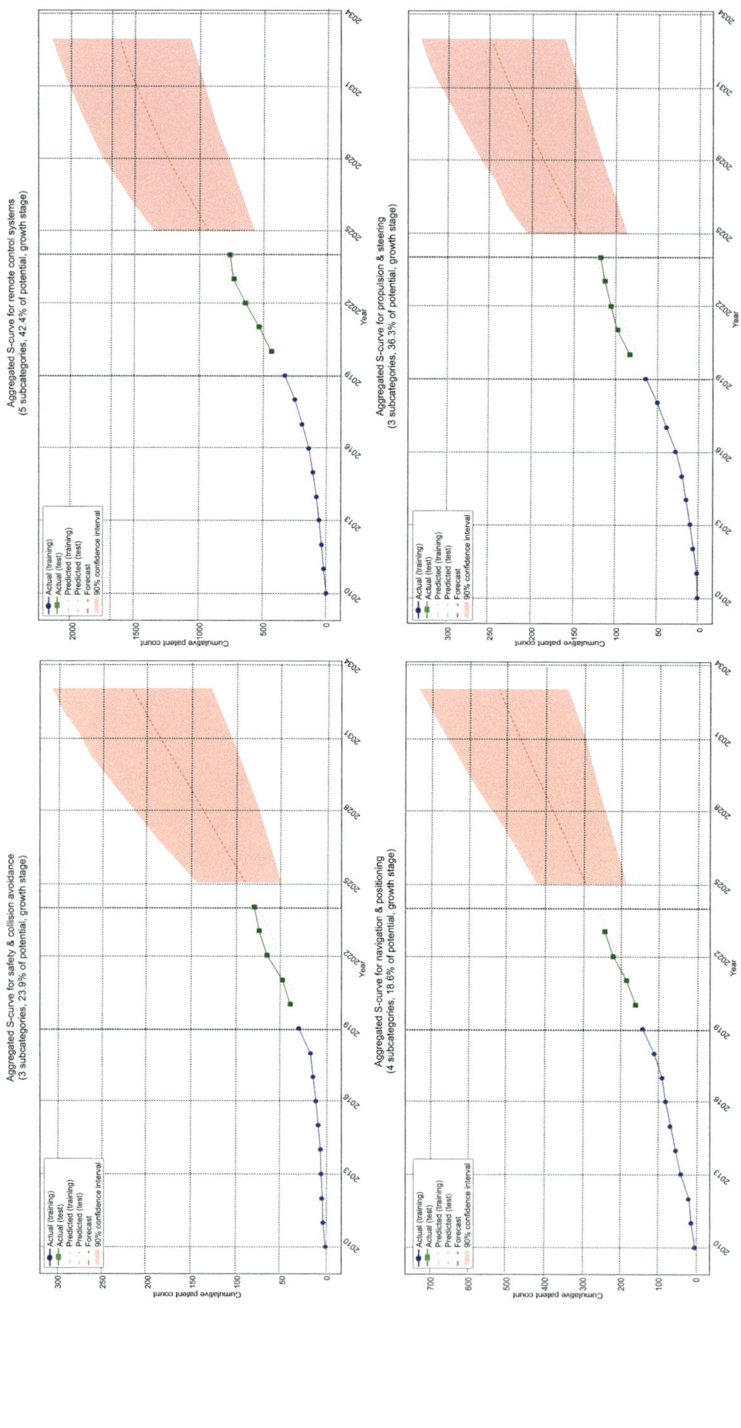

FIGURE 1.7 (Continued)

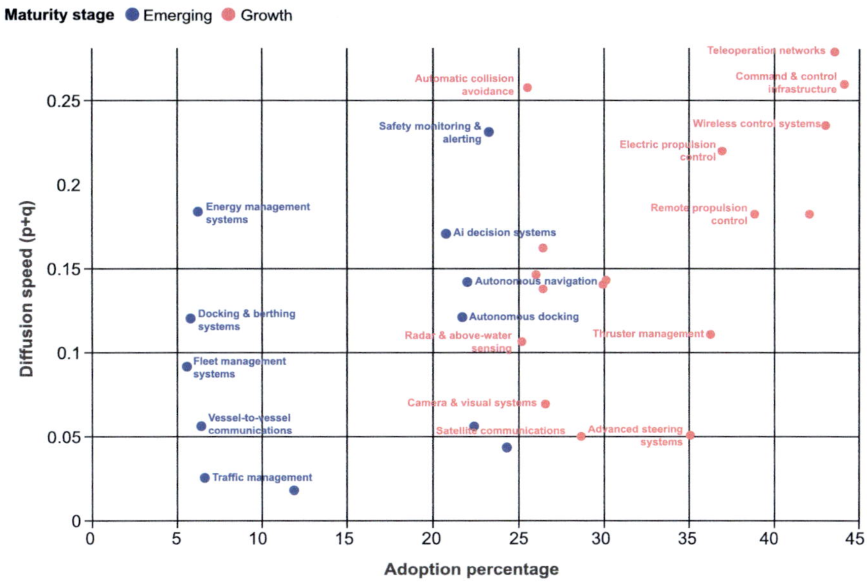

FIGURE 1.8 Diffusion speed ($p + q$) versus current adoption (some technology labels may be omitted due to space constraints)

Moreover, Figure 1.8 (Diffusion speed ($p + q$)[1] versus current adoption) shows four technology clusters based on market penetration and diffusion dynamics. Overall, of all technologies (subcategories), 65.5% are in the growth stage while 34.5% are in the merging stage.

The upper-right quadrant (high diffusion/high adoption) includes technologies like "Teleoperation Networks", "Command & Control Infrastructure" and "Wireless Control Sysltems". These technologies have reached widespread adoption (40–60% of market potential) while maintaining high diffusion speeds (0.24–0.28), suggesting they are established but still actively evolving.

On the other hand, the lower-left quadrant contains technologies like "Traffic Management", "Positioning Systems" and "Vessel-to-Vessel Communications" with both low adoption rates (<10%) and slow diffusion speeds (<0.06). These represent either highly specialised niches or very early-stage innovations that haven't yet gained significant traction.

Finally, Figure 1.9 (Innovation versus imitation parameters) offers complementary insights by revealing the dominant adoption mechanisms. Technologies positioned higher on the y-axis (q coefficient), like "Teleoperation Networks" and "Wireless Control Systems" ($q > 0.22$), spread primarily through imitation effects where companies adopt technologies based on competitive pressures and established successes. These technologies benefit from network effects and industry standardisation.

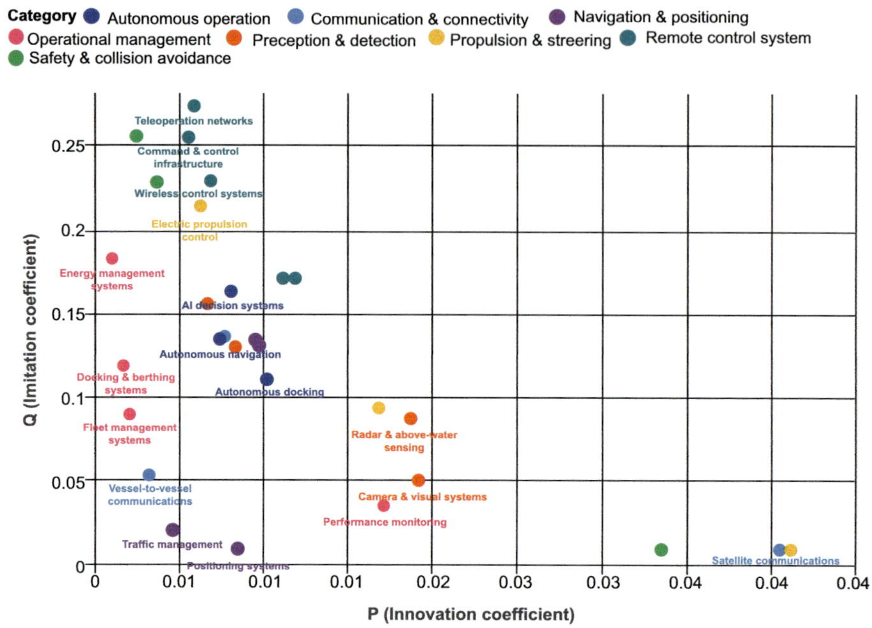

FIGURE 1.9 Innovation versus imitation parameters (some technology labels may be omitted due to space constraints)

Technologies with higher innovation coefficients (p) like "Advanced Steering Systems" and "Satellite Communications" ($p > 0.04$), but low imitation effects spread through breakthrough innovation rather than mimetic adoption. Their development is driven by pioneer companies rather than industry-wide imitation.

Most technologies cluster in the middle-left region with moderate imitation coefficients (0.10–0.20) and low innovation coefficients (<0.02), suggesting balanced development patterns with greater emphasis on incremental improvements than radical innovation (breakthroughs).

Looking at maturity stages across both visualisations, several patterns can be observed:

- **"Remote-Control Systems"** category shows the most mature technologies, with three subcategories in the widespread adoption phase.
- **"Navigation & Positioning"** technologies show moderate adoption (30–40%) with varied diffusion mechanisms.
- **"Autonomous Operation"** technologies remain largely in early adoption phases despite moderate diffusion speeds.
- **"Safety & Collision Avoidance"** technologies show some differences, with some reaching widespread adoption (**"Safety Monitoring"**) while others remain in early phases (**"Collision Risk Assessment"**).

The complete absence of technologies in the market maturity and saturation phases confirms that maritime remote-control technology as a field has not reached maturity. Even the most established technologies still have high growth potential while the numerous technologies in early adoption phases suggest considerable innovation activity remains ahead.

5 Discussion and Conclusion

5.1 Discussion

This study mapped and forecasted the technological landscape of maritime remote-control systems using patent data and advanced modelling techniques. Patent filings surged from 2010, peaking in 2022 before a recent decline, while publications continue to rise, reflecting sustained momentum. Leading contributors include traditional maritime firms, tech innovators and academic institutions, with China dominating geographically, followed by Korea and the United States.

The topic modelling indicated "Remote-Control Systems" as the dominant category, with "Remote Navigation Interfaces" leading the charge. These systems are necessary for shore-based vessel control. "Perception & Detection" technologies, essential for situational awareness, rely on multi-sensor integration, while "Navigation & Positioning" systems, specifically "Route Planning & Optimisation", anchor operational precision. "Safety & Collision Avoidance" technologies show varied integration and "Communication & Connectivity" are the basis of all remote functions. "Emerging Operational Management" systems signal a shift to shore-based roles, while "Autonomous Operation" technologies remain at early stages, suggesting a future of hybrid human-machine operations. Network analysis highlights the centrality of "Route Planning & Optimisation" and the influence of "Safety Monitoring & Alerting" yet technologies such as "Emergency Response Systems" remain isolated.

The maturity analysis conclusively demonstrates that maritime remote-control technology remains in early developmental stages, with 65.5% of technologies in the growth phase and 34.5% in the emerging phase. None have reached maturity or saturation, confirming the sector remains in active evolution rather than standardisation. The Bass diffusion modelling indicates different adoption mechanisms across technologies: "Remote-Control Systems" show predominantly imitation-driven diffusion (high q values), while "Autonomous Operation" technologies demonstrate more innovation-driven patterns (higher p values).

5.2 Implications

This chapter provides several key implications.

The network analysis shows **"Route Planning & Optimisation"** has the highest degree centrality and significant betweenness centrality, positioning it as a critical bridge technology. This suggests route planning systems serve as integration hubs that connect various maritime technologies. Developers should prioritise open APIs and standardised data exchange formats for route planning systems to facilitate integration with collision avoidance, propulsion control and sensor systems.

"Safety Monitoring & Alerting" shows the highest eigenvector centrality (0.389), indicating its connections to other influential technologies. This central position suggests safety systems require extensive integration with numerous vessel systems to function effectively. When implementing remote-control technologies, organisations should ensure safety systems can access data from navigation, propulsion and perception systems. For instance, a safety alert about potential collision risks should automatically integrate data from radar systems, vessel positioning and environmental conditions to provide operators with complete situational awareness.

The network analysis identified several technologies with zero connections, including **"Emergency Response Systems"**, **"Automatic Collision Avoidance"** and **"Human-Autonomous Interaction"**. This isolation suggests these critical technologies are developing independently of the main innovation ecosystem. Industry stakeholders should create focused integration initiatives to connect these isolated technologies with the broader network. For emergency response systems, this might involve developing standardised emergency protocols that can be triggered by multiple systems and coordinated through the command infrastructure.

It's particularly concerning that **"Human-Autonomous Interaction"** appears disconnected from other technologies, as this interface will be crucial during the transition to more autonomous operations. The isolation of "Human-Autonomous Interaction" technologies presents significant risks for maritime safety and operational effectiveness. This disconnection suggests that these systems are being developed independently from other critical technologies such as navigation, safety monitoring and communication systems. Such isolation could lead to poor integration when these systems are deployed together, potentially resulting in loss of situational awareness as operators struggle to understand autonomous system decisions. This could also lead to inappropriate trust calibration where operators either over-rely on or under-trust autonomous capabilities and ineffective intervention capabilities when human oversight is required. The lack of integration may also indicate that current development is not adequately considering the broader technological ecosystem in which these interfaces must operate. Design guidelines should mandate that autonomous systems maintain clear communication channels with human operators, providing transparency about system status, decision-making processes and requesting intervention when appropriate.

Beyond technological infrastructure, this patent analysis has important workforce implications. The emergence of hybrid remote-autonomous systems indicated by the network analysis suggests maritime education must move past traditional seamanship. As Belabyad et al. (2025a) emphasise, successful implementation of these technologies requires workforce transformation, with operators needing hybrid competencies that combine traditional knowledge with digital proficiency. Training institutions should develop programmes specifically addressing the cognitive demands of transitioning between observation and intervention roles. Certification frameworks will need restructuring to recognise these new competencies that blend maritime expertise with digital literacy. As a result, industry partnerships between technology developers, operators and educators will be essential to align skill development with technological trajectories identified in this forecast, which shows all clusters remain in growth phases without approaching saturation.

5.3 Limitations and Future Research

The reliance on patent data may overlook unpatented innovations, skewing the technological landscape. Maturity assessments based on patent counts do not fully reflect operational considerations, as some technologies may be widely used despite fewer filings. Network connections show relationships but not their practical strength; an "isolated" "Emergency Response System" might still be effective as a standalone. These gaps call for field studies on operator experiences and deeper subcategory analysis to validate this chapter's findings.

Furthermore, future research should specifically investigate why human-autonomous interaction appears as an isolated technology cluster despite its critical importance for safe maritime operations. Research priorities should include examining the barriers preventing its integration with other maritime technologies, developing frameworks for seamless human-machine collaboration in maritime contexts, and establishing design principles that ensure these systems can effectively interface with navigation, safety and communication technologies.

5.4 Conclusion

This patent analysis of maritime remote-control technologies showcases a dynamic and rapidly evolving field. Through the analysis of 1,875 patents using BERTopic modelling, network analysis and Bass diffusion forecasting, eight core technology clusters were identified, with "Route Planning & Optimisation" serving as a critical bridge technology and "Safety Monitoring & Alerting" as highly influential within the innovation ecosystem.

The forecasting results indicate that all identified technologies remain in growth or emerging phases, with none nearing saturation, projecting significant expansion through 2033. This finding, combined with the network analysis highlighting isolated yet critical technologies such as "Human-Autonomous Interaction", emphasises the need for stakeholders to prioritise technological interoperability and integration strategies.

For industry practitioners, these insights provide a roadmap for strategic technology investments and partnership decisions. For researchers, the identified gaps in technology integration present opportunities for future investigation, particularly in bridging isolated but critical capabilities such as emergency response systems and human-machine interaction interfaces. As the maritime industry continues its digital transformation, understanding these technological trajectories becomes essential for shaping the future of shore-based maritime operations.

Acknowledgements

This work is supported by the Reframing Education and Competence Model for Remote Maritime Operations (REFRAME) project, funded by the Research Council of Norway; the ERC project Towards Resilient and Sustainable Container Supply Chains (TRUST), funded by the European Research Council; and a doctoral scholarship from Liverpool John Moores University.

Note

1 "$p + q$" represents the total diffusion speed of a technology, combining both innovation (p) and imitation (q) effects. Technologies with higher $p + q$ values will spread more rapidly through the market regardless of whether adoption is primarily driven by external factors (p) or internal factors (q).

References

Andersen, B. (1999). The hunt for S -shaped growth paths in technological innovation: A patent study. *Journal of Evolutionary Economics*, 9(4), 487–526.

Aristodemou, L., & Tietze, F. (2018). The state-of-the-art on Intellectual Property Analytics (IPA): A literature review on artificial intelligence, machine learning and deep learning methods for analysing intellectual property (IP) data. *World Patent Information*, *55*, 37–51. https://www.sciencedirect.com/science/article/pii/S0172219018300103

Asche, G. (2017). '80% of technical information found only in patents' – Is there proof of this [1]? *World Patent Information*, *48*, 16–28.

Bass, F. M. (1969). A new product growth model for consumer durables. *Management Science*, *15*, 215–227.

Belabyad, M., Kontovas, C., Pyne, R., & Chang, C. H. (2025a). Skills and competencies for operating maritime autonomous surface ships (MASS): A systematic review and bibliometric analysis. *Maritime Policy & Management*, 1–26.

Belabyad, M., Pyne, R., Paraskevadakis, D., Chang, C.-H., & Kontovas, C. (2025b). Technology evolution in maritime autonomous systems: A patent-based analysis. *Ocean & Coastal Management*, *267*, 107744.

Burmeister, H.-C., Constapel, M., Ugé, C., & Jahn, C. (2020). From sensors to MASS: Digital representation of the perceived environment enabling ship navigation. *IOP Conference Series Materials Science and Engineering*, *929*(1), 012028–012028.
Burt, R. S. (1999). The social capital of opinion leaders. *The ANNALS of the American Academy of Political and Social Science*, *566*(1), 37–54.
Campbell, R. S. (1983). Patent trends as a technological forecasting tool. *World Patent Information*, *5*(3), 137–143.
Chen, C.-J., Huang, Y.-F., & Lin, B.-W. (2012). How firms innovate through R&D internationalization? An S-curve hypothesis. *Research Policy*, *41*(9), 1544–1554.
Cho, R. L.-T., Liu, J. S., & Ho, M. H.-C. (2021). The development of autonomous driving technology: Perspectives from patent citation analysis. *Transport Reviews*, *415*, 1–27.
Christensen, C. M. (1992). Exploring the limits of the technology s-curve. Part I: Component technologies. *Production and Operations Management*, *1*(4), 358–366.
Clott, C., & Hartman, B. C. (2022). Do maritime innovation centers produce results?. *WMU Journal of Maritime Affairs*, *Springer Science+Business Media*, *21*(3), 283–326.
Clunie, T., DeFilippo, M., Sacarny, M., & Robinette, P. (2021). Development of a perception system for an autonomous surface vehicle using monocular camera, LIDAR, and marine RADAR. *2021 IEEE International Conference on Robotics and Automation (ICRA),* 14112–14119.
Daim, T., & Suntharasaj, P. (2009). Technology diffusion: Forecasting with bibliometric analysis and Bass model. *Foresight*, *11*(3), 45–55.
de Oliveira, M. N., Mosquéra, L. R., Helena, P., Luiz, A., Bispo, G. D., Vergara, G. F., Saiki, G. M., Neumann, C., & Gonçalves, V. P. (2024). Tracking biofuel innovation: A graph-based analysis of sustainable aviation fuel patents. *Energies*, *1715*, 3683. https://www.mdpi.com/1996-1073/17/15/3683
DNV. (2024). Class guidelines: Autonomous and remotely operated vessels – DNV-CG-0264. https://standards.dnv.com/explorer/document/61F34A49A17F4929A6BE38765C68A19B (Accessed 27 January 2025).
Egger, R., & Yu, J. (2022). A topic modeling comparison between LDA, NMF, Top2Vec, and BERTopic to demystify Twitter posts. *Frontiers in Sociology*, *7*. https://www.frontiersin.org/articles/10.3389/fsoc.2022.886498/full
EMSA. (2024). *CMOROC final report – identification of competences for MASS operators in remote operations centres*. EMSA. https://www.emsa.europa.eu/publications/reports/download/7675/5089/23.html
Foster, R. N. (1986). Innovation: the attacker's advantage. Summit Books.
Ghaffari, M., Aliahmadi, A., Khalkhali, A., Zakery, A., Daim, T. U., & Zamani, M. (2024). Exploring the technological leaders using tire industry patents: A topic modeling approach. *Technology in Society*, Pergamon, *78*, 102664. https://www.sciencedirect.com/science/article/pii/S0160791X24002124
Gomez, J. C., & Moens, M.-F. (2014). A survey of automated hierarchical classification of patents. In G. Paltoglou, F. Loizides and P. Hansen, eds., Professional search in the modern world. Springer. https://doi.org/10.1007/978-3-319-12511-4_11
Grootendorst, M. (2022). BERTopic: Neural topic modeling with a class-based TF-IDF procedure. arXiv preprint arXiv:2203.05794.
Hoyhtya, M., Huusko, J., Kiviranta, M., Solberg, K., & Rokka, J. (2017). Connectivity for autonomous ships: Architecture, use cases, and research challenges. *2017 International Conference on Information and Communication Technology Convergence (ICTC),* 345–350.
Ivanova, A., Butsanets, A., Breskich, V., & Zhilkina, T. (2021). Autonomous shipping means: The main areas of patenting research and development results. *Transportation Research Procedia*, *54*, 793–801.

Karetnikov, V., Ol'Khovik, E., Ivanova, A., & Butsanets, A. (2020). Technology level and development trends of autonomous shipping means. *International Scientific Conference Energy Management of Municipal Facilities and Sustainable Energy Technologies EMMFT, 2019*, 421–432.

Li, X., Fan, M., Zhou, Y., Fu, J., Yuan, F., & Huang, L. (2020). Monitoring and forecasting the development trends of nanogenerator technology using citation analysis and text mining. *Nano Energy*, *71*, 104636.

Lin, Y., Wang, X., Yang, J., & Wang, S. (2024). Core technology topic identification and evolution analysis based on patent text mining – A case study of unmanned ship. *Applied Sciences*, *14*(11), 4661–4661.

Liu, W., Yao, J., & Bi, K. (2024). Identifying emerging technologies to foresee the future of intelligent ships: A machine learning approach to patent data. *International Journal of Technology Policy and Management*, *24*(4), 417–442.

McLaren, C. D., Bruner, M. W. (2022). Citation network analysis. *International Review of Sport and Exercise Psychology*, *15*(1), 179–198.

Meade, N., & Islam, T. (2006). Modelling and forecasting the diffusion of innovation – A 25-year review. *International Journal of Forecasting*, *22*(3), 519–545. https://www.sciencedirect.com/science/article/pii/S0169207006000197

Miwornunyuie, N., Mao, G., Benani, N., Ampah, J. D., & Hunter, J. (2024). Investigating the research and development status and trends of constructed wetlands: A bibliometric and patent analysis. *Journal of Water Process Engineering*, *63*, 105430–105430.

Muller, E., & Peres, R. (2019). The effect of social networks structure on innovation performance: A review and directions for research. *International Journal of Research in Marketing*, *36*(1), 3–19. https://www.sciencedirect.com/science/article/pii/S0167811618300284#s0005

Nelson, R. R., & Winter, S. G. (1982). An evolutionary theory of economic change. Harvard University Press.

Porathe, T., Hoem, Å., Rødseth, Ø., Fjørtoft, K., & Johnsen, S. O. (2018). At least as safe as manned shipping? Autonomous shipping, safety and 'human error'. *Safety and Reliability – Safe Societies in a Changing World*, 417–425.

Porathe, T., Prison, J., & Man, Y. (2014). Situation awareness in remote control centres for unmanned ships. *Proceedings of Human Factors in Ship Design & Operation*, 26–27 (p. 93).

Qiu, Z., & Wang, Z. (2022). Technology forecasting based on semantic and citation analysis of patents: A case of robotics domain. *IEEE Transactions on Engineering Management*, *Institute of Electrical and Electronics Engineers*, *69*(4), 1216–1236.

Ramos, M. A., Utne, I. B., & Mosleh, A. (2019). Collision avoidance on maritime autonomous surface ships: Operators' tasks and human failure events. *Safety Science*, *116*, 33–44.

Rao, K. U., & Kishore, V. V. N. (2010). A review of technology diffusion models with special reference to renewable energy technologies. *Renewable and Sustainable Energy Reviews*, *14*(3), 1070–1078.

Razmjooei, D., Alimohammadlou, M., Ranaei Kordshouli, H.-A., & Askarifar, K. (2023). Industry 4.0 research in the maritime industry: A bibliometric analysis. *WMU Journal of Maritime Affairs*, *22*.

Ringbom, H. (2019). Regulating autonomous ships – Concepts, challenges and precedents. *Ocean Development & International Law*, *50*(2–3), 141–169.

Rødseth, Ø., & Nordahl, H. (2017). Definitions for autonomous merchant ships. 10.13140/RG.2.2.22209.17760.

Stępień, B. (2024). Navigating new waters: IMO's efforts to regulate autonomous shipping. *Chinese Journal of International Law*, *23*(3). https://academic.oup.com/chinesejil/article/23/3/599/7758205

Stokey, N. L. (2020). Technology diffusion. *Review of Economic Dynamics*, *42*, 15–36.
Sun, M., Tong, T., Jiang, M., & Zhu, J. X. (2024). Innovation trends and evolutionary paths of green fuel technologies in maritime field: A global patent review. *International Journal of Hydrogen Energy*, *71*, 528–540.
Wang, F., Yan, F., & Hou, Y. (2007). The influence of network externality on technology diffusion. *2007 International Conference on Wireless Communications, Networking and Mobile Computing*, *IEEE*, 5783–5786.
Wang, H., & Sun, B. (2021). Diffusion mechanism of leading technology in the new energy industry based on the bass model. *Frontiers in Energy Research*, 9.
Wang, J., Hu, R., & Xu, H. (2024). Coupled simultaneous evolution of policy, enterprise innovation awareness, and technology diffusion in multiplex networks. *Mathematics*, *12*(13), 2078.
Wasserman, S., & Faust, K. (1994). Social network analysis: Methods and applications. Cambridge University Press.
WIPO (n.d.) Module 6 – Patent Information [online]. https://www.wipo.int/export/sites/www/sme/en/documents/pdf/ip_panorama_6_learning_points.pdf.
Yang, X., Liu, C., & Lan, J. (2023). Sustainable technology diffusion manufacturing outwards FDI firms: Evidence from China using numerical simulation methods. *Sustainability*, *15*(4), 3108–3108.
Yu, Z. H. (2011). Diffusion channel of generic technology in equipment manufacturing industry. *Advanced Materials Research*, *328–330*, 708–716. https://doi.org/10.4028/www.scientific.net/amr.328-330.708
Yusup, M. F. B. (2024). The role of business incubators in encouraging maritime technology start-up innovation. *Maritime Park: Journal of Maritime Technology and Society*, *3*(3), 158–162.
Zhang, Y., Zhang, D., & Jiang, H. (2023). A review of artificial intelligence-based optimization applications in traditional active maritime collision avoidance. *Sustainability*, *15*(18), 13384–13384.

2

CYBERSECURITY RESEARCH ON MARITIME AUTONOMOUS SURFACE SHIPS, UNMANNED AIRCRAFT SYSTEMS, AND CONNECTED AND AUTONOMOUS VEHICLES

Sofie Irene Nygard Branstad, Tae Eun Kim and Are Kristoffer Sydnes

1 Introduction

The potential safety benefits and reduction in human error offered by autonomous transport systems depend on the extent to which the security of underlying information and operational technologies is enhanced to address evolving threat landscapes (Lehto, 2020; Tusher et al., 2022). To enhance cyber safety and security, which prevents unauthorised access that could take control of an operating system and threaten its safe operation, substantial research and development have been carried out in identifying and classifying potential vulnerabilities and cyber risks (Pizzi, 2020) as well as exploring firewalls and cyber-attack countermeasures (Al-Zahrani, 2022; Roopesh, 2024). Maritime autonomous surface ships (MASS), unmanned aircraft systems (UAS) and connected and autonomous vehicles (CAV) represent three major transport sectors. While they clearly operate in different contexts and use distinct operating systems, autonomous ships, aerial drones and autonomous cars rely on many of the same technologies, such as GPS, radar, cameras and sensor systems and, in some cases, communication with remote or ground control centres (Lynch et al., 2023; Kim et al., 2020). Consequently, it might be expected that similar types of threats and attacks could affect these systems and components across industries. However, it remains unclear which aspects of cybersecurity research from other sectors are applicable to autonomous shipping and how these similarities can be operationalised to support cross-sectoral learning.

In an initial review of the current literature, we identified several bibliometric analysis studies. For example, Kim and Schröder-Hinrichs (2025)

DOI: 10.4324/9781003586883-2

carried out a comparative analysis of MASS and autonomous vehicles with particular emphasis on regulatory aspects, Tabish and Chaur-Luh (2024) reviewed cybersecurity challenges in MASS, Tanaji and Roychowdhury (2024) conducted a survey on cybersecurity challenges and mitigation techniques for CAVs, and Manesh and Kaabouch (2019) examined cyber-attacks on unmanned aerial system networks. While bibliometric analyses exist for individual sectors, a comprehensive comparison across these three sectors is not available as of March 2025 to the author's knowledge.

To that end, this chapter begins by conducting three individual bibliometric analyses of research on cybersecurity in autonomous ships, aerial drones and autonomous vehicles, respectively. Following this, a comparative analysis is carried out. The same methods and metrics are applied across all three research domains to highlight both differences and similarities. The results of each analysis, along with the topics addressed in the most cited articles within each industry, serve as the basis for comparing and discussing the implications for future research on cybersecurity in autonomous systems, with a primary focus on autonomous ships.

This chapter has three objectives. The first is to provide an overview of the developments, themes and trends within the literature on cybersecurity in three different industries through a comparative bibliometric analysis of the literature conducted on MASS, UAS and CAV. The second is to identify emerging themes and future research directions. The third is to investigate how autonomous ship cybersecurity can be enhanced by considering perspectives from other industries.

1.1 Definitions

To refer to the three different types of autonomous systems, the acronyms MASS, UAS and CAV will be used throughout. MASS stands for *maritime autonomous surface ship* and refers to "a ship which, to a varying degree, can operate independent of human interaction" (IMO, 2021, p. 3), ranging from decision support to remotely controlled or fully autonomous unmanned ships. UAS is an acronym for *unmanned aircraft system,* a term which encompasses both the unmanned aerial vehicle (UAV), commonly referred to as "drone", and the components that enable its unmanned operation, such as the ground station (ICAO, 2011). CAV refers to *connected and autonomous vehicle* and is a vehicle which partially or fully replaces the human for driving tasks, ranging from driver assistance functions to full automation (Limbasiya et al., 2022), and is often referred to as "driverless cars" or "self-driving cars".

2 Methodology

2.1 Literature Collection

This section addresses how literature was identified, screened and selected for the analysis. The systematic process of collecting relevant literature consisted of four steps: (1) literature search, (2) initial screening, (3) second screening and (4) inclusion, with each step described in more detail below. This method was carried out three separate times to collect literature relevant to MASS, UAS and CAV respectively, as illustrated in Figure 2.1.

2.1.1 Literature Search

Three databases were utilised for the identification and collection of relevant publications: Web of Science, Oria (a Norwegian university library database) and Science Direct. The searches were further restricted to English publications only. To identify publications related to cybersecurity within the specified industry, advanced searches were conducted using a cyber-related term and an industry-specific term, combined with the Boolean operator AND. The three terms "cybersecurity", "cybersecurity" and "cyber risk" were combined with the Boolean operator OR in all three industry-specific searches. For MASS, the terms "autonomous ship", "autonomous surface ship" and

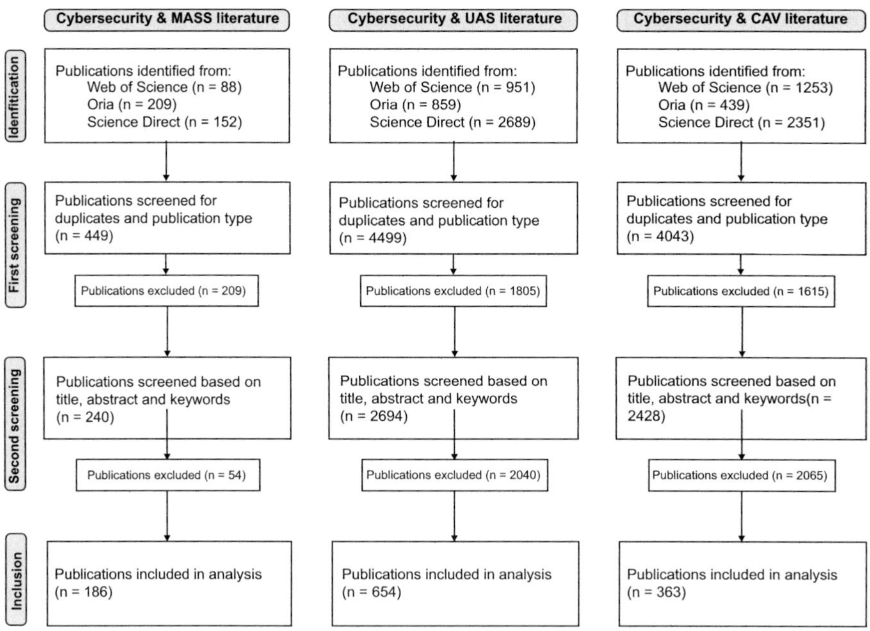

FIGURE 2.1 Literature collection process for all three industries

"autonomous surface vessel" were used. For UAS, the terms "unmanned aerial vehicle", "unmanned aircraft system" and "drone" were utilised, while for CAV the terms were "autonomous vehicle", "self-driving car" and "driverless car". For example, in the Science Direct database, the search for literature on cybersecurity in autonomous ships was conducted as *("cyber-security" OR "cyber security" OR "cyber risk") AND ("autonomous ship" OR "autonomous surface ship" OR "autonomous surface vessel").*

2.1.2 First Screening

The next step consisted of screening the identified publications against a set of surface-level criteria. Duplicates were removed, forming a significant portion of publications due to the use of multiple databases. Publications that were not of an article type (e.g. books or conference papers) were also removed, as were those publications marked as articles but clearly belonging to a newspaper rather than an academic journal. This first screening reduced the number of publications to a more manageable amount for further consideration.

2.1.3 Second Screening

The second screening consisted of a more thorough review of the remaining articles based on their relevance to the topic at hand. The title and, if necessary, the keywords and abstract were reviewed to ensure that each publication was relevant to both cybersecurity and the autonomous system in question.

2.1.4 Inclusion

For each industry, the remaining articles deemed relevant were retained in a database for further analysis. The amount of relevant literature for each sector was considerably different: 186 articles were identified for MASS, 654 for UAS and 363 for CAV.

2.2 Bibliometric Analysis

The selection of suitable bibliometric analysis methods was based on the purpose of the chapter, which was to explore the trends and themes of the literature rather than the authors and institutions within the industries. Four different analysis methods were used, with the open-source software VOSviewer employed for the last three analyses:

1 Year-wise distribution of publications: Using the publication year of the identified articles, starting with the earliest year of publication in the data.

2 Percentage of publications by country: Number of co-authored publications by country, using fractional counting, including countries with a minimum of one publication.
3 Keyword co-occurrence network analysis: Number of occurrences and co-occurrences of keywords in publications, using fractional counting, merging similar keywords.
4 Keyword co-occurrence publication analysis: Average publication year of articles containing each keyword, using fractional counting and merging similar keywords

Further, to complement the analysis with qualitative insights, the three most cited articles from each sector were selected from the screened articles to represent their respective fields and reviewed in depth.

3 Results

3.1 Year-Wise Distribution of Publications

Figure 2.2 depicts the number of published articles per year for each of the industries. What is evident from Figure 2.2 is that research in all three sectors is on the rise, although the MASS literature appears to have flattened out between 2023 and 2024. For UAS, the yearly rise in studies on cybersecurity in UAS is the most evident, followed by research on connected and autonomous vehicles. The amount of literature related to cybersecurity in UAS is

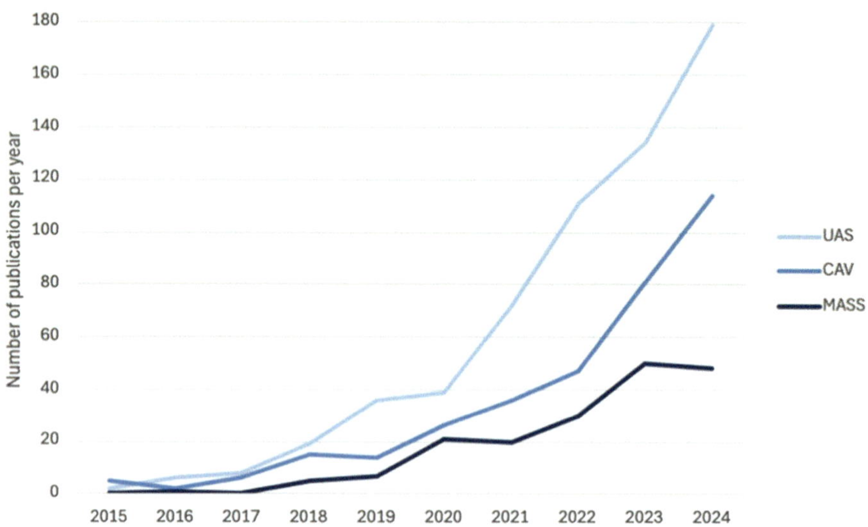

FIGURE 2.2 Year-wise distribution of publications by industry

more than three times that of the literature on MASS, while the CAV research output is about twice the size of the MASS literature.

This is not surprising considering that drones are already a consumer-grade commercial craft and autonomous cars are slowly being implemented on the roads in certain locations (Scanlon et al., 2021), while unmanned ships are still in a trial phase with regulatory gaps (Kim and Schröder-Hinrichs, 2021).

3.2 Leading Countries

In addition to illustrating which countries produce the most publications regarding a topic, the overview of the leading countries within a research field can indicate where the innovation hubs are located, who is most likely to influence international regulations or policies, and who is prioritising and investing most heavily in these industries. As indicated in Figure 2.3, Norway accounts for 20% of the research output regarding cybersecurity in MASS, with England second and China third. These three countries combined make up 43% of research in this field. The USA is the leading country in both UAS and CAV cybersecurity research, while China is second in both industries. However, they diverge at their third most publishing country; Saudi Arabia is a major player in the UAS industry, while England makes up a significant share of the publication outputs for CAVs.

3.3 Research Topics and Communities

3.3.1 MASS

In terms of research topics, in the network visualisation of keyword co-occurrences, the size of a node represents the number of occurrences of a keyword. The most frequently occurring keywords in the MASS literature are, unsurprisingly, the two search terms used to collect literature: cybersecurity and autonomous ship. Other keywords occurring frequently are risk

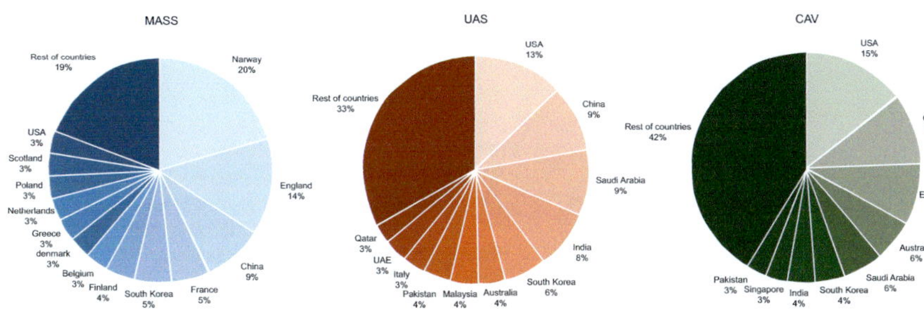

FIGURE 2.3 Percentage of publications by country, separated by industry

assessment, engineering, safety, automation, shipping, maritime industry, maritime safety and navigation. Additionally, this visualisation illustrates how the keywords are linked to each other and how they belong to different categories or clusters, which illustrate specific themes or communities within the research. In Figure 2.4, the network model shows that there are five distinct clusters in the MASS cybersecurity literature.

By studying the composition of keywords in each cluster, the clusters can be given titles that illustrate their research themes, as shown in Figure 2.4 and Table 2.1. The first cluster (red) emerged surrounding the topic of technologies. Aside from generic terms, this largest cluster of the dataset contains keywords focusing on autonomy and the technology involved, such as algorithms, big data, blockchain and internet of things. The second cluster is entitled assessment and modelling cluster (green) and contains keywords focusing more on science, engineering, risk assessment and analysis models such as STPA and Bayesian networks. The third cluster, security and

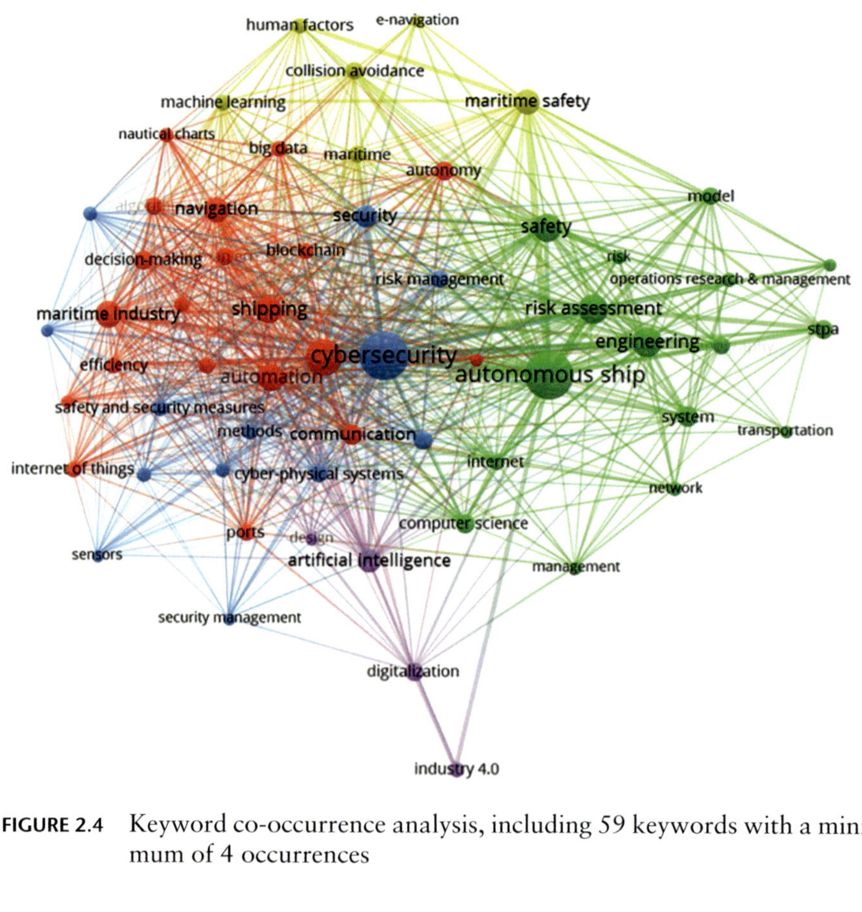

FIGURE 2.4 Keyword co-occurrence analysis, including 59 keywords with a minimum of 4 occurrences

TABLE 2.1 Overview of keyword clusters in MASS literature

Cluster	*No. of keywords*	*Keywords*
Cluster 1 (red): Technology	20	algorithms, automation, autonomous vehicles, autonomy, big data, blockchain, communication, decision-making, efficiency, environmental protection, human error, internet of things, literature reviews, maritime industry, nautical charts, navigation, ports, ship, shipping, trends
Cluster 2 (green): Assessment & modelling	16	autonomous ship, Bayesian network, computer science, engineering, internet, management, model, network, oceanography, operations research and management science, risk, risk assessment, safety, STPA, system, transportation
Cluster 3 (blue) Security and management	13	cyber-physical systems, cybersecurity, cyberterrorism, information systems, methods, passenger ships, remote control, risk management, safety and security measures, security, security management, sensors, software
Cluster 4 (yellow): E-navigation	6	collision avoidance, e-navigation, human factors, machine learning, maritime, maritime safety
Cluster 5 (purple): Artificial intelligence	4	artificial intelligence, design, digitalisation, Industry 4.0

management cluster (blue), focuses primarily on safety and security and their associated management and measures. The fourth cluster (yellow) is centred on e-navigation and collision avoidance, while the fifth (purple), the smallest of the five, contains the keywords *artificial intelligence*, *design*, *digitalisation and Industry 4.0*, which revolves around intelligent systems.

3.3.2 UAS

When it comes to the literature on UAS, as illustrated in Figure 2.5 and Table 2.2, the most common keywords, as evident from the size of their associated nodes, are unmanned aircraft system, wireless communication, safety and security, computer science, cybersecurity, engineering, internet of things and blockchain. This dataset also produced five thematic clusters, which can be categorised into five groups.

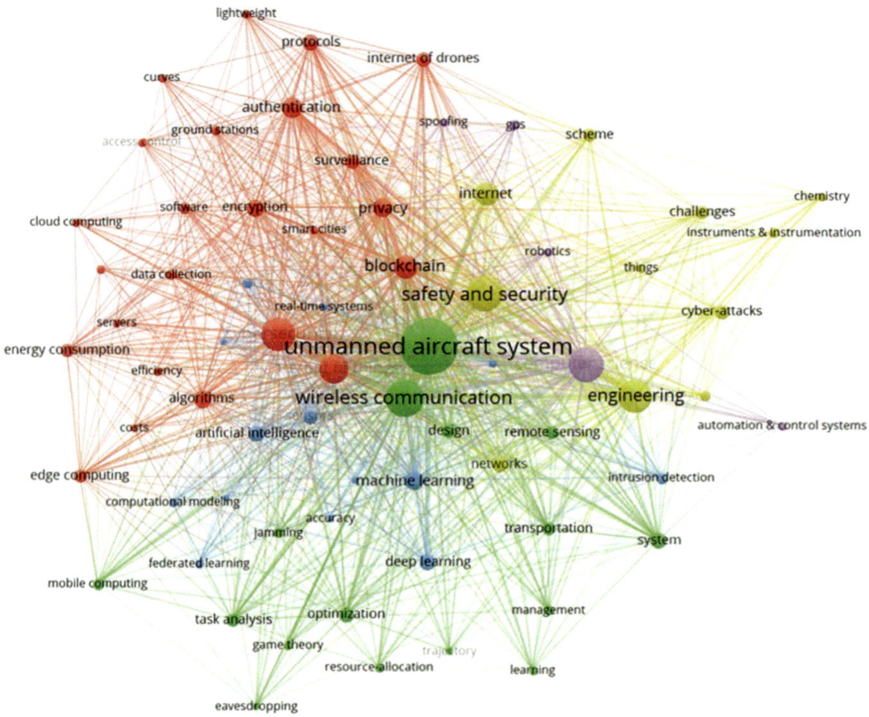

FIGURE 2.5 Keyword co-occurrence analysis, including 70 keywords with a minimum of 10 occurrences

The first cluster (red) focuses on cybersecurity measures and mainly discusses the technologies used for security purposes, such as access control, authentication, blockchain, encryption and protocols. The second cluster (green) is centred on optimal and threat-centric design, which concentrates on elements central to the design of the UAS, such as mobile computing, remote sensing, resource allocation and wireless communication, as well as anticipatory threat-centric notions such as game theory, eavesdropping and jamming. The blue cluster focuses on AI and its subsets, such as machine learning, feature extraction, federated learning and deep learning, as well as monitoring, accuracy and real-time systems. The yellow cluster contains one of the major keywords – *safety* and *security* – along with challenges and cyber-attacks, and the immediate referent objects of security, which are networks and cyber-physical systems. The GPS spoofing cluster (purple) highlights GPS and a critical threat to this system called spoofing, indicating that this is an important cybersecurity concern for the UAS.

TABLE 2.2 Overview of keyword clusters in UAS literature

Cluster	*No. of keywords*	*Keywords*
Cluster 1 (red): Cybersecurity measures	24	access control, algorithms, authentication, blockchain, cloud computing, costs, curves, cybersecurity, data collection, edge computing, efficiency, encryption, energy consumption, ground stations, internet of drones, internet of things, lightweight, performance evaluation, privacy, protocols, servers, smart cities, software, surveillance
Cluster 2 (green): Optimal and threat-centric design	16	design, eavesdropping, game theory, jamming, learning, management, mobile computing, optimisation, remote sensing, resource-allocation, system, task analysis, trajectory, transportation, unmanned aircraft system, wireless communication
Cluster 3 (blue): Artificial intelligence	14	accuracy, artificial intelligence, collaboration, computational modelling, data models, deep learning, denial of service attacks, feature extraction, federated learning, intrusion detection, machine learning, monitoring, real-time systems, sensors
Cluster 4 (yellow): Safety and security	13	challenges, chemistry, cyber-attacks, cyber-physical systems, engineering, instruments and instrumentation, internet, networks, safety and security, scheme, things
Cluster 5 (purple): GPS spoofing	5	automation and control systems, computer science, GPS, robotics, spoofing

3.3.3 CAV

The most common keywords in the CAV literature, as illustrated in Figure 2.6 and Table 2.3, are autonomous vehicle, cybersecurity, engineering, safety and security, computer science, communication, transportation, system, privacy and artificial intelligence. Just as in the two previous cases, the keywords were distributed into five distinct thematic clusters. Judging by the keywords this red cluster is composed of, there is no specific theme. Rather, it

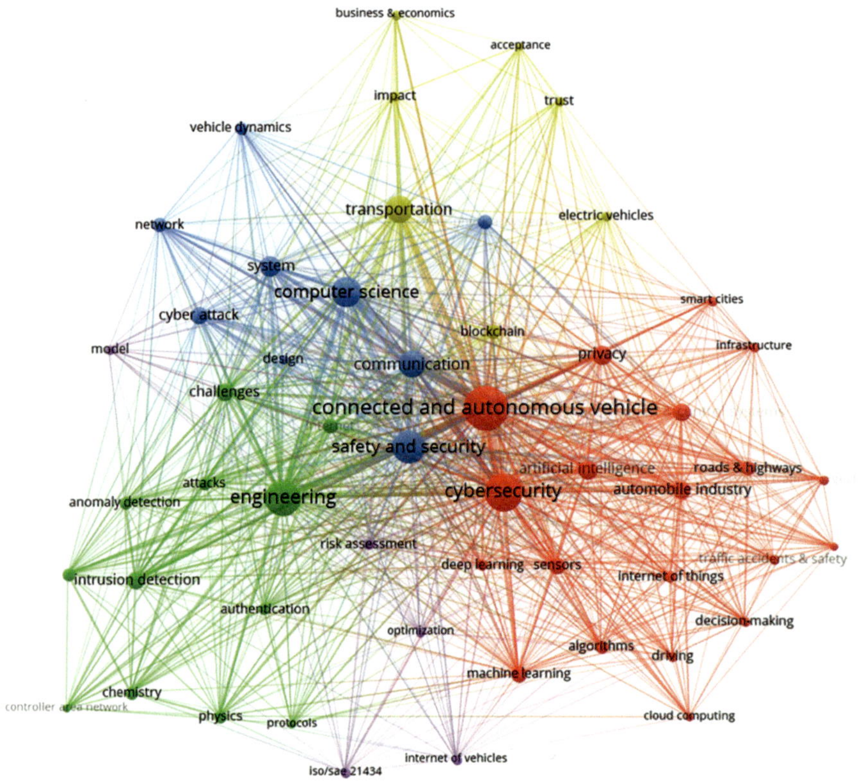

FIGURE 2.6 Keyword co-occurrence analysis, including 53 keywords with a minimum of 8 occurrences

contains keywords related to the technologies used in CAVs, such as artificial intelligence, sensors and the internet of things, as well as CAV-related terms like *smart cities* and *infrastructure*, and important issues such as cybersecurity, privacy and traffic concerns.

This threat detection and measures cluster (green) contains keywords focusing on anomaly and intrusion detection, as well as potential controls such as authentication and protocols. The design cluster (blue) focuses on a blend of both physical aspects and systems/networks, illustrating how a CAV is a cyber-physical system. The user-centric cluster (yellow) consists of keywords related to the human operating the vehicle, such as acceptance and trust, as well as some novel (in this context) technologies such as blockchain and electric vehicles. The risk assessment and management cluster (purple) mentions risk assessment and the road vehicle cybersecurity standard ISO/SAE 21434, along with model, optimisation and internet of vehicles.

TABLE 2.3 Overview of keyword clusters in CAV literature

Cluster	*No. of keywords*	*Keywords*
Cluster 1 (red): General CAV	20	algorithms, artificial intelligence, automation and control systems, automobile industry, cloud computing, connected and autonomous vehicles, cybersecurity, decision-making, deep learning, driving, infrastructure, internet of things, machine learning, privacy, roads and highways, sensors, smart cities, software, traffic accidents and safety, traffic congestion
Cluster 2 (green): Threat detection and measures	12	anomaly detection, attacks, authentication, challenges, chemistry, controller area network, engineering, instruments and instrumentation, internet, intrusion detection, physics, protocols
Cluster 3 (blue): Design	9	communication, computer science, cyber-attack, cyber-physical systems, design, network safety and security, system, vehicle dynamics
Cluster 4 (yellow): User-centric	7	acceptance, blockchain, business and economics, electric vehicles, impact, transportation, trust
Cluster 5 (purple): Risk assessment and management	5	internet of vehicles, ISO/SAE 21434, model, optimisation, risk assessment

3.4 Emerging Research Trends

3.4.1 MASS

The overlay visualisation in VOSviewer plots the co-occurrences of the keywords using the same structure as the network visualisation, but instead of separating them into clusters, the nodes are categorised according to their average year of publication, as shown in Figure 2.7. While the literature in this study ranges in publication year between 2016 and 2025, the average publication years of the keywords primarily range between 2021 and 2023.5, and this forms the basis for the colour range; adjusting the range to cover a larger span of years led to minimal variation in the colours and therefore a nearly indecipherable model. Considering that most of the MASS literature

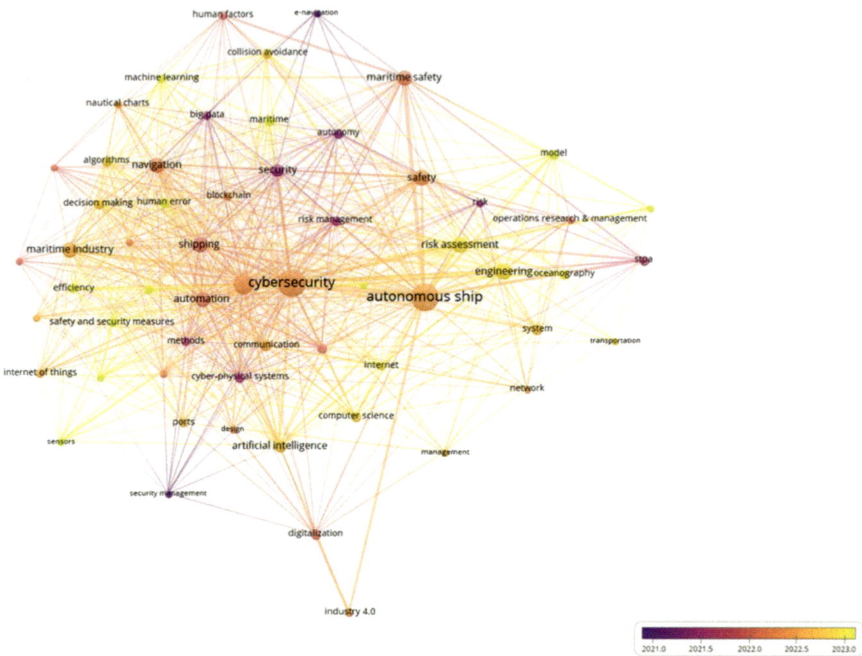

FIGURE 2.7 Average publication year per keyword in MASS literature

has been published within the last five years, it cannot be claimed that any of the keywords are outdated, but some terms can be identified as belonging to more recent publications and therefore also likely to provide some indication of emerging research trends in the literature. Among the keywords in this network, topics such as *machine learning*, *human error*, *safety and security measures*, *cyberterrorism*, *literature reviews* and *sensors* have an average publishing year of 2023 or later. On the other end of the scale, keywords belonging to articles with an average publishing year below 2021.5 include *e-navigation*, *big data*, *cyber-physical systems* and *security management*.

3.4.2 UAS

The UAS literature, as shown in Figure 2.8, displays much of the same behaviour as that of MASS in that there are very few keywords with an average publishing year earlier than 2021 or later than 2024. However, some terms stand out in both directions. *Efficiency*, *accuracy*, *computational modelling*, *data models* and *real-time systems* all have an average publishing year later than 2023.5. Keywords with an average publishing year earlier than 2021 are *cloud computing*, *GPS* and *cyber-physical systems*.

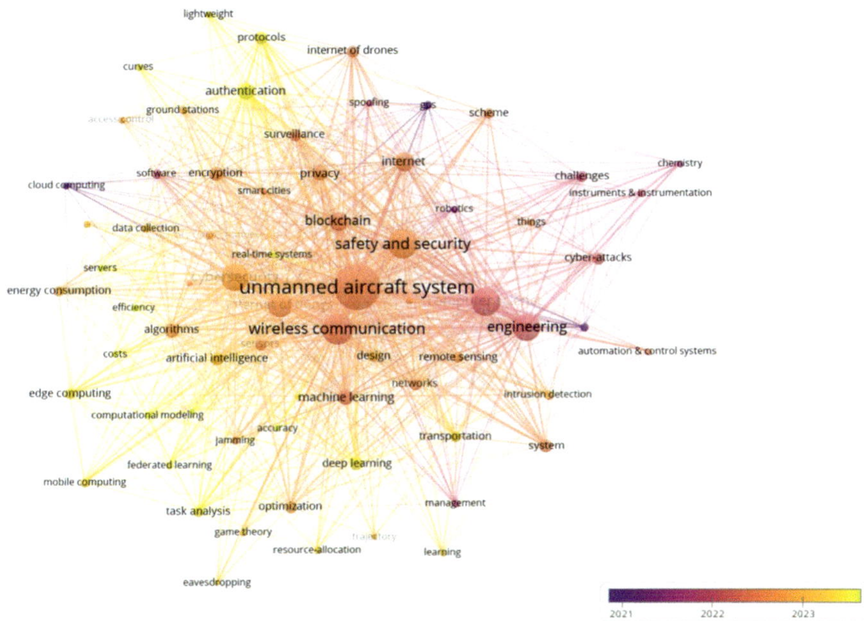

FIGURE 2.8 Average publication year per keyword in UAS literature

3.4.3 CAV

The CAV literature in Figure 2.9 appears to have a higher share of keywords with an average year in the lower range (i.e. 2021 and 2022) compared to the two other industries. This might indicate that questions about these topics have already been resolved, or it might simply suggest that these topics have been a primary focus since the beginning of research on autonomous vehicles. The keywords with the lowest average publishing years are *automobile industry*, *driving*, *traffic congestion*, *privacy*, and *roads and highways*, all with an average below 2021.5. On the other hand, keywords with an average publishing year above 2023 include *ISO/SAE 21434*, *risk assessment*, *protocols* and *anomaly detection.*

3.5 Insights From the Most Cited Articles

Statistical results from the bibliometric analysis can only get us so far in grasping of the essence of the literature. To gain further insight into the research from each industry, the actual contents of the literature must also be considered. This makes it possible to compare and verify the findings of the bibliometric analysis. The three most cited articles from each industry are

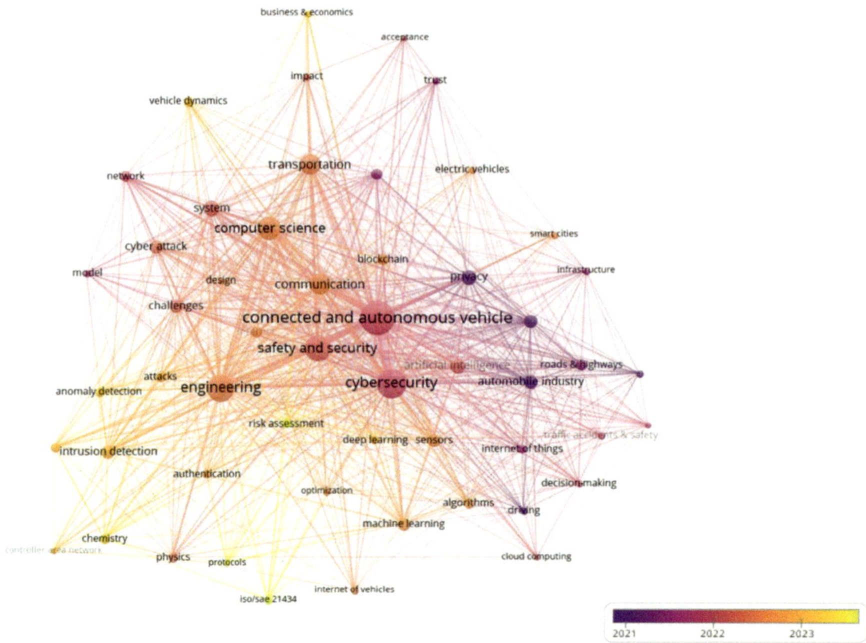

FIGURE 2.9 Average publication year per keyword in CAV literature

reviewed in detail to identify the cybersecurity risks, challenges and proposed recommendations.

3.6 Cybersecurity Concerns and Challenges

In the maritime domain, threats to cybersecurity are considered a major hazard to the operational safety of autonomous ships. In Chang et al. (2021), an expert survey found cyber-attacks to be the second most critical hazard category (after "interaction with manned vessels and detection of objects"), with concerns that hacker attacks can lead to a communication breakdown between the ship and the Shore Control Centre (SCC) or to a failure of the operating system. Bolbot et al. (2020) conducted a cyber risk assessment and found that attacks on the SCC and ship control station to obtain privileged access would have the highest safety implications, followed by malware installation on the situation awareness system and collision avoidance system. Akdag et al. (2022) argue that while manipulation and spoofing attacks on the autonomous ship can be addressed similarly to those of automotive vehicular communications, radio jamming attacks are a somewhat unique threat for the maritime sector and are also difficult to prevent. It is also found that current collaborative collision avoidance algorithms are vulnerable to attacks because they do not consider the presence of malicious actors (Akdag et al., 2022).

In UAS research, cybersecurity is a major topic as these crafts often collect and transmit sensitive or critical data (He et al., 2017). Similarly to MASS, there are concerns regarding the vulnerability of the communication between the vessel and the ground station, and the potential for GPS spoofing (He et al., 2017). Eavesdropping, replay, man-in-the-middle and insider attacks are some of the main threats which impact the confidentiality of the data, while jamming, data tampering or manipulation, backdoor malware and denial of service attacks are threats to the availability and control of the craft itself (Al-Turjman et al., 2020; Tsao et al., 2022). There are also concerns regarding commercial and civilian drone usage, especially that costly security measures might be neglected by individuals and that the drones themselves can be used to conduct cyber-attacks (Al-Turjman et al., 2020; He et al., 2017).

The CAV literature is also rife with concerns about how safe operation can be disrupted by cyber-attacks. Autonomous vehicles are considered vulnerable to various cyber threats, some fairly similar to autonomous ships such as GPS jamming and spoofing, denial of service (DoS) attacks and radar or lidar jamming, while others are more unique to the road transport sector such as attacks on road infrastructure (e.g. signs) or injection of fake messages (Parkinson et al., 2017; Petit and Shladover, 2015). Concerns about the privacy of the human operator are raised in relation to what data is generated and stored about the behaviours and journeys of the driver, and who owns this data, how it is used and who is responsible for securing it (Parkinson et al., 2017; Taeihagh and Lim, 2019). Furthermore, there are key issues regarding how responsibility and control should be passed back and forth between the vehicle system and the driver in case of a cyber-attack and how (and to what extent) human users should be informed of such situations (Parkinson et al., 2017). While some countries, especially the United States, have begun exploring and addressing cybersecurity risks to autonomous vehicles through regulatory means, there appears to be little regulatory cooperation between countries or at the international level (Taeihagh and Lim, 2019).

3.7 Cybersecurity Recommendations

From the maritime domain, some general recommendations for addressing risks and enhancing cybersecurity are setting up standardised operating procedures, focusing on cybersecurity awareness and training and establishing a public key infrastructure (PKI) for maritime applications (Akdag et al., 2022; Chang et al., 2021). To secure the communication between the ship and the SCC, Bolbot et al. (2020) recommend the use of a secure network and cutting the SCC connection to the internet. To protect the collision avoidance system and situation awareness system from malware, firewalls, intrusion detection and antivirus software should be installed, and it is also recommended that the situation awareness system continuously carries out "sanity checks" or cross-checking of the sensor data it receives (e.g. speed and position) (Bolbot et al., 2020). Because radio jamming attacks at sea are considered difficult to prevent, Akdag et al. (2022) suggest that collaborative collision avoidance algorithms should have an inherently predictable and reliable mode of operation in case of signal interference or blockage.

The cybersecurity recommendations in the UAS literature are often highly technical and specific, focusing primarily on securing communication links. He et al. (2017) suggest encrypting the data and using cryptographic keys to protect the confidentiality of the data in case of an attack, but note that trust set-ups can be challenging to manage in, for example, inter-organisational contexts. Tsao et al. (2022) identify ten different potential security solutions which can defend against multiple threats to flying ad-hoc networks (FANET) but also note that they did not find any solutions for backdoor malware in this context, which signals a critical vulnerability and an area that needs further research. They recommend that FANET security solution design takes into account its limitations instead of relying on mobile or vehicular ad-hoc network characteristics (Tsao et al., 2022). Al-Turjman et al. (2020) suggest applying the software-defined networking (SDN) paradigm to multi-UAV communication – primarily for flexibility purposes, but they argue that it will also mitigate cybersecurity threats by isolating control units and thereby minimising unauthorised access attempts. SDN potentially makes the system more flexible and also helps improve security by keeping the control parts separate, which makes it harder for hackers to break in. However, the implementation of SDN requires numerous measures such as secure information registration and data exchange between drones, operators and ground objects, and advanced facilities for data protection (Al-Turjman et al., 2020).

The CAV cybersecurity recommendations from the selected literature are less developed than the others. To mitigate attacks on sensors, Petit and Shladover (2015) recommend ensuring enough redundancy in the sources of data so that anomalous data from a compromised sensor can be detected by comparing it to the remaining uncorrupted data sources. Authentication is recommended to protect against intrusions and the injection of fake messages, while misbehaviour detection is proposed as a solution to detect internal or unintentional incidents (Parkinson et al., 2017; Petit and Shladover, 2015). Multiple authors suggest adapting technologies from the military domain to protect against jamming and spoofing, although it is unclear how these technologies will be afforded or even accessed for commercial use (Parkinson et al., 2017; Petit and Shladover, 2015). According to Parkinson et al. (2017), DoS attacks will always be a possible threat to CAVs, and it is unclear how to detect these attacks and avoid unwanted consequences. Overall, there appears to be much uncertainty regarding how to address cyber threats. However, more recent publications may have addressed these issues in further depth.

4 Key Findings and Discussion

The bibliometric analysis of literature on cybersecurity of MASS revealed that risk assessment is a frequently occurring term, with STPA and Bayesian networks being two frequently applied analytical methods. Navigation, collision avoidance and sensors are among the systems most frequently mentioned, while artificial intelligence, big data, blockchain and internet of things are the most popular information technologies. Risk assessment and human error appear to be emergent topics found in the most recent articles (2023 or later). Notably, the only cybersecurity threat mentioned frequently is cyberterrorism, while other threats, attack types or malicious actors do not appear in their analysis. Overall, the trend in the MASS literature appears to focus on the technology and system components related to the design, construction and safe operation of these vessels. This is not surprising, considering that autonomous ships are still a recent phenomenon in terms of implementation.

The research on UAS consisted of a much larger body of literature than that of MASS. A larger number of keywords were identified even with twice the occurrence threshold, suggesting a far more developed field of research. Artificial intelligence and its subtypes are a recurring theme which forms a cluster within the network of keywords. With regard to cybersecurity specifically, the most common cyber threats addressed in the literature are eavesdropping, jamming, denial of service attacks and spoofing, the latter particularly related to GPS. More recent trends in the UAS literature appear to be related to topics such as efficiency, accuracy, modelling and real-time systems, indicating that the research is moving away from design and implementation considerations and towards optimisation and advancement.

Within the CAV literature, some of the most frequently occurring keywords are *communication*, *privacy* and *AI*. While no specific threats, attack types or malicious actors were identified in this analysis, the literature was nonetheless concerned with anomaly and intrusion detection as well as security-related measures such as authentication and blockchain. Additionally, although human factors or human error were not explicitly mentioned, important related concepts such as trust and acceptance appear to play an essential role. Several articles mentioned risk assessment and ISO/SAE 21434, which is a standard that specifies cybersecurity risk management engineering requirements for the electrical and electronic systems in road vehicles.

Some themes were common across all three industries. Artificial intelligence and its related subtypes formed a keyword cluster in the MASS and UAS literature and were a frequently occurring keyword in the CAV research. However, there was little mention of artificial intelligence in the most cited articles in either industry, making it difficult to draw further conclusions. Risk assessment and risk/security management were also important themes, forming clusters within all three keyword networks. It is worth noting that in the MASS literature, security/risk *management* appears to be a somewhat older term, while risk *assessment* is more frequently applied in recent publications. This may suggest that research is evaluating new risks that will, in turn, become the focus of future studies of risk management.

4.1 Implications of Cybersecurity Threats and Challenges

One of the main findings of this analysis is that the three industrial sectors appear to face many of the same cybersecurity threats, such as GPS spoofing, jamming, DoS, data manipulation or theft and disruption to communication links. This has two main implications. The first is that the three industries share a similar cyber threat landscape which, in turn, differs somewhat from the broader cyber threat landscape. According to ENISA (2024), the current prime threats to cybersecurity in the EU are ransomware, malware and social engineering, followed by data breaches and leaks, DoS and disinformation. While there are some similarities, spoofing, jamming and other disruptions to communication links are threats of a cyber-physical nature and appear to be a much larger concern for autonomous systems than in the general cybersecurity domain. This means that for academics, policymakers or regulators, it might be necessary to redefine what the term *cybersecurity* means when discussing these types of domain-specific systems rather than relying on mainstream approaches.

The second implication is that, as the threats or attack types are so similar across industries, low-level actors with limited resources, such as script kiddies, might use programmes or techniques that have been successfully weaponised by others for one type of autonomous system and leverage them against another. The threats can be highly transferable and may diffuse across the three industries. To prevent this, the MASS, UAS and CAV industries might benefit from a shared reporting system or database in which known vulnerabilities, threats or attacks are reported when discovered so that pre-emptive action can be taken. However, the successful implementation of this system hinges on companies' willingness to share known vulnerabilities. This can be a challenge, especially in competitive environments rich in trade secrets, such as those analysed in this study. As a consequence, policy or regulatory incentives and oversight may be required to realise the opportunities for achieving common gains in the face of the joint threats posed by cybersecurity.

4.2 Future Research Areas on MASS

The bibliometric analysis provided an overview of the current state and trends of research for each industry sector. This can aid in informing and directing future research, as well as outlining potential avenues for cross-industry learning. Both the UAS and CAV literature appear to have more developed research on cybersecurity threats and measures than MASS, the former regarding attack types and the latter regarding intrusion detection, which can serve as useful reference points for future MASS cybersecurity research. Furthermore, the road vehicle standard ISO/SAE 21434 might provide examples of how a standard should be developed for equivalent or similar MASS systems.

In one of the most cited MASS articles, Akdag et al. (2022) argued that autonomous ships could address manipulation and spoofing attacks on the autonomous ship in a similar way to the automotive industry. However, it was unclear from the reviewed CAV research which measures were considered effective for dealing with such attacks, except for a suggestion to adapt military-grade anti-spoofing technology (SAASM) (Petit and Shladover, 2015). On the other hand, it can be expected that more research and testing have been conducted on cybersecurity for autonomous vehicles since this review. Future researchers wishing to explore how to prevent these types of attacks on MASS might benefit from examining more recent CAV research and reports.

Another issue that requires further research is the role of human factors in cybersecurity. In the MASS literature, human error was identified as an emerging theme, and although it appeared in the same cluster as the term *decision-making*, it remains somewhat unclear from this study's findings what role human error plays in cybersecurity on autonomous ships. Furthermore, in the UAS research, human factors or human error did not even appear as common keywords, nor were they discussed to any notable extent in the most cited articles. Considering the relative maturity of the UAS research, this raises the question of why human factors are not addressed in the current literature. Is it because it has already been addressed and is not considered important to cybersecurity by research outside the scope of this study, or is it because it has not been explored thoroughly by science? On the other hand, the CAV literature has raised the concepts of trust and important questions regarding the shared responsibility and control between the operator and the autonomous system. These general issues are critical to all autonomous systems and may be addressed in the context of each of the three autonomous systems.

5 Conclusion

While the literature suggests that the three systems face many of the same threats to cybersecurity, the UAS and CAV literature appear to have developed both further and for longer than MASS. UAS cybersecurity research hints at progressing towards optimalisation rather than focusing on implementation-level issues, while CAV research shows promise in human factors such as trust and acceptance. There remains potential to combine research across the different industries, particularly to explore how autonomous systems can withstand common and inevitable attacks such as spoofing, jamming and DoS. Additionally, there appears to be untapped potential in research on the relationship between human factors and cybersecurity in autonomous systems, especially for MASS and UAS. Based on the observed increasing publication trends within all three industries, it is likely that new discoveries will be abundant in the coming years, and intentional, directed efforts to share and collaborate on research, solutions and regulations can help all three industries reap these benefits.

References

Akdag, M., Solnor, P., & Johansen, T. A. (2022). Collaborative collision avoidance for maritime autonomous surface ships: A review [Review]. *Ocean Engineering*, *250*, 17, Article 110920. https://doi.org/10.1016/j.oceaneng.2022.110920

Al-Turjman, F., Abujubbeh, M., Malekloo, A., & Mostarda, L. (2020). UAVs assessment in software-defined IoT networks: An overview. *Computer Communications*, *150*, 519–536. https://doi.org/10.1016/j.comcom.2019.12.004

Al-Zahrani, A. (2022). Assessing and proposing countermeasures for cyber-security attacks. *International Journal of Advanced Computer Science and Applications*, *13*(1).

Bolbot, V., Theotokatos, G., Boulougouris, E., & Vassalos, D. (2020). A novel cyber-risk assessment method for ship systems. *Safety Science*, *131*, 104908. https://doi.org/10.1016/j.ssci.2020.104908

Chang, C.-H., Kontovas, C., Yu, Q., & Yang, Z. (2021). Risk assessment of the operations of maritime autonomous surface ships. *Reliability Engineering & System Safety*, *207*, 107324. https://doi.org/10.1016/j.ress.2020.107324

ENISA. (2024). ENISA threat landscape 2024. ENISA. https://www.enisa.europa.eu/publications/enisa-threat-landscape-2024

He, D. J., Chan, S., & Guizani, M. (2017). Drone-assisted public safety networks: The security aspect. *IEEE Communications Magazine*, *55*(8), 218–224. https://doi.org/10.1109/mcom.2017.1600799cm

ICAO. (2011). Unmanned Aircraft Systems (UAS) (ICAO Cir 328 AN/190). ICAO. https://skybrary.aero/bookshelf/icao-circular-328-unmanned-aircraft-systems-uas

IMO. (2021). Outcome of the regulatory scoping exercise for the use of Maritime Autonomous Surface Ships (MASS) (MSC.1/Circ.1638). IMO. https://wwwcdn.imo.org/localresources/en/MediaCentre/HotTopics/Documents/MSC.1-Circ.1638%20-%20Outcome%20Of%20The%20Regulatory%20Scoping%20ExerciseFor%20The%20Use%20Of%20Maritime%20Autonomous%20Surface%20Ships.%20(Secretariat).pdf

Kim, M., Tae-Hwan, J., Byongug, J., & Park, H.-S. (2020). Autonomous shipping and its impact on regulations, technologies, and industries. *Journal of International Maritime Safety, Environmental Affairs, and Shipping*, *4*(2), 17–25. https://doi.org/10.1080/25725084.2020.1779427

Kim, T.E., & Schröder-Hinrichs, J.-U. (2025). Comparative analysis of regulatory focus in Autonomous Vehicles (AVs) and Maritime Autonomous Surface Ships (MASS). In: *Proceedings of the IEEE International Conference on Industrial Engineering and Engineering Management (IEEM)*. Melbourne, Australia.

Kim, T. E., & Schröder-Hinrichs, J. U. (2021). Research developments and debates regarding maritime autonomous surface ship: Status, challenges and perspectives.

New Maritime Business: Uncertainty, Sustainability, Technology and Big Data, 175–197. Springer Nature.

Lehto, M. (2020). Cyber security in aviation, maritime and automotive. In: Diez, P., Neittaanmäki, P., Periaux, J., Tuovinen, T., Pons-Prats, J. (eds) *Computation and Big Data for Transport. Computational Methods in Applied Sciences*, *54*. Springer, Cham. https://doi.org/10.1007/978-3-030-37752-6_2

Limbasiya, T., Teng, K. Z., Chattopadhyay, S., & Zhou, J. Y. (2022). A systematic survey of attack detection and prevention in connected and autonomous vehicles. *Vehicular Communications*, *37*, 23, Article 100515. https://doi.org/10.1016/j.vehcom.2022.100515

Lynch, K. M., Banks, V. A., Roberts, A. P. J., Radcliffe, S., & Plant, K. L. (2023). Maritime autonomous surface ships: Can we learn from unmanned aerial vehicle incidents using the perceptual cycle model? *Ergonomics*, *66*(6), 772–790. https://doi.org/10.1080/00140139.2022.2126896

Manesh, M. R., & Kaabouch, N. (2019). Cyber-attacks on unmanned aerial system networks: Detection, countermeasure, and future research directions. *Computers & Security*, *85*, 386–401.

Parkinson, S., Ward, P., Wilson, K., & Miller, J. (2017). Cyber threats facing autonomous and connected vehicles: Future challenges. *IEEE Transactions on Intelligent Transportation Systems*, *18*(11), 2898–2915. https://doi.org/10.1109/tits.2017.2665968

Petit, J., & Shladover, S. E. (2015). Potential cyberattacks on automated vehicles. *IEEE Transactions on Intelligent Transportation Systems*, *16*(2), 546–556. https://doi.org/10.1109/tits.2014.2342271

Pizzi, G. (2020). Cybersecurity and its integration with safety for transport systems: Not a formal fulfillment but an actual commitment. *Transportation Research Procedia*, *45*, 250–257.

Roopesh, M. (2024). Cybersecurity solutions and practices: Firewalls, intrusion detection/prevention, encryption, multi-factor authentication. *Academic Journal on Business Administration, Innovation & Sustainability*, *4*(3), 37–52.

Scanlon, J. M., Kusano, K. D., Daniel, T., Alderson, C., Ogle, A., & Victor, T. (2021). Waymo simulated driving behavior in reconstructed fatal crashes within an autonomous vehicle operating domain. *Accident Analysis & Prevention*, *163*, 106454.

Taeihagh, A., & Lim, H. S. M. (2019). Governing autonomous vehicles: Emerging responses for safety, liability, privacy, cybersecurity, and industry risks. *Transport Reviews*, *39*(1), 103–128. https://doi.org/10.1080/01441647.2018.1494640

Tanaji, B. A., & Roychowdhury, S. (2024). A survey of cybersecurity challenges and mitigation techniques for connected and autonomous vehicles. *IEEE Transactions on Intelligent Vehicles,* 1–18. https://doi.org/10.1109/TIV.2024.3493938

Tsao, K. Y., Girdler, T., & Vassilakis, V. G. (2022). A survey of cyber security threats and solutions for UAV communications and flying ad-hoc networks. *Ad Hoc Networks*, *133*, 39, Article 102894. https://doi.org/10.1016/j.adhoc.2022.102894

Tusher, H. M., Munim, Z. H., Notteboom, T. E., Kim, T. E., & Nazir, S. (2022). Cyber security risk assessment in autonomous shipping. *Maritime Economics & Logistics*, *24*(2), 208–227.

Tabish, N., & Chaur-Luh, T. (2024). Maritime autonomous surface ships: A review of cybersecurity challenges, countermeasures, and future perspectives. *IEEE Access*, *12*, 17114–17136.

3

HUMAN OVERSIGHT IN SHIP AUTONOMY

Koen van de Merwe and Erik Veitch

1 Introduction

Maritime autonomous surface ships (MASS) are increasingly adopted as compelling ways to promote greener shipping, enhance the attractiveness of maritime careers, mitigate the impacts of piracy and improve safety records. Over the last decade, the industry has worked towards developing technologies in which autonomous ships execute their voyages without the need for human involvement, including performing collision avoidance. This way, the industry aims to enable alternative and efficient ship designs, explore new ways of operating, facilitate the use of alternative energy sources and potentially remove seafarers from hazardous operations altogether (Kretschmann et al., 2017; Kurt & Aymelek, 2022). To enable this, proposed ship concepts typically use technologies that can recognise objects in the ship's vicinity, create a world model of the ship's surroundings, estimate collision risks with charted and uncharted objects, determine avoidance manoeuvres in accordance with the collision regulations, and implement these safely and efficiently (Chang et al., 2024; Kim et al., 2022). In these systems, components employing AI play an important role.

For example, object-recognition systems deploy machine learning algorithms trained on large image datasets to detect uncharted objects in the ship's surroundings (Brandsæter et al., 2020). Also, machine learning algorithms trained on traffic patterns for a specific area may be used to predict the future path of target vessels as input to collision avoidance manoeuvring. However, although such systems excel at recognising patterns in data, they may easily be misled (Akhtar & Mian, 2018), do not have an understanding of what is possible in the world (Littman et al., 2021) and lack a model of

DOI: 10.4324/9781003586883-3

causation (Pearl & Mackenzie, 2018). Consequently, these systems may be brittle in the face of novel situations, have limited ability to predict how their avoidance manoeuvres might change the overall traffic situation, or understand what may have happened under different circumstances. Therefore, due to the safety-critical nature of maritime navigation, such systems must exhibit high reliability and robustness across a broad range of scenarios and situations. Careful design, development, implementation, management and operation are therefore necessary when deploying novel autonomous ship concepts in dynamic and real-world environments. Considering this uncertainty, humans are poised to play a critical role here.

The recently introduced European Union's (EU) AI Act stipulates expectations regarding the role of humans in the supervision of AI-enabled systems (European Commission, 2024). For example, the act states that "high-risk AI systems should be designed and developed in such a way that natural persons can oversee their functioning" (European Commission, 2024, p. 21). Furthermore, humans should be able to "correctly interpret the high-risk AI system's output", "decide, in any particular situation, not to use the high-risk AI system" and "intervene in the operation of the high-risk AI system or interrupt the system through a 'stop' button or a similar procedure that allows the system to come to a halt in a safe state" (European Commission, 2024, pp. 60, 61). Similarly, preliminary results from the development of the International Maritime Organisation (IMO) MASS code also point towards the need to appoint a human master (onboard the ship or elsewhere) to intervene when necessary (IMO, 2023). Although work is ongoing to understand the implications of the EU AI Act on the European maritime industry (Lee et al., 2024; Schütte, 2024), this should make it clear that humans are expected to play an important role in overseeing the functioning and performance of autonomous ships.

Overseeing autonomous ships implies interpreting information provided by the system, based on which people can make a judgement about its performance. This ability, in turn, depends primarily on the operators' effectiveness in interpreting the information provided by the autonomous ship and other sources. Enabling human operators to perform effective and meaningful oversight of MASS implies providing a supportive environment that allows operators to understand the system's capacities and limitations, monitor its operations, correctly interpret its output, intervene in the system's operations, or otherwise decide not to use it (European Commission, 2024). In other words, providing oversight of MASS operations entails interpreting potentially complex AI-enabled systems by human operators. In addition, the black-box nature of these systems complicates their monitoring and prediction compared to "traditional" control systems and makes them difficult to understand and predict (Endsley, 2023; Hollnagel, 2012; Loyola-González,

2019). It therefore follows that exerting meaningful human oversight of autonomous ships requires ensuring that system design features support the supervisor's cognitive processes needed to perform this task.

This chapter discusses relevant themes from the literature on human oversight and addresses pertinent topics concerning the cognitive aspects related to this task. This includes practical guidance on implementing appropriate design solutions for the remote supervision of autonomous ships, as well as avoiding pitfalls. The chapter concludes with a discussion of the consequences of continuous technological advancements and how these may shape new ways in which humans and autonomous systems interact.

2 Principles for Interacting With Autonomous Systems

Understanding the consequences of introducing systems that perform tasks previously carried out by humans has long interested scholars (Endsley, 2017; Fitts, 1951; Licklider, 1960; Parasuraman & Riley, 1997; Rasmussen, 1986; Sheridan & Verplank, 1978). In engineering, the objective of automation systems is typically to improve a process by supporting or substituting human behaviour (perceived as unreliable) with automation (perceived as reliable). Although tremendous improvements in automation have been achieved over the years, discrepancies may still exist between the intended design of a system and its actual implementation.

Roseborough acutely described the challenge engineers face when developing control and safety systems (see Figure 3.1) (Roseborough, 1988; Sheridan, 2002). In a complex control system, it is typically assumed that the controlled process cannot be fully modelled, nor can its optimal state be accurately defined. Therefore, engineers typically rely on human operators to complement any limitations of the system. However, given the complexity of the controlled process, operators may require decision support from the system in performing this task. To provide operators with reliable decision support, a system function is needed that has a relatively complete model of the controlled process. Given that this conflicts with the initial assumption, such systems are incomplete in themselves (and if they weren't, a human operator might not have been needed in the first place). Therefore, Roseborough (1988) argued that the value of human operators lies in their use of supplementary information, knowledge and experience, that is, information not explicitly modelled in the system, which allows them to decide when to use, adjust, or not use the supervised system. Furthermore, control systems may not be able to compute the optimal state of the system and therefore require humans to do so, considering the operational context. Finally, human sensory abilities, such as hearing, motion sensing and sight, are valuable complementary assets in a safety-critical operational context where only limited automated functions are yet available.

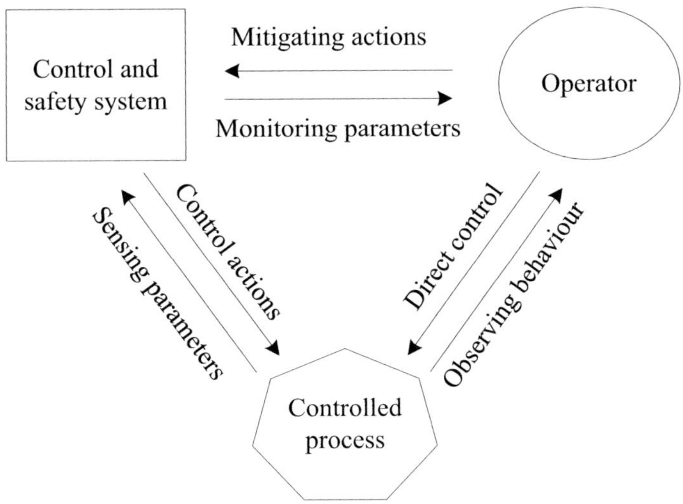

FIGURE 3.1 The interaction between a controlled process, a control and safety system and a human operator

In the autonomous and remotely operated shipping context, human oversight is thus foreseen to play an important role in enabling operations for ships with reduced manning (e.g. on periodically or completely unmanned bridges). This implies that supervisors are required to "follow along" with the operations of the ship, understand how the system is performing in its operational context and can take action when this is needed. For example, if an autonomous collision avoidance system encounters a situation outside, or at the limits of its operational design domain, the supervisor may be required to take an intervening action (Rødseth et al., 2021). This means that supervisors should be able to evaluate the sufficiency of the system's awareness of the situation, the adequacy of its decisions and the satisfactoriness of the system's execution of its plan. Here, the knowledge, skills, training and experience of the supervisor play an important role in interpreting the information provided by the system, in addition to mentally integrating any information provided by independent sources (van de Merwe et al., 2024b).

2.1 Information Processing and Human Oversight

In academic and applied research, oversight is associated with the activities humans perform when interacting with automated or autonomous systems to ensure that system goals are achieved. Human oversight has been extensively studied, and decades of research have culminated in extensive knowledge regarding the psychological aspects involved in this.

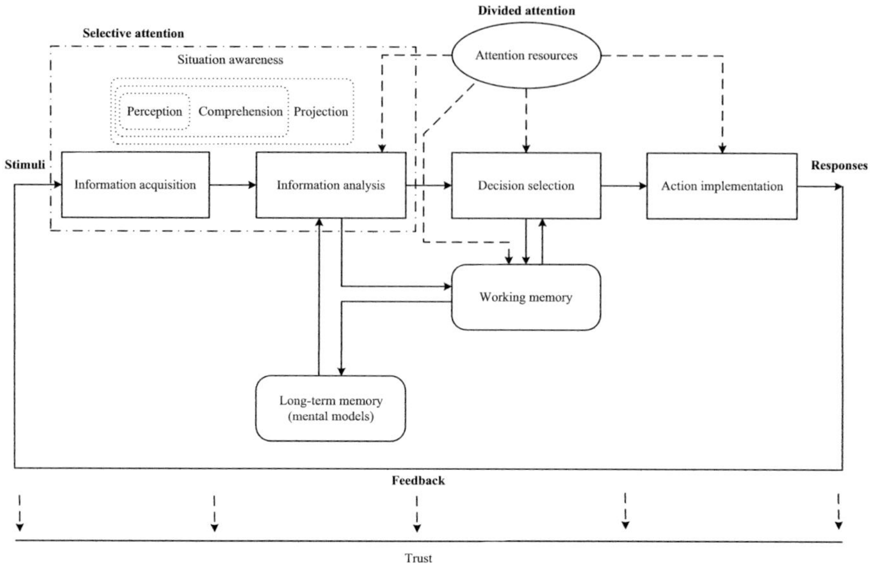

FIGURE 3.2 Human information processing model

Source: Adapted from Lee et al. (2017) and Parasuraman et al. (2000).

Figure 3.2 depicts a simple model of human information processing where the roles of working memory, long-term memory and attentional resources are crucial factors (Lee et al., 2017; Parasuraman et al., 2000). Working memory refers to the transient and vulnerable form of information storage that is capable of retaining a limited amount of information, such as images, symbols and locations (Wickens & Carswell, 2021). Due to the finite capacity of working memory, maintaining information active in working memory while minimising distraction from competing elements is essential for achieving and sustaining performance (Haberlandt, 1999). The manipulation of information elements and the prevention of their decay requires attentional resources and is what makes such tasks mentally demanding. Given that attentional resources are similarly limited, dividing attention between multiple activities is mentally taxing (Kahneman, 1973). Consequently, as demands increase, the quality of action execution may deteriorate. As a coping strategy, the adoption of more efficient, resource-conserving methods and the prioritisation of tasks may be chosen (Hancock et al., 2021). However, when demands exceed capacity and coping strategies are exhausted altogether, performance will ultimately degrade (Wickens, 2008). These mechanisms underscore the importance of the underlying memory and attentional processes within dynamic environments such as the (remote) supervision of autonomous ships.

2.2 Mental Models, Situation Awareness and Trust

When operators interact with and oversee control and safety systems, they require some kind of understanding of how the system works to supervise it correctly. Likewise, understanding the controlled process is important to grasp what is being controlled. This internal representation of the external world is called a "mental model". Mental models are conceptual analogues of the external world, enabling its understanding and prediction (Mogford, 1997) and "mechanisms whereby humans are able to generate descriptions of system purpose and form, explanations of system functioning and observed system states, and predictions of future system states" (Rouse & Morris, 1986). Mental models reside in long-term memory, are generated through training and experience, and serve as an essential mechanism in humans' ability to filter and integrate substantial amounts of information, comprehend their meaning and anticipate their future implications. In the context of autonomous shipping, supervisors will require mental models of the environment in which their vessels operate, the systems with which they interact, and the autonomous ships they are overseeing. Furthermore, mental models shape the perception of information and allow supervisors to generate an awareness of "what is going on" in the situation, that is, situation awareness (SA). SA is defined as "the perception of the elements in the environment within a volume of time and space, the comprehension of their meaning, and the projection of their status in the near future" (Endsley, 1988, 1995). Within this framework, SA can be understood in terms of the knowledge produced and the processes used to generate that knowledge, which are essential for decision-making and action execution (Endsley, 1995; van Doorn et al., 2017).

There is a close relationship between SA and mental models. In complex and dynamic environments, human perceptual limitations severely constrain the amount of information that can be perceived, comprehended and projected. To assist operators in making sense of this vast information flow, mental models are crucial for directing attention to pertinent information, developing an understanding of this information, and projecting it into the future, that is, building SA. This means that a proper mental model helps operators know what information to look for, how to interpret it, and decide what to do with it. For example, in the context of autonomous collision avoidance systems, operators need to understand the system's limitations, capabilities, reliability, functioning and logic (Endsley, 2023). This way, operators will be able to assess the performance of the system given its current operational context or determine whether extra mitigating actions are needed. Hence, mental models and SA are the mechanisms that support operators in actively perceiving, making sense of and predicting the status of the system, thereby facilitating sound decision-making. Furthermore, understanding how the system works, experiencing the activities of the system over time, and recognising the system's abilities and limitations allow operators to know when to trust the system and when not to.

Trust is a central construct when humans interact with autonomous systems. Trust can be defined as "the attitude that an agent will help achieve an individual's goals in a situation characterized by uncertainty and vulnerability" (Lee & See, 2004, p. 51). Trust is important because humans tend to rely on systems that they trust and reject systems that they do not trust. In other words, systems that are trustworthy are more likely to be used compared to untrustworthy systems. In many ways, trust between humans and systems is similar to trust between humans; it develops when humans are reliable and honest, disappears quickly when they are let down or betrayed, and is slow to redevelop.

As depicted in Figure 3.2, trust is not identified as a component of the human information processing system but rather emerges as a result of interactions between humans and systems in their operational context (Chiou & Lee, 2023; Hancock et al., 2023). That is, trust emerges when humans interact with systems and can evaluate their reliability. Not surprisingly, systems that are reliable tend to be trusted more than less reliable systems. In terms of human oversight, this implies that trust is an important construct to establish and maintain, as it directly relates to the extent to which autonomous systems are used appropriately in their operational context.

3 Interacting With Autonomously Operated Ships

When interacting with and overseeing autonomous ships, the ability of supervisors to adequately perform their tasks depends on the responsibilities assigned to them, the operating conditions in which these are performed, and the design and characteristics of the systems with which they interact. As autonomous ships continue to develop, the characteristics of introduced concepts also evolve. Considering IMO's taxonomy (IMO, 2018), the highest degree of autonomation (full autonomy, independent of human involvement) remains visionary for the present. Still, the industry is actively working on creating products that fit one or more of the first three categories. For example, products are being developed that implement collision and grounding avoidance (CAGA) systems on conventional ships as a decision support system for navigators (Avikus, 2024), may allow for periodically unmanned or unattended bridge operations (ABB, 2018), or even enable unmanned ship operations with supervision from remote operation centres (Massterly, 2023). Although such solutions help the industry to meet its goals, the consequences for the supervisory role – be it from the bridge or from a remote operating station – are under continued investigation (van de Merwe et al., 2024b). This means that, based on the preceding discussion of the cognitive aspects related to supervision, several aspects are important to consider in relation to these developments.

3.1 Explaining How the System Works

As supervisors are tasked with providing oversight of autonomous systems, their mental models of the ship in its operating environment play an important role in their ability to make sound decisions regarding the system's performance. Earlier, it was stated that supervisors, through experience, construct working models of the system to assist in comprehension and projection of system states. Additionally, formal training and instruction assist supervisors in creating initial mental models of the systems and ships they interact with (Mueller et al., 2019). However, a number of elements related to ship autonomy challenge operators in building mental models.

AI systems adopting machine learning algorithms are typically classified as "black box" models and are inherently challenging to understand (Loyola-González, 2019). Also, machine learning uses statistical methods to learn from data and generalise to unseen data (Alpaydin, 2020). For example, an AI-enabled system may be trained on very large datasets consisting of pictures of sailboats, thereby enabling camera-based detection of sailing vessels in real-life operations. However, considering the probabilistic nature of machine learning algorithms, there is a degree of uncertainty associated with object classification (Zhang et al., 2022), and while the algorithm may perform well in detecting sailing vessels, it may perform poorly in detecting kite-surfers. This means that, from a supervisor's point of view, the performance of the detection system may vary unpredictably depending on the objects and circumstances encountered. Combined, these issues make it challenging for a supervisor to describe how the system is constructed, explain how it works and predict its functioning (Rouse & Morris, 1986). This means that developing accurate mental models is difficult and may require more time, experience and training for the supervisor to understand how the system performs under different circumstances.

3.2 Understanding What the System Is Doing

SA in the context of autonomous ships means understanding what the ship is doing, why it is doing it and what it will do next, in real time (Endsley, 2017). In contrast to mental models, SA is concerned with the real-time understanding of the decisions and planned actions of the system within its operating environment. For supervisors of autonomous systems, SA is essential, as it forms the basis for monitoring strategies and for deciding when and how to intervene.

Considering that ship navigation is an activity performed in a continuously evolving dynamic context, ship-to-ship encounters may occur at any moment.

In terms of navigation, transitioning from conventional to supervised collision avoidance has consequences for the locus of decisions and actions associated with this task. In conventional collision avoidance, decisions and avoidance actions are performed by the navigator. In supervised autonomous shipping, these are now outsourced to an AI-enabled system. In turn, the supervisor is left with the task of overseeing the system's decision-making and actions. Earlier research has demonstrated that supervising automation affects human performance because of, among other factors, reduced vigilance (because of depleted mental resources) (Finomore et al., 2013; Warm et al., 1996), passive information processing (Metzger & Parasuraman, 2001), and complacency issues (Parasuraman & Manzey, 2010; Wickens et al., 2015). In short, when supervisors are not part of the information and decision-making loop, their SA will deteriorate and supervisory performance will degrade (Endsley & Kiris, 1995).

When extending these issues to a remote supervisory context, dividing attention between multiple ships poses additional challenges to SA. As noted earlier, humans have limited attentional and memory capacities that constrain the amount of information they can handle simultaneously. Therefore, monitoring multiple ships at the same time will pose a significant burden on the supervisor and will require strategies that support this activity. An important question in this context concerns the number of ships supervisors can monitor simultaneously. Previous research has attempted to estimate this, but the answer is likely domain- and case-specific (Cummings & Guerlain, 2007; Porathe, 2014). For example, in high-intensity periods (e.g. a ship experiencing an emergency), the supervisor's capacity may be limited to a single ship only. Conversely, in periods of low intensity with little activity, supervisors may monitor multiple ships simultaneously. Still, in all of these cases, supervisors need to follow what their ships are doing, evaluate their performance and intervene if required. Considering the cognitive challenges of doing this adequately, the organisation of work, the design of tasks and the design of control systems should be carefully considered to support establishing and maintaining SA in all relevant circumstances.

3.3 Relying on the System

In contrast with mental models and SA, the goal of trust is not to maximise it but rather to calibrate it (Lee & See, 2004). That is, operators should not trust a system more than it is worthy of trust, as overtrust can lead to misuse and distrust may lead to disuse of the system (Parasuraman & Riley, 1997). Therefore, trust should be appropriate to the degree of trustworthiness such that an operator with a calibrated trust relationship with the system should be able to know when to rely on the system and when not to.

Trust calibration is related to the degree of knowledge operators have about the system under supervision and the extent to which they can explain it

(Tatasciore & and Loft, 2025). Knowing more about a system benefits the understanding of it, which, in turn, supports trust calibration (Kraus et al., 2020). Conversely, this implies that, initially, when operators have limited knowledge about the system, trust in the system is limited or, at least, inappropriate (Hoffman et al., 2019). Consequently, an operator may not be able to explain the actions of the system, which makes it difficult to predict the system's behaviour.

Mental models of the system play an important role in establishing and maintaining trust in the system. By learning about the system's abilities, capabilities, functioning, components and limitations, operators can at least explain its functioning and understand where its limits lie. Furthermore, SA of the system also plays an important role in establishing a real-time understanding of the system in its operating environment (National Academies of Sciences, Engineering and Medicine, 2022). That is, by understanding what the system is doing, why it is doing it and what it will do next, SA of the system is maintained, and operators are better equipped to predict system behaviour and know when to intervene or not. This, in turn, contributes to calibrating trust in the system (see Figure 3.3).

However, as discussed earlier, establishing and maintaining mental models and SA for AI-enabled systems is challenging due to their opaqueness and the brittleness of their performance when operating at the limits of, or outside, their operational design domain. This means that effort should be directed towards designing systems that are understandable and predictable to their users such that an appropriate trust relationship can be established.

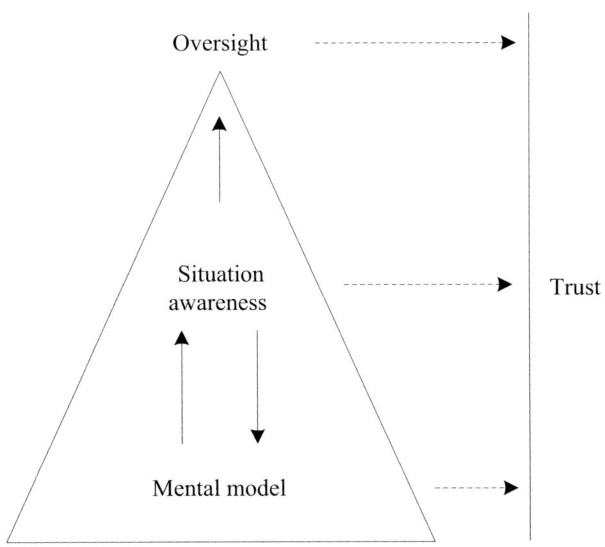

FIGURE 3.3 Mental models, SA and trust in relation to human oversight (based on National Academies of Sciences, Engineering and Medicine (2022))

4 Designing for Human Oversight

To facilitate interaction between humans and autonomous systems, display-based human–machine interfaces (HMI) are common in most modern systems. The HMI enhances human-machine interactions by providing relevant feedback to support SA and enabling appropriate input commands for action execution. Norman (1990) emphasised the importance of suitable feedback during interactions with automation, arguing that the issue with maintaining human involvement is not the automation itself but the lack of adequate information provided to users.

Human-centred design (HCD) focuses on incorporating human needs and capabilities in system design (ISO, 2019). Unlike technology-centred design, HCD takes into account the user's tasks, context and abilities to inform system design. This approach aims to create more effective systems by reducing errors, improving productivity and increasing user acceptance and satisfaction. HCD also requires an interdisciplinary approach, in which end users, in this case supervisors of autonomous ships, play a central role. Key activities in the HCD process include understanding the system's context of use, specifying user requirements, producing design solutions and evaluating the design (see Figure 3.4) (ISO, 2019). Iterative improvements and evaluations ensure that the final solution meets user requirements.

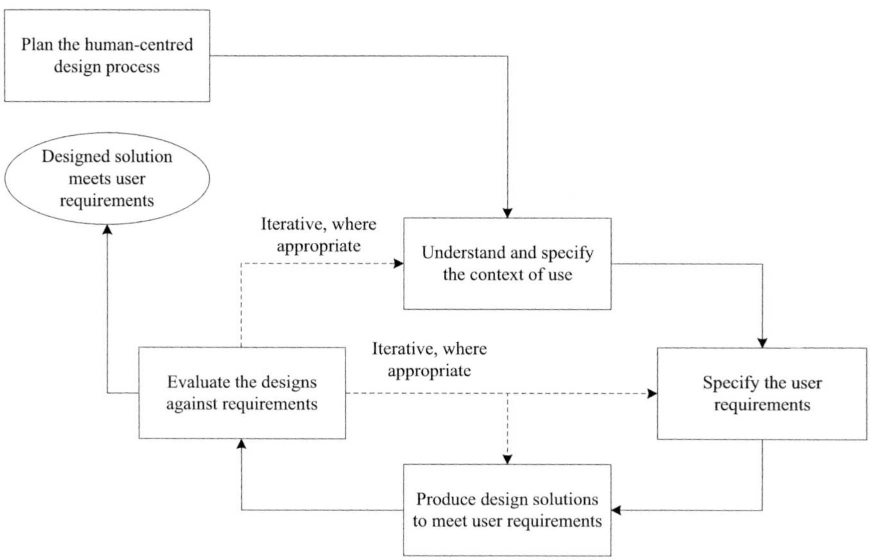

FIGURE 3.4 The human-centred design process

Source: Adopted from ISO (2019).

4.1 Understanding the Context of Use

The first step of the HCD process defines the context in which the technology will be used, including understanding the characteristics of the users and the tasks they will perform. An important element in defining the context of use is understanding the goals operators aim to achieve when working with the new system, the critical decisions they make and the challenges they may encounter. In the ship autonomy context, this means understanding how the conventional way of operating ships is affected by the introduction of autonomous technologies. For example, when introducing decision support systems to assist navigators in performing collision avoidance, an analysis should be carried out of how the availability of such a system may affect the navigator's decision-making. Likewise, for unmanned ships that are supervised from a remote location, it is important to understand how safe and efficient operations can be achieved and what the challenges and opportunities are in achieving this goal with the new technology. In other words, technology changes the role of the operator and therefore a thorough understanding of the context in which the technology will be used is an important prerequisite for designing systems that support human work.

4.2 Specifying the User Requirements

Human oversight of AI-enabled systems implies that operators are enabled "to properly understand the relevant capacities and limitations of the high-risk AI system and be able to duly monitor its operation, including in view of detecting and addressing anomalies, dysfunctions and unexpected performance" (European Commission, 2024, p. 60). In the context of ship autonomy, this implies that operators supervising autonomous ships should have sufficient and specific information available to do so. But what information does this entail? What information is necessary to successfully perform this task?

Task analysis (TA) is a method commonly used to describe and evaluate the interaction between humans and other actors within a system (Kirwan & Ainsworth, 1992; Stanton, 2006). Goal-directed task analysis (GDTA) is a type of cognitive TA that focuses on the goals, decisions and information needs of humans when performing a task (Endsley & Jones, 2025). GDTA is a technology-agnostic technique, which means that the analysis aims to determine what operators ideally would like to know to perform a task, without specifying which technology provides this information. In addition, the analysis aims to understand how the operator integrates the information to derive decisions. In this way, systems can be designed that support the cognitive needs of the operator and thereby enhance decision-making and performance.

4.3 Producing Design Solutions

Considering that most modern systems deploy visual display units, designing for human oversight of autonomous systems entails developing HMIs that are suitable for this task. The information requirements identified in the previous phase guide the development of design solutions. Note that the GDTA is a technology-agnostic approach, which means that the requirements identified do not describe *how* the information should be made available, only *that* the information is important in meeting overall goals. Therefore, the interdisciplinary design team tasked with developing solutions should consider which medium is best suited to support operators in providing that information. Although a plethora of design recommendations can be made with regard to supporting human interaction with autonomous systems (see Endsley & Jones, 2025; ISO, 2019), there are two design principles that warrant specific attention when designing for human supervision of autonomous systems.

Autonomous systems, especially those that use AI components, have their own particular challenges when it comes to human oversight. Specifically, the opaqueness of the underlying model is a key challenge in building and maintaining accurate mental models. This means that effort should be directed towards developing solutions that "open up the black box" (Loyola-González, 2019). Explainable AI is the field of study that aims to create solutions to make AI systems interpretable to their users (Gunning, 2016). Explainability refers to the "property of an AI system to express important factors influencing the AI system results in a way that humans can understand" (ISO, 2022, p. 12) and "provides information in a backward-looking manner on the logic, process, factors, or reasoning upon which the system's actions or recommendations are based" (National Academies of Sciences, Engineering and Medicine, 2022, p. 31). An important assumption for designing HMIs is that they shall be used by operators who are likely not specialists in machine learning. Therefore, autonomous systems should provide insight into their reasoning "in a human understandable format" (DNV, 2024, p. 28). In this way, operators are supported in establishing and maintaining their mental model of the system under supervision, which, in turn, improves human–AI performance (Rieger et al., 2025).

Transparency "provides a real-time understanding of the actions of the AI system, as a part of SA" (National Academies of Sciences, Engineering and Medicine, 2022, p. 31) (Figure 3.5). In other words, a transparent autonomous system keeps operators in the loop by constantly informing them about its planned actions (Endsley, 2017). For example, a collision avoidance system can be considered transparent when it presents the target ships it has detected, identifies which targets form a collision risk, which relative priorities are assigned to own ship and the target ships (i.e. give-way and/or stand-on), and plots the avoidance manoeuvre it plans to perform (van de Merwe et al., 2023a, 2023b). In this way, operators gain insight into the

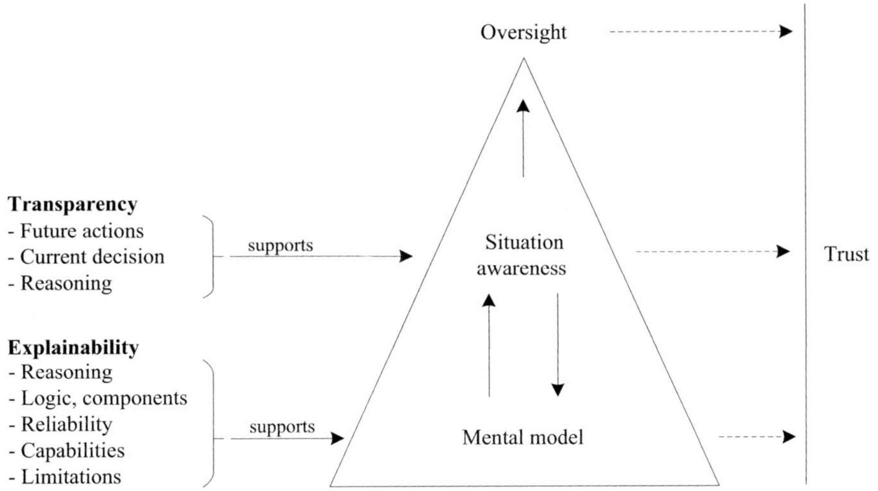

FIGURE 3.5 Designing for human oversight with explainability and transparency (based on Endsley (2023) and National Academies of Sciences, Engineering and Medicine (2022)

reasoning of the system and can follow along with its actions, thereby maintaining SA of the system in its operational context and being able to calibrate their trust in it.

4.4 Evaluating the Design

The type and depth of evaluation depend on the maturity of the concept and the readiness of the technology for human use (HFES, 2021). Nevertheless, user-centred evaluation is an important aspect of HCD. Even in the early stages of developing design solutions, evaluations can be performed to determine whether the design is on the right track and/or where adjustments are needed to achieve more user-oriented solutions. However, as real-life testing can be complex and costly, simpler approaches using mock-ups, drawings, prototypes, or talk-throughs can be effective. An evaluation of the final product is still essential to assess whether the end-user requirements are met or whether further iterations are necessary.

Evaluations also provide an initial opportunity for end-users to become familiar with the system. Here, operators of autonomous ships can learn how the system works, understand its capabilities and limitations, and experience how it keeps them informed about its functioning. Throughout the design of the system, the evaluation may also be more sophisticated, such as experimental testing in desktop, real-time and dynamic simulators, as well as in real-life settings (see Figure 3.6).

FIGURE 3.6 Evaluating human oversight using a real-time simulator

Source: Adopted from Alsos et al. (2022).

4.5 Case study: Collision and Grounding Avoidance System

This section illustrates the HCD process by discussing a case study in which an HMI was developed that aimed to support supervisors in understanding a CAGA system's decisions, planned actions and the reasoning behind them.

Understanding the context of use: To establish the context in which the CAGA system was to be deployed, multiple in-situ interviews were performed onboard passenger ferries with navigators who were on duty (van de Merwe et al., 2024b). The interviews addressed the actions navigators perform to observe and make sense of their surroundings, how they determine collision risk and which actions they take to avoid collisions. In addition, in-situ observations were performed while interviewing the navigators, and real-world encounters with other ships could be used as examples of how collisions were avoided, providing an opportunity to experience these situations first-hand (see Figure 3.7).

Specifying the user requirements: The interviews and observations provided the primary information basis for understanding the goals, decisions and tasks of navigators when performing collision avoidance manoeuvres. In addition, company procedures and a detailed analysis of the COLREG were used as input sources. Based on these sources, a GDTA was established

FIGURE 3.7 Observations and interviews performed onboard a passenger ferry

Source: Adopted from van de Merwe (2024).

for "conventional" collision avoidance and served as the basis for identifying requirements for "supervised" collision avoidance (van de Merwe et al., 2022, 2024b). This analysis identified that the supervisor's primary task was to verify that the CAGA system is performing according to their expectations. If the supervisor finds that the planned behaviour of the ship is not in accordance with expectations, an intervention may be relevant.

For example, upon detecting a collision situation with another ship, a supervisor may notice that their own ship does not plan to make an avoidance manoeuvre, plans to execute it too late, plans for too little distance to the target ship, or plans a manoeuvre that is not in accordance with the collision regulations (e.g. a port manoeuvre where starboard is prescribed). Such deviations between actual and expected ship behaviour may prompt a supervisor to scrutinise the system's behaviour more closely, adjust the system's parameters, or otherwise intervene in the system's functioning. This means that, for a supervisor to be able to stay informed about system performance and make appropriate decisions in a dynamic context, the system should continuously inform the supervisor about its (planned) actions and the reasons behind them so that appropriate and sufficient SA can be maintained. Examples of this type of information include depicting the system's detection of other ships, terrain and objects, indicating the target ship's type,

TABLE 3.1 Example information requirements for supervising a collision avoidance system

Autonomous collision avoidance system	*Information requirements (examples)*
1. Risk identification	• Identified target ship • Target ship type and size • Identified target relative motion
2. Risk analysis	• Target ships that pose a risk • Risk target priority (give-way/stand-on) • Risk target course and speed • Risk target estimated trajectory • Risk object conflict type (head-on/crossing/overtaking)
3. Decision-making and planning	• Own ship priority (give-way/stand-on) • Own ship intended track and speed
4. Collision avoidance manoeuvring	N/A: only action implementation, that is, the information given earlier is continuously shown during navigation

Source: Adopted from van de Merwe et al. (2024b).

size and activity, and identifying which of the target ships pose a collision risk. Finally, the system should provide information about its intended avoidance actions and the time required to perform these actions. Together, this information forms the inputs for designing the system. Table 3.1 provides examples of the information requirements identified through the GDTA for a CAGA system (van de Merwe et al., 2024b).

Producing design solutions: Figure 3.8 depicts an example illustration of how a CAGA system could be made transparent to its supervisor based on the requirements identified through the GDTA (van de Merwe et al., 2023a). Situated on a conventional radar screen from a popular maritime equipment manufacturer, the information shows a traffic situation in which own ship, at the centre of the radar screen, is involved in a crossing situation with the orange target. However, own ship is "boxed in" since there is a target on the starboard side that prevents an unrestricted avoidance manoeuvre. Since own ship is required to give way, the target on the immediate starboard side becomes the highest risk target while performing the avoidance manoeuvre. Regarding how the CAGA system intends to resolve this situation: own ship depicts its intended avoidance manoeuvre by drawing its planned track for the next 18 minutes (3 × 6-minute vectors) in white. It also depicts "GW" next to own ship, indicating it has interpreted that the own ship needs to give way. Furthermore, own ship indicates the conflict situation and type of vessel for each target it has identified (e.g. CR for crossing and MV for motor vessel for the orange target). Moreover, all targets have received identifiers (green

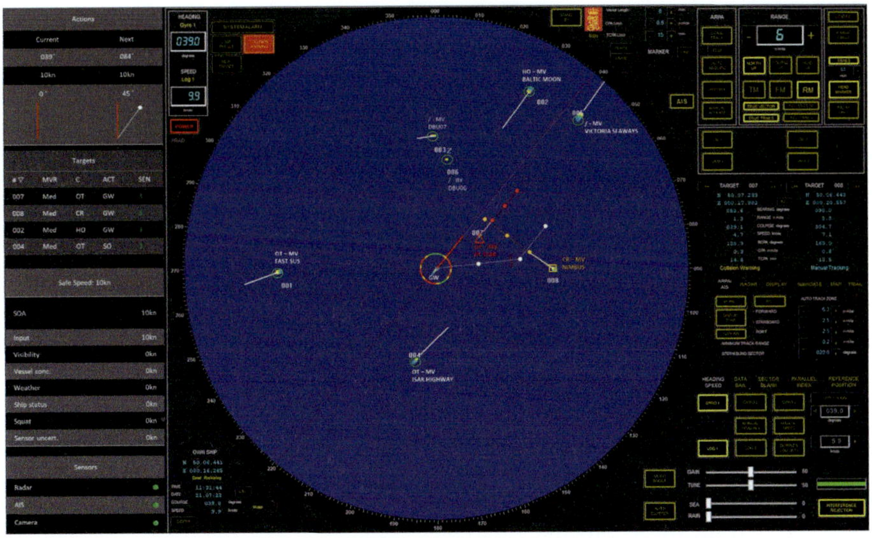

FIGURE 3.8 A conceptual illustration of a radar screen depicting symbology to represent the CAGA system's decisions, planned actions and reasoning

Source: Adopted from van de Merwe et al. (2024c).

circles, orange square and red triangle) and initial classifications (ship types and relevant conflict-type indicators). Finally, additional target, speed and sensor information is depicted on the left side of the screen to assist in further comprehension of the parameters the CAGA system is using in determining collision avoidance solutions.

Evaluating the design: In developing a transparent CAGA system, a desktop evaluation platform was used to experimentally assess the effect of transparency on SA, mental workload and task performance with 34 licensed navigators (van de Merwe et al., 2024c). For this experiment, four types of transparency information were developed to explore how different types and amounts of information affected the dependent variables. Furthermore, two levels of traffic complexity were used to assess whether the effects of transparency depended on the density of information depicted on the HMI. The results showed that transparency improves SA and that the additional information, depicting the CAGA system's (planned) actions and reasoning, did not lead to additional mental workload. However, navigators did spend more time understanding the traffic situation and the intended actions of the CAGA system, especially when higher levels of transparency were presented. In other words, more information about the CAGA system's intended actions aided its understanding but came at the cost of information processing time. These results demonstrate that providing navigators with transparency information

FIGURE 3.9 Simple, paper-based desktop evaluation of different concept illustrations for a collision avoidance system

can enhance SA, but care should be taken when applying these principles in conditions where additional transparency information may cause unwanted delays in decision-making. Finally, when the participants were asked to qualitatively rank which levels of transparency they preferred and why, they indicated that they were most interested in understanding how the CAGA system evaluated the traffic situation's risk picture (see Figure 3.9) (van de Merwe et al., 2024a). This finding emphasises the safety-critical nature of collision avoidance manoeuvring, including the supervisor's role herein, to ensure that the CAGA system performs as it should. It also highlights the need to provide supervisors with appropriate information regarding the system's reasoning in support of their SA. Finally, since the HMIs were developed through a structured and systematic user-centred design process, the lack of any effect on mental workload emphasises the importance of integrating transparency information into primary task displays (van de Merwe et al., 2024c, 2024a).

5 Towards Teaming With Autonomous Ships

Ongoing developments within AI and autonomous systems have resulted in impressive applications in the maritime domain, across industries and society at large. Looking to the future, what will be the result of these fast-paced and increasingly rapid developments in designing ever more sophisticated systems? Recent developments point towards the creation of intelligent agents able to exert goal-directed behaviour using observation through sensors and executing actions through actuators in a dynamic environment and independently of human involvement (Russell et al., 2010). Considering the level of sophistication of such agents and the degree of human involvement, the relationship between humans and automation may need to be revisited. That is, rather than approaching autonomous ships as automation that operators *interact* with, in the future, autonomous systems may need to be viewed as entities that operators *team up* with.

Human-autonomy teaming (HAT) may be the next frontier for human oversight of autonomous ships. The reasoning behind this is twofold. The first reason stems from the commonly held "levels of autonomy", which do not sufficiently describe the end goals of machine autonomy. In their preliminary taxonomy for MASS, the IMO assigned four such levels to describe ship autonomy, where machine control advances in degrees towards a "fully autonomous ship" (IMO, 2021). While this is typical for such taxonomies, it is problematic because such a one-dimensional model necessarily implies that each gain in machine control results in an equal loss in human control. Why should human control of autonomous systems be complicit in such a zero-sum game? (See Shneiderman, 2022, for a discussion.) We intuitively understand that this is not desirable – at least not for complex, safety-critical systems such as ships. Thus, a shift away from the "levels" approach and towards models for joint machine and human autonomy is needed. Such models can be spawned from a HAT approach, which is specifically tuned to the needs of teaming with autonomous systems – no matter how autonomous the machine may be.

The second reason for why HATs are the way forward for human oversight of autonomous ships stems from the role of social mechanisms in coordination and control. It is well established that in control rooms, social cues such as shouts and gestures (and even expletives) continuously serve to guide the focal point of collective attention (Heath & Luff, 1992). In this respect, simply looking where another person is looking is a fundamentally important cue. In fact, it has been postulated that human behaviour is unique in this regard and helps explain why humans as a species are remarkably adept at cooperating. According to the "cooperative eye hypothesis", humans evolved to have the largest sclera (white areas of the eyes) of any other mammal precisely because this trait allows them to indicate – with a mere glance – where another person is looking and thus where to direct one's own attention (Tomasello et al., 2007). However, social behaviours are challenging for machines to simulate, as they seem to rely on ineffably biological hardware and tacit cultural experience. The challenge in a control room context is therefore assessing how the introduction of machine autonomy affects these social mechanisms. Adopting a HAT approach can manage this challenge by framing such social mechanisms as distinguishable team processes (e.g. cooperation and communication) that can be modelled, predicted and assessed.

Kozlowski and Bell (2013) define teams as two or more individuals who share common goals, exhibit task interdependencies, interact socially, maintain and manage boundaries, and are embedded within a larger organisational context. This definition also fits a human-autonomy team, with the caveat that the human-machine coupling must not hinder these defining features. Lyons et al. (2021) label HATs as a "force multiplier", as they should, in theory, serving to execute a mission with fewer people required. Indeed, some scholars make no special distinction between human-human teams using autonomy and human-autonomy teams, since autonomous technology is, at its core, intended to work with humans as teammates (McNeese et al., 2018). Thus, a HAT is like a team composed of humans – only that at least one human is substituted by a machine. In the maritime autonomy domain, the team can be composed of one or more operators at an ROC who maintain oversight of one or more autonomous ships.

So how can work be aimed towards HATs that successfully orchestrate autonomous ship oversight? While research on HATs is relatively new, it has the advantage of standing on the shoulders of a century of research on human-automation interaction and human-human teaming. By the same token, there are at least two aspects that distinguish HATs from these two previous research topics. First, where automation was *assistive* (e.g. tools and decision support), autonomy is now *assertive* (e.g. it has the agency to make its own decisions). Second, whereas human-human teams were composed of a species with highly evolved social cooperation skills, human-machine teams are premised on fewer humans in the team.

HCD methods, for one, can be extended into a team-oriented approach (see the earlier section for an overview). For human-automation interaction, HCD methods have been successful in parlaying human factors concepts into practical design specifications and recommendations. This can also be the case for HATs. Practically speaking, this may begin by translating fundamental concepts like mental models, SA and trust (introduced in Section 2) to a team context. Luckily, this translation already has a well-established research precedent. *Shared* mental models (Cannon-Bowers et al., 2015), *shared* SA (specifically in a HAT context; Endsley, 2023) and trust of new autonomous team members (de Visser et al., 2018) can be used as building blocks in a team-oriented HCD approach. Whereas HCD focuses on understanding requirements for individuals' taskwork, a team-oriented approach extends this understanding to human-machine partnerships underpinning teamwork.

In this way, oversight of autonomous ships describes a direct case of HAT. Take the straightforward case of a single operator teaming with a single autonomous ship. Until roles can be interdependent (e.g. like an officer of the watch and lookout), and until the two can interact socially (e.g. follow each other's gaze) and co-inhabit roles within a larger organisation, we remain in the realm of human-automation interaction. The distinction between assistive (automatic) and assertive (autonomous) machines is not trivial and represents the biggest step-change in maritime technology in the past century.

This is because it will no longer be sufficient just to "use" machine autonomy – rather, the key to human oversight will lie in teaming with it.

6 Conclusion

This chapter discussed human oversight in the context of autonomous ships. We argued that, given the challenge of developing reliable and predictable systems capable of operating in dynamic real-world environments, human supervision is essential to ensure operational and safety goals are met. As modern technology continuous to evolve, and the pace of technological progress accelerates, we may eventually see autonomous systems become extremely safe, reliable and accurate – up to a point where human oversight becomes redundant. However, for the foreseeable future, humans are expected (and required; IMO, 1978, 2011) to play a central role in designing, developing, deploying, managing and overseeing their performance. This implies that AI-enabled autonomous systems, operating in high-risk environments, should be designed and developed in a way that allows people to effectively supervise and perform oversight of their functioning (European Commission, 2024). To this end, a number of recommendations are made to support this goal.

First, follow a structured and multidisciplinary HCD process, taking into account the context in which the system will be used (ISO, 2019; Margetis et al., 2021). Second, focus on understanding the goals of the overall system, the role of the human within it, the tasks they are intended to perform and the information they require (Endsley & Jones, 2025; Kirwan & Ainsworth, 1992). Third, consider human cognitive capabilities and limitations when designing for human oversight (Wickens & Carswell, 2021). Fourth, develop systems that are understandable and predictable so that humans can provide meaningful human oversight (National Academies of Sciences, Engineering and Medicine, 2022). Finally, keep humans engaged, in control and in the loop by designing systems that are explainable, transparent and worthy of trust (Lee & See, 2004; Sanneman & Shah, 2022).

References

ABB. (2018). *B0 – a conditionally and periodically unmanned bridge*. https://new.abb.com/marine/media-center/articles-and-highlights/b0-a-conditionally-and-periodically-unmanned-bridge

Akhtar, N., & Mian, A. (2018). Threat of Adversarial Attacks on Deep Learning in Computer Vision: A Survey. *IEEE Access*, *6*, 14410–14430. IEEE Access. https://doi.org/10.1109/ACCESS.2018.2807385

Alpaydin, E. (2020). *Introduction to Machine Learning* (4th edition). MIT Press.

Alsos, O., Veitch, E., Pantelatos, L., Vasstein, K., Eide, E., Petermann, F.-M., & Breivik, M. (2022). NTNU Shore Control Lab: Designing Shore Control Centres in the Age of Autonomous Ships. *Journal of Physics: Conference Series*, *2311*, 012030. https://doi.org/10.1088/1742-6596/2311/1/012030

Avikus. (2024). *HiNAS navigation*. https://avikus.ai/hinas-navigation
Brandsæter, A., Smefjell, G., van de Merwe, G. K., & Kamsvåg, V. (2020). Assuring Safe Implementation of Decision Support Functionality Based on Data-Driven Methods for Ship Navigation. *Proceedings of the 30th European Safety and Reliability Conference and the 15th Probabilistic Safety Assessment and Management Conference, 8*. https://doi.org/978-981-14-8593-0
Cannon-Bowers, J. A., Salas, E., & Converse, S. (2015). Shared Mental Models in Expert Team Decision Making. In N. J. Castellan (Ed.), *Individual and Group Decision Making: Current Issues* (1st edition). Psychology Press.
Chang, C.-H., Wijeratne, I. B., Kontovas, C., & Yang, Z. (2024). COLREG and MASS: Analytical Review to Identify Research Trends and Gaps in the Development of Autonomous Collision Avoidance. *Ocean Engineering, 302*, 117652. https://doi.org/10.1016/j.oceaneng.2024.117652
Chiou, E. K., & Lee, J. D. (2023). Trusting Automation: Designing for Responsivity and Resilience. *Human Factors, 65*(1), 137–165. https://doi.org/10.1177/00187208211009995
Cummings, M. L., & Guerlain, S. (2007). Developing Operator Capacity Estimates for Supervisory Control of Autonomous Vehicles. *Human Factors, 49*(1), 1–15. https://doi.org/10.1518/001872007779598109
de Visser, E. J., Pak, R., & Shaw, T. H. (2018). From 'Automation' to 'Autonomy': The Importance of Trust Repair in Human–Machine Interaction. *Ergonomics, 61*(10), 1409–1427. https://doi.org/10.1080/00140139.2018.1457725
DNV. (2024). *Rules for classification, part 6 additional class notations, chapter 12 autonomy and remote operation (DNV-RU-SHIP Pt.6 Ch.12)* (No. DNV-RU-SHIP Pt.6 Ch.12). rules.dnv.com
Endsley, M. R. (1988). Design and Evaluation for Situation Awareness Enhancement. *Proceedings of the Human Factors Society Annual Meeting, 32*(2), 97–101. https://doi.org/10.1177/154193128803200221
Endsley, M. R. (1995). Toward a Theory of Situation Awareness in Dynamic Systems. *Human Factors, 37*(1), 217–249. https://doi.org/10.4324/9781315092898-13
Endsley, M. R. (2017). From Here to Autonomy: Lessons Learned from Human-Automation Research. *Human Factors, 59*(1), 5–27. https://doi.org/10.1177/0018720816681350
Endsley, M. R. (2023). Supporting Human-AI Teams: Transparency, Explainability, and Situation Awareness. *Computers in Human Behavior, 140*, 107574. https://doi.org/10.1016/j.chb.2022.107574
Endsley, M. R., & Jones, D. G. (2025). *Designing for Situation Awareness: An Approach to User-Centered Design* (3rd edition). CRC Press.
Endsley, M. R., & Kiris, E. O. (1995). The Out-of-the-Loop Performance Problem and Level of Control in Automation. *Human Factors, 37*(2), 381–394. https://doi.org/10.1518/001872095779064555
European Commission. (2024). *Regulation (EU) 2024/1689 of the European Parliament and of the council of 13 June 2024 laying down harmonised rules on artificial intelligence and amending regulations (EC) No 300/2008, (EU) No 167/2013, (EU) No 168/2013, (EU) 2018/858, (EU) 2018/1139 and (EU) 2019/2144 and Directives 2014/90/EU, (EU) 2016/797 and (EU) 2020/1828 (Artificial Intelligence Act)*. http://data.europa.eu/eli/reg/2024/1689/oj/eng
Finomore, V. S., Shaw, T. H., Warm, J. S., Matthews, G., & Boles, D. B. (2013). Viewing the Workload of Vigilance Through the Lenses of the NASA-TLX and the MRQ. *Human Factors, 55*(6), 1044–1063. https://doi.org/10.1177/0018720813484498
Fitts, P. M. (1951). *Human engineering for an effective air-navigation and traffic-control system* (pp. 1–109). https://apps.dtic.mil/dtic/tr/fulltext/u2/b815893.pdf

Gunning, D. (2016). *Explainable artificial intelligence (XAI)* (No. DARPA-BAA-16–53; p. 52). Defense Advanced Research Projects Agency. https://www.darpa.mil/attachments/DARPA-BAA-16–53.pdf

Haberlandt, K. (1999). *Human Memory: Exploration and Application.* Allyn and Bacon.

Hancock, P. A., Kessler, T. T., Kaplan, A. D., Stowers, K., Brill, J. C., Billings, D. R., Schaefer, K. E., & Szalma, J. L. (2023). How and Why Humans Trust: A Meta-Analysis and Elaborated Model. *Frontiers in Psychology, 14.* https://doi.org/10.3389/fpsyg.2023.1081086

Hancock, G. M., Longo, L., Young, M. S., & Hancock, P. A. (2021). Mental Workload. In G. Salvendy & W. Karwowski (Eds.), *Handbook of Human Factors and Ergonomics* (5th edition, pp. 203–226). John Wiley & Sons, Ltd. https://doi.org/10.1002/9781119636113.ch7

Heath, C., & Luff, P. (1992). Collaboration and Control Crisis Management and Multimedia Technology in London Underground Line Control Rooms. *Computer Supported Cooperative Work (CSCW), 1*(1), 69–94. https://doi.org/10.1007/BF00752451

HFES. (2021). *Human readiness level scale in the system development process* (No. ANSI/HFES 400–2021). Human Factors and Ergonomics Society.

Hoffman, R. R., Mueller, S. T., Klein, G., & Litman, J. (2019). *Metrics for Explainable AI: Challenges and Prospects* (No. arXiv:1812.04608). arXiv. https://doi.org/10.48550/arXiv.1812.04608

Hollnagel, E. (2012). Coping with Complexity: Past, Present and Future. *Cognition, Technology & Work, 14*(3), 199–205. https://doi.org/10.1007/s10111-011-0202-7

IMO. (1978). *International convention on standards of training, certification and watchkeeping for seafarers.* https://www.imo.org/en/OurWork/HumanElement/Pages/STCW-Conv-LINK.aspx

IMO. (2011). *Resolution A.1047(27) Principles of safe manning.* https://www-cdn.imo.org/localresources/en/KnowledgeCentre/IndexofIMOResolutions/AssemblyDocuments/A.1047(27).pdf

IMO. (2018, December 3). *Maritime Safety Committee (MSC), 100th session, 3–7 December 2018.* https://www.imo.org/en/MediaCentre/MeetingSummaries/Pages/MSC-100th-session.aspx

IMO. (2021). *MSC.1/Circ.163 – Outcome of the regulatory scoping exercise for the use of Maritime Autonomous Surface Ships (MASS).* International Maritime Organisation. https://wwwcdn.imo.org/localresources/en/MediaCentre/HotTopics/PublishingImages/Pages/Autonomous-shipping/MSC.1-Circ.1638%20-%20Outcome%20Of%20The%20Regulatory%20Scoping%20ExerciseFor%20The%20Use%20Of%20Maritime%20Autonomous%20Surface%20Ships.%20(Secretariat).pdf

IMO. (2023). *MSC 107/5/1 development of a goal-based instrument for maritime autonomous surface ship (MASS)* (No. MSC 107/5/1). International Maritime Organisation. https://wwwcdn.imo.org/localresources/en/MediaCentre/HotTopics/Documents/MSC%20107-5-1-Report%20of%20the%20MSC-LEG-FAL%20Joint%20Working%20Group.pdf

ISO. (2019). *ISO 9241–210:2019 ergonomics of human-system interaction – Part 210: Human-centred design for interactive systems.* International Organization for Standardization.

ISO. (2022). *ISO/IEC 22989:2022 information technology – Artificial intelligence – Artificial intelligence concepts and terminology.* International Organization for Standardization.

Kahneman, D. (1973). *Attention and Effort.* Prentice Hall.

Kim, D., Kim, J.-S., Kim, J.-H., & Im, N.-K. (2022). Development of Ship Collision Avoidance System and Sea Trial Test for Autonomous Ship. *Ocean Engineering*, *266*, 113120. https://doi.org/10.1016/j.oceaneng.2022.113120

Kirwan, B., & Ainsworth, L. K. (Eds.). (1992). *A guide to task analysis*. Taylor & Francis.

Kozlowski, S. W. J., & Bell, B. S. (2013). *Work groups and teams in organizations*. https://ecommons.cornell.edu/server/api/core/bitstreams/42df91e0-eb80–406b-8647–6c5adb353ed5/content#page=5.39

Kraus, J., Scholz, D., Stiegemeier, D., & Baumann, M. (2020). The More You Know: Trust Dynamics and Calibration in Highly Automated Driving and the Effects of Take-Overs, System Malfunction, and System Transparency. *Human Factors*, *62*(5), 718–736. https://doi.org/10.1177/0018720819853686

Kretschmann, L., Burmeister, H. C., & Jahn, C. (2017). Analyzing the Economic Benefit of Unmanned Autonomous Ships: An Exploratory Cost-Comparison Between an Autonomous and a Conventional Bulk Carrier. *Research in Transportation Business and Management*, *25*, 76–86. https://doi.org/10.1016/j.rtbm.2017.06.002

Kurt, I., & Aymelek, M. (2022). Operational and Economic Advantages of Autonomous Ships and Their Perceived Impacts on port operations. *Maritime Economics & Logistics*, *24*(2), 302–326. https://doi.org/10.1057/s41278-022-00213-1

Lee, J. D., & See, K. A. (2004). Trust in Automation: Designing for Appropriate Reliance. *Human Factors*, *46*(1), 50–80. https://doi.org/10.1518/hfes.46.1.50_30392

Lee, J. D., Wickens, C. D., Liu, Y., & Boyle, L. N. (2017). *Designing for People: An Introduction to Human Factors Engineering* (3rd edition, revision 1). CreateSpace.

Lee, Y.-G., Lee, C.-H., Jeon, Y.-H., & Bae, J.-H. (2024). Transformative Impact of the EU AI Act on Maritime Autonomous Surface Ships. *Laws*, *13*(5), Article 5. https://doi.org/10.3390/laws13050061

Licklider, J. C. R. (1960). Man-Computer Symbiosis. *IRE Transactions on Human Factors in Electronics*, *HFE-1*(1), 4–11. https://doi.org/10.1109/THFE2.1960.4503259

Littman, M., Ajunwa, I., Berger, G., Boutilier, C., Currie, M., Doshi-Velez, F., Hadfield, G., Horowitz, M., Isbell, C., Kitano, H., Levy, K., Lyons, T., Mitchell, M., Shah, J., Sloman, S., Vallor, S., & Walsh, T. (2021). *Gathering Strength, Gathering Storms: The One Hundred Year Study on Artificial Intelligence (AI100) 2021 Study Panel Report*. Stanford University. http://ai100.stanford.edu/2021-report

Loyola-González, O. (2019). Black-Box vs. White-Box: Understanding Their Advantages and Weaknesses From a Practical Point of View. *IEEE Access*, *7*, 154096–154113. https://doi.org/10.1109/ACCESS.2019.2949286

Lyons, J. B., Sycara, K., Lewis, M., & Capiola, A. (2021). Human–Autonomy Teaming: Definitions, Debates, and Directions. *Frontiers in Psychology*, *12*, 589585. https://doi.org/10.3389/fpsyg.2021.589585

Margetis, G., Ntoa, S., Antona, M., & Stephanidis, C. (2021). Human-Centred Design of Artificial Intelligence. In G. Salvendy & W. Karwowski (Eds.), *Handbook of Human Factors and Ergonomics* (5th edition, pp. 1085–1106). Wiley. https://doi.org/10.1002/9781119636113.ch42

Massterly. (2023). *A snapshot of some of the projects we are involved in*. https://www.massterly.com/news-1

McNeese, N. J., Demir, M., Cooke, N. J., & Myers, C. (2018). Teaming With a Synthetic Teammate: Insights into Human-Autonomy Teaming. *Human Factors*, *60*(2), 262–273. https://doi.org/10.1177/0018720817743223

Metzger, U., & Parasuraman, R. (2001). The Role of the Air Traffic Controller in Future Air Traffic Management: An Empirical Study of Active Control Versus Passive Monitoring. *Human Factors*, *43*(4), 519–528. https://doi.org/10.1518/001872001775870421

Mogford, R. H. (1997). Mental Models and Situation Awareness in Air Traffic Control. *The International Journal of Aviation Psychology*, *7*(4), 331–341. https://doi.org/10.1207/s15327108ijap0704_5

Mueller, S. T., Hoffman, R. R., Clancey, W. J., Emery, A. K., & Klein, G. (2019). *Explanation in Human-AI Systems: A Literature Meta-Review Synopsis of Key Ideas and Publications and Bibliography for Explainable AI*. Florida Institute for Human and Machine Cognition. https://apps.dtic.mil/sti/citations/AD1073994

National Academies of Sciences, Engineering and Medicine. (2022). *Human-AI Teaming: State of the Art and Research Needs*. The National Academies Press. https://doi.org/10.17226/26355

Norman, D. A. (1990). The "Problem" with Automation: Inappropriate Feedback and Interaction, Not "Over-Automation." *Philosophical Transactions of the Royal Society of London. Series B, Biological Sciences*, *327*(1241), 585–593. https://doi.org/10.1098/rstb.1990.0101

Parasuraman, R., & Manzey, D. H. (2010). Complacency and Bias in Human Use of Automation: An Attentional Integration. *Human Factors: The Journal of the Human Factors and Ergonomics Society*, *52*(3), 381–410. https://doi.org/10.1177/0018720810376055

Parasuraman, R., & Riley, V. (1997). Humans and Automation: Use, Misuse, Disuse, Abuse. *Human Factors*, *39*(2), 230–253. https://doi.org/10.1518/001872097778543886

Parasuraman, R., Sheridan, T. B., & Wickens, C. D. (2000). A Model for Types and Levels of Human Interaction with Automation. *IEEE Transactions on Systems, Man, and Cybernetics Part A: Systems and Humans*, *30*(3), 286–297. https://doi.org/10.1109/3468.844354

Pearl, J., & Mackenzie, D. (2018). *The Book of Why: The New Science of Cause and Effect* (1st edition). Basic Books.

Porathe, T. (2014). Remote Monitoring and Control of Unmanned Vessels –The MUNIN Shore Control Centre. *Proceedings of the 13th International Conference on Computer Applications and Information Technology in the Maritime Industries (COMPIT '14), May*, 460–467.

Rasmussen, J. (1986). *Information Processing and Human-Machine Interaction: An Approach to Cognitive Engineering*. North-Holland.

Rieger, T., Schindler, H., Onnasch, L., & Roesler, E. (2025). Explaining AI Weaknesses Improves Human-AI Performance in a Dynamic Control Task. *International Journal of Human-Computer Studies*, 103505. https://doi.org/10.1016/j.ijhcs.2025.103505

Rødseth, Ø. J., Lien Wennersberg, L. A., & Nordahl, H. (2021). Towards Approval of Autonomous Ship Systems by Their Operational Envelope. *Journal of Marine Science and Technology*. https://doi.org/10.1007/s00773-021-00815-z

Roseborough, J. B. (1988). *Aiding Human Operators with State Estimates* [Thesis, Massachusetts Institute of Technology]. https://dspace.mit.edu/handle/1721.1/14550

Rouse, W. B., & Morris, N. M. (1986). On Looking Into the Black Box: Prospects and Limits in the Search for Mental Models. *Psychological Bulletin*, *100*(3), 349–363. https://doi.org/10.1037/0033-2909.100.3.349

Russell, S. J., Norvig, P., & Davis, E. (2010). *Artificial Intelligence: A Modern Approach* (3rd edition). Prentice Hall.

Sanneman, L., & Shah, J. A. (2022). The Situation Awareness Framework for Explainable AI (SAFE-AI) and Human Factors Considerations for XAI Systems. *International Journal of Human–Computer Interaction*. https://www.tandfonline.com/doi/abs/10.1080/10447318.2022.2081282

Schütte, B. (2024). *Chapter 11: Damage Caused by Autonomous Ships: Towards Regulation for Civil Liability in EU Waters?* https://doi.org/10.4337/9781035321469.00018

Sheridan, T. B. (2002). *Humans and Automation: System Design and Research Issues* (1st edition). Wiley-Interscience.

Sheridan, T. B., & Verplank, W. L. (1978). *Human and Computer Control of Undersea Teleoperators*. Defense Technical Information Center. https://doi.org/10.21236/ADA057655

Shneiderman, B. (2022). *Human-centered AI*. Oxford University Press.

Stanton, N. A. (2006). Hierarchical Task Analysis: Developments, Applications, and Extensions. *Applied Ergonomics*, *37*(1), 55–79. https://doi.org/10.1016/j.apergo.2005.06.003

Tatasciore, M., & Loft, S. (2025). Calibrating Reliance on Automated Advice: Transparency and Trust Calibration Feedback. *International Journal of Human–Computer Interaction*, *0*(0), 1–11. https://doi.org/10.1080/10447318.2025.2487861

Tomasello, M., Hare, B., Lehmann, H., & Call, J. (2007). Reliance on Head Versus Eyes in the Gaze Following of Great Apes and Human Infants: The Cooperative Eye Hypothesis. *Journal of Human Evolution*, *52*(3), 314–320. https://doi.org/10.1016/j.jhevol.2006.10.001

van de Merwe, K. (2024). Agent Transparency and Human Performance in Supervisory Control [Doctoral Thesis, University of South-Eastern Norway]. https://openarchive.usn.no/usn-xmlui/handle/11250/3145497

van de Merwe, K., Mallam, S. C., Engelhardtsen, Ø., & Nazir, S. (2022). Exploring Navigator Roles and Tasks in Transitioning Towards Supervisory Control of Autonomous Collision Avoidance Systems. *Journal of Physics: Conference Series*, *2311*(1), 012017. https://doi.org/10.1088/1742-6596/2311/1/012017

van de Merwe, K., Mallam, S. C., Engelhardtsen, Ø., & Nazir, S. (2023a). Operationalising Automation Transparency for Maritime Collision Avoidance. *TransNav, International Journal on Marine Navigation and Safety of Sea Transportation*, *17*(2). https://doi.org/10.12716/1001.17.02.09

van de Merwe, K., Mallam, S. C., Engelhardtsen, Ø., & Nazir, S. (2023b). Towards an Approach to Define Transparency Requirements for Maritime Collision Avoidance. *Proceedings of the Human Factors and Ergonomics Society Annual Meeting*, *67*(1), 483–488. https://doi.org/10.1177/21695067231192862

van de Merwe, K., Mallam, S. C., Nazir, S., & Engelhardtsen, Ø. (2024a). Navigators' Perspective on Information Requirements for Supervisory Control of Autonomous Ships. *Proceedings of the Human Factors and Ergonomics Society Annual Meeting*, *68*(1), 416–422. https://doi.org/10.1177/10711813241261686

van de Merwe, K., Mallam, S. C., Nazir, S., & Engelhardtsen, Ø. (2024b). Supporting Human Supervision in Autonomous Collision Avoidance Through Agent Transparency. *Safety Science*, *169*, 13. https://doi.org/10.1016/j.ssci.2023.106329

van de Merwe, K., Mallam, S. C., Nazir, S., & Engelhardtsen, Ø. (2024c). The Influence of Agent Transparency and Complexity on Situation Awareness, Mental Workload, and Task Performance. *Journal of Cognitive Engineering and Decision Making*, *18*(2), 156–184. https://doi.org/10.1177/15553434241240553

van Doorn, E., Rusák, Z., & Horváth, I. (2017). A Situation Awareness Analysis Scheme to Identify Deficiencies of Complex Man-Machine Interactions. *International Journal of Information Technology and Management*, *16*(1), 53–72. https://doi.org/10.1504/IJITM.2017.080958

Warm, J. S., Dember, W. N., & Hancock, P. A. (1996). Vigilance and Workload in Automated Systems. In *Automation and Human Performance: Theory and Applications* (pp. 183–200). Lawrence Erlbaum Associates, Inc.

Wickens, C. D. (2008). Multiple Resources and Mental Workload. *Human Factors: The Journal of the Human Factors and Ergonomics Society*, *50*(3), 449–455. https://doi.org/10.1518/001872008X288394

Wickens, C. D., & Carswell, C. M. (2021). Information Processing. In G. Salvendy & W. Karwowski (Eds.), *Handbook of Human Factors and Ergonomics* (5th edition, p. 1603). John Wiley & Sons, Incorporated.
Wickens, C. D., Clegg, B. A., Vieane, A. Z., & Sebok, A. L. (2015). Complacency and Automation Bias in the Use of Imperfect Automation. *Human Factors: The Journal of the Human Factors and Ergonomics Society*, *57*(5), 728–739. https://doi.org/10.1177/0018720815581940
Zhang, X., Chan, F. T. S., & Mahadevan, S. (2022). Explainable Machine Learning in Image Classification Models: An Uncertainty Quantification Perspective. *Knowledge-Based Systems*, *243*, 108418. https://doi.org/10.1016/j.knosys.2022.108418

4

COGNITIVE CHALLENGES OF HUMAN-TECHNOLOGY INTERACTION IN REMOTE MARITIME AUTONOMOUS OPERATIONS

Engy Awad and Steven C. Mallam

1 Introduction

Early automation initiatives in the maritime sector focused on mechanical aids such as gyrocompasses (1908) and autopilots (1910s), which were designed to assist navigation with minimal human input (Jaskólski et al., 2019; Skrobonja et al., 2020). The 20th century marked a significant shift with the introduction of electronic control systems, radar-based collision avoidance technologies and digital communication tools, all of which gradually reduced the need for direct human involvement in vessel operation (Wang et al., 2024). In the 21st century, the integration of advanced technologies such as artificial intelligence (AI) and machine learning (ML) has further transformed maritime operations, enabling the transition from manually controlled vessels to semi-autonomous and fully autonomous models (Mallam et al., 2019a). This growing adoption of automation aims to enhance safety, improve productivity, increase efficiency and security, reduce operational costs, and minimise the risk of human error (Porathe et al., 2018). However, the maritime domain's transition towards greater automation also presents significant complexities, including the redefinition of human-technology interaction and the disruption or replacement of long-established industry norms (Wright, 2020; Woods et al., 2017; Kim & Mallam et al., 2020; Porathe et al., 2018; Ringbom, 2019; Boehm-Davis et al., 2015).

These innovations further impose new cognitive demands on human operators, necessitating continuous adaptation and a reimagining of human oversight roles within automated systems (Endsley, 1995; Wickens et al., 2004; Wickens et al., 2021). Henceforth, the maritime domain's transition towards greater automation brings forth both opportunities and challenges inherent in this technological evolution.

DOI: 10.4324/9781003586883-4

As the maritime industry navigates the transition towards increasingly autonomous operations, understanding the cognitive and human factors shaping remote vessel monitoring is essential. This chapter provides a comprehensive analysis of how remote operators perceive, process and respond to dynamic maritime scenarios. It further explores the multifaceted challenges associated with human-technology interaction in remote autonomous environments, highlighting critical themes including decision-making under uncertainty, cognitive workload, trust calibration issues, cognitive bias and the pivotal role of situation awareness (SA). To mitigate these challenges, the chapter emphasises the importance of adaptive automation, predictive situation awareness (PSA) tools, signal detection theory (SDT) frameworks and targeted training to support cognitive resilience, decision quality and human-system collaboration. These insights lay the foundation for the case study that follows, illustrating how these challenges can be addressed in real-world autonomous vessel operations. As reliance on automation increases, it becomes essential to address emerging challenges to ensure that technology complements human expertise while upholding safety, reliability and regulatory compliance.

2 Human Factors in Autonomous Operations

2.1 Human-System Integration and Decision-Making

Autonomous vessel operations require a balance between automation and human monitoring, with human input available to intervene when system limitations or unexpected conditions arise. The interaction between operators and the autonomous ship involves decision-making, which is generally defined as "a task requiring an individual to choose among several alternatives with some uncertainty regarding which choice is the best one. . . . Using whatever information may be available" (Stone et al., 2018).

Decision-making research is commonly divided into three main approaches: normative, descriptive and naturalistic. The **normative approach** outlines how decisions should be made to achieve optimal outcomes, assuming rational evaluation of all options without cognitive limitations (Simon, 1957). Expected value theory, a key normative model, suggests individuals assess probabilities and values to guide their choices (Payne et al., 1988), though its real-world applicability is limited due to human cognitive constraints (Anderson et al., 2000). In contrast, the **descriptive approach** examines how people actually make decisions. Research by Kahneman et al. (1982) showed that individuals often use heuristics, mental shortcuts that reduce cognitive load but can introduce biases. Strategies such as elimination by aspects and satisficing (Simon, 1957; Payne, 1976) illustrate this trade-off between efficiency and optimality. The **naturalistic decision-making** (NDM) approach examines how experts make decisions in real-world, high-stakes environments (Klein et al., 1993). Models such as recognition-primed decision-making (Klein, 1998) emphasise intuitive, experience-based processes, where individuals rapidly recognise patterns and simulate outcomes rather than relying solely on analytical reasoning. Models such as recognition-primed decision-making (Klein, 1998) illustrate how experienced individuals rapidly identify patterns and mentally simulate outcomes, highlighting intuitive, experience-based decision-making rather than purely analytical methods.

One way to improve decision-making is using **decision aids**, which help individuals evaluate alternatives more systematically. **Decision trees** and automated systems are common tools that guide users through a structured decision process, reduce cognitive load and mitigate biases (Bekker et al., 2003; Wickens, 2014). In aviation, for example, decision aids are used to optimise flight plans and generate emergency trajectories (Chen & Pritchett, 2001).

In the maritime domain, decision-making relies on a suite of data collection systems that enhance perception, situational awareness (SA) and navigation. These systems include technologies such as radio detection and ranging (RADAR), light detection and ranging (LIDAR), sonar, global positioning system (GPS), automatic identification system (AIS), inertial measurement units (IMUs), edge computing units, various environmental and navigational sensors and high-resolution cameras. However, SA extends beyond data acquisition; it also involves system interface design, cognitive workload management and training at both individual and team levels (Stanton et al., 2001). Training that develops practical knowledge and tacit skills, such as "ship sense" – the perceptual and cognitive fluency required for safe and efficient manoeuvring – is especially critical (Stone et al., 2018).

The literature increasingly supports the view that autonomy should augment rather than replace human expertise, emphasising human-centred system design and AI transparency as key to future maritime safety and effectiveness. This is echoed by Prison et al. (2013), who define the operator's goal as achieving "harmony" – a balanced control between the ship and its environment. They identify three categories influencing this harmony: environmental (e.g. weather, context), vessel-specific (e.g. inertia, navigation tools) and personal (e.g. spatial awareness, knowledge, experience) prerequisites. Intuitive system design can help reduce cognitive workload and support effective human-machine collaboration (Schmidt et al., 2018), whereas poorly designed interfaces may increase cognitive strain, leading to errors, reduced SA and ultimately suboptimal decision-making (Endsley & Jones, 2012).

Building on this foundation, Porathe et al. (2014) extend the discussion to shore-based unmanned ship operations through the EU's Maritime Unmanned Ship through Intelligence in Networks (MUNIN) projects. They argue that the loss of direct sensory input – visual, auditory and kinesthetic – when shifting from onboard to onshore disrupts the operator's ability to maintain harmony. Their findings highlight challenges such as information overload, reduced stress responses, potential complacency and the need for revised mental models to support remote decision-making.

Ultimately, the success of maritime autonomous operations depends not only on technological sophistication but also on ensuring that humans remain effectively "in the loop". Achieving this balance requires rethinking interface design, training paradigms and reengineering organisational structures to maintain harmony in both traditional and emerging operational settings.

2.2 Cognitive Workload in Remote Monitoring

Cognitive workload is a foundational concept in engineering psychology and human factors, critical to understanding and optimising human performance in complex environments. It refers to the demands placed on the limited information-processing capacity of the human brain during task execution (Wickens et al., 2021). Cognitive workload is conceptualised through a **resource-demand model** (**RDM**), in which task demands are matched against the individual's available cognitive resources. When demands exceed capacity, crossing the so-called "red line", performance begins to decline. This zone is characterised by cognitive workload, whereas demands beneath the red line fall within the "reserve capacity" zone, where performance remains stable despite variations in effort or complexity (Wickens, 2008; Wickens et al., 2021). The **multiple resource theory** (**MRT**) provides a framework for understanding how tasks compete for cognitive resources. It posits that individuals have multiple pools of cognitive resources based on modality (visual, auditory), processing stages (perceptual, cognitive, motor) and codes (verbal, spatial). Tasks that share the same resource pool interfere more than tasks using different pools, guiding system design to reduce such overlaps (Wickens et al., 2021).

Cognitive overload occurs when the volume of incoming information exceeds an individual's processing capacity. A high workload impairs decision-making and SA and increases the risk of error, while a workload that is too low may cause vigilance decrements and disengagement (Wickens et al., 2004; Wickens et al., 2021).

In addition to work overload, the impact of **stress and fatigue** on cognitive decision-making must also be considered. Stress can significantly impair decision-making, particularly in high-pressure situations such as emergency response. Empirical evidence suggests that under stress, individuals tend to narrow their focus (**cognitive tunnelling**), consider fewer alternatives, and make quicker decisions, often relying on cognitive shortcuts or heuristics (Janis & Mann, 1977; Wickens et al., 2021). While such adaptive responses

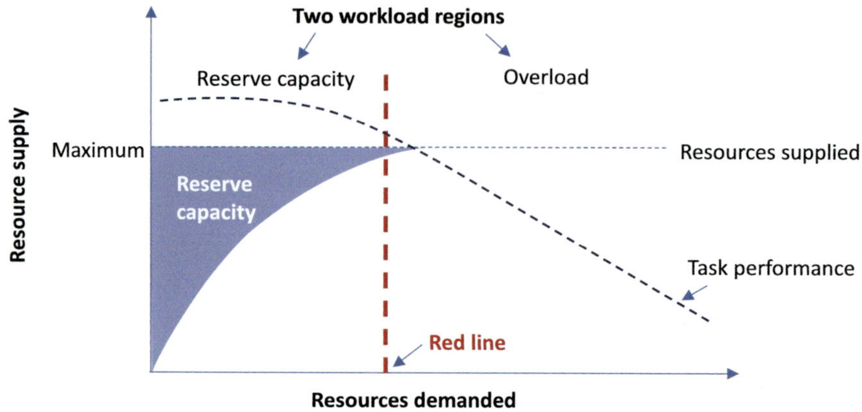

FIGURE 4.1 Resource demand model – mental workload for task resource demand, resources supplied and performance, indicating the "red line" of workload (Wickens et al., 2012).

may be beneficial in time-sensitive scenarios, they can also result in rigid thinking and suboptimal outcomes.

However, stress does not invariably produce negative effects. Klein et al. (1993) suggest that experienced decision-makers adapt to stress by employing simplified strategies and concentrating on the most critical information, which makes them less susceptible to its adverse cognitive effects. A prominent example of this is US Airways Flight 1549, in which pilots successfully executed an emergency landing on the Hudson River after a dual engine failure. This case illustrates how expertise and training can mitigate the effects of acute stress (Driskell & Salas, 1991).

Operators of remote autonomous vessels are required to process large volumes of real-time data, monitor system alerts and make rapid, high-stakes decisions. Prolonged monitoring tasks may lead to vigilance decrement, a phenomenon in which the ability to detect critical signals diminishes over time (Endsley et al., 2018). To counter this, Wickens et al. (2021) recommend implementing **workload management strategies**, including rotational shifts, intelligent alerting mechanisms, task redesign and adaptive automation systems that respond to real-time cognitive states.

2.3 Situation Awareness in Autonomous Systems

SA first emerged conceptually during World War I, when Oswald Boelke highlighted the importance of understanding an enemy's position and intentions in combat (Gilson, 1995). However, SA did not gain substantial academic and technical attention until the late 1980s, largely due to advancements in aviation technology and automation (Stanton et al., 2001; Norman, 1991). Stanton et al. (2001) broadly defined SA as the ability to perceive, comprehend and anticipate critical environmental information to guide effective decision-making.

Several theoretical frameworks have shaped the understanding of SA. Endsley's (1995) **three-level model** remains one of the most influential, conceptualising SA as a hierarchical process involving perception of relevant cues, comprehension of their meaning and projection of future states. This model has been widely applied in fields such as aviation, maritime navigation and military operations, particularly for diagnosing SA failures and developing targeted training programmes (Stanton et al., 2013).

Alternatively, Bedny and Meister (1999) proposed the **interactive subsystems approach**, viewing SA as an emergent property of the dynamic interactions between cognitive processes and task demands. This perspective highlights the role of goals, environmental constraints and system design in shaping situational understanding, offering valuable insights for human-centred system development.

Additionally, Neisser's (1976) **perceptual cycle model** presents SA as a continuous, iterative process involving the interaction between mental models and environmental feedback (Stanton et al., 2001). This model emphasises how individuals actively shape their perception through existing knowledge structures and adjust their actions based on new information.

While these models differ in emphasis – process versus product – their integration offers a more comprehensive understanding of SA. Endsley's model is concerned primarily with the product of SA (i.e. the end state of awareness), whereas the interactive subsystems and perceptual cycle models focus more on the process by which SA is developed and maintained.

Gaba and Howard (1995) emphasised that enhanced SA can improve decision-making under uncertainty. Drawing from dynamic and high-risk domains such as anaesthesiology, they considered SA a **teachable skill**. To address decision-making challenges, PSA tools offer data-driven support that can help mitigate bias. Examples include collision avoidance systems with predictive path modelling, predictive maintenance platforms, and anomaly detection and threat prediction systems (Postolache et al., 2024; Stone et al., 2018; Endsley, 2021; Stanton et al., 2001; Wickens et al., 2021). Moreover, training programmes that focus on pattern recognition, multitasking and attention management can help operators sustain high levels of SA, even in time-critical scenarios (Sharma et al., 2019).

The impact of shared displays and task load on **team situation awareness** (TSA) in complex dynamic environments was investigated by Bolstad and Endsley (2000). Their study demonstrated that **abstracted shared displays**, which present only essential shared information, significantly enhance team performance under high workload conditions, whereas **full shared displays**, which replicate all team members' information, can be detrimental due to information overload. The findings support the **TSA model**, emphasising the importance of shared SA requirements, devices, mechanisms and processes in optimising team coordination. Furthermore, the study revealed that teams rely more on implicit coordination through shared displays rather than direct verbal communication as workload increases, reinforcing the necessity of well-designed SA tools in high-stakes decision-making environments. These insights contribute to the broader literature on team cognition, providing empirical evidence that shared displays must be carefully structured to enhance rather than hinder performance in complex operational settings.

Stanton et al. (2001) and Endsley (1995) identified the negative effects of losing SA, including errors in detecting critical cues, slower detection of system problems, delayed responses, ineffective remediation strategies and failures in communication, all of which can result in serious safety incidents. Drawing on evidence from aviation studies, researchers found that key strategies for improving SA include enhanced system design, training in multitasking and pattern recognition. Further research by Jones and Endsley (1996) revealed that the majority of SA-related errors in aviation occur at Level 1 SA, where operators fail to perceive relevant information. In contrast, air traffic controllers tend to experience more errors at Level 3 SA, likely due to the predictive nature of their tasks, which require accurate anticipation of future system states.

Supporting these findings, Durso et al. (1998) observed that air traffic controllers who had lost SA were more prone to errors in data entry and communication, whereas those who maintained SA were more likely to make errors in judgement and decision-making (Stanton et al., 2001). These results emphasise the importance of system design and targeted training to reduce cognitive workload and enhance both perceptual accuracy and decision quality.

To that end, **SA** can be significantly improved through effective interface design, real-time feedback loops and adaptive automation strategies, all of which contribute to safer and more effective maritime operations (Endsley & Jones, 2012). Additionally, the integration of **AI** and **ML** algorithms holds great promise for further advancing SA by optimising real-time decision-making and data interpretation (Goerlandt, 2020).

2.4 AI and Machine Learning in Autonomous Decision-Making

AI-driven predictive analytics enables proactive maintenance by analysing historical data to anticipate equipment failures, thereby reducing downtime, mental workload (MWL) and optimising fleet performance (Kabashkin & Susanin, 2024). Additionally, ML algorithms enhance autonomous navigation by processing past navigational data to optimise routes, incorporating factors such as weather conditions, sea traffic and fuel efficiency (Fossen, 2011). These advancements reduce human intervention and the likelihood of errors while improving vessel performance and cost-effectiveness.

AI-enhanced anomaly detection and system monitoring are also transforming maritime operations by ensuring real-time assessment of vessel performance. Advanced ML models detect deviations in sensor data, signalling potential system failures before they escalate (Simion et al., 2024). This capability enhances operational reliability and safety by allowing timely interventions. However, despite these benefits, AI systems introduce concerns related to transparency and interpretability, as the complexity of AI-driven decisions often limits human operators' ability to understand or challenge them (Endsley & Jones, 2012). Moreover, ethical concerns arise regarding the delegation of decision-making autonomy to AI, particularly in high-stakes scenarios such as collision avoidance (Goodall et al., 2014).

Addressing these challenges requires the development of explainable AI models and regulatory frameworks that balance automation with human oversight. Ensuring that AI aligns with industry regulations and maritime safety protocols is critical for widespread adoption. Overall, while AI and ML offer significant improvements in maritime autonomy, their successful implementation depends on overcoming challenges related to transparency, ethics and regulatory compliance.

3 Method

This chapter employed a multi-method qualitative research approach to examine cognitive and human-system integration (HSI) challenges in remote maritime autonomous operations. The methodology consisted of two interconnected components: a systematic literature review and a case study analysis of the Canadian autonomous surface vehicle (ASV). The literature review encompassed a broad range of scholarly research, theories, technical reports and methodologies related to autonomous maritime systems, with a particular focus on remote operators and HSI. It identified key cognitive and operational challenges, including decision-making under uncertainty, cognitive workload, trust calibration, cognitive biases and the critical role of SA. To address these challenges, the chapter highlights the value of adaptive automation, PSA tools, SDT and targeted training strategies aimed at enhancing cognitive resilience, decision accuracy and effective human-system collaboration. To ensure a structured and transparent analysis, this chapter applies a structured approach that facilitates the identification of research gaps and informs the development of the chapter's objectives and theoretical framework.

The literature search was conducted electronically using the Scopus, Elsevier Freedom Collection and ProQuest Central databases. A carefully selected set of keywords was used to capture the chapter's core themes: HSI, SA, remote vessel operation, autonomous maritime systems, SDT, trust in automation, cognitive workload, multiple resource theory and PSA. Following the removal of duplicate and non–peer-reviewed records, documents were screened based on type, language and title to ensure relevance. Abstracts of the remaining records were then reviewed to exclude non-original research and studies outside the scope of the investigation.

In total, 92 articles met the eligibility criteria and were included in this review. These sources form the analytical foundation of the chapter, providing critical insights into the cognitive demands, system design challenges and decision-making considerations associated with human-system collaboration within the maritime autonomous domain.

To complement the theoretical insights, a qualitative case study was conducted using empirical data collected from structured field trials of the Canadian ASV. Data collection methods included observational field notes from real-time ASV operations, post-trial debriefings with operators and technical staff, and user feedback from structured training sessions and manual override exercises. These data were analysed using thematic coding to identify recurring patterns in operator behaviour, cognitive load, trust calibration and system interaction.

4 Analytical Procedure

This chapter adopts a structured analytical approach rooted in the three-step CAR technique of "challenge", "action" and "result" (Abugohar & Yassin, 2020). This approach serves as the analytical lens through which cognitive challenges in autonomous maritime operations are examined. By structuring the analysis around identified operational and cognitive problems (challenges), corresponding mitigation strategies (actions), and their anticipated or observed effectiveness (results), the chapter ensures a coherent thread from theoretical constructs to practical interventions. The CAR framework not only contextualises each challenge within established human factors theory but also illustrates the actionable steps required to strengthen human-autonomy collaboration in maritime settings. This structured approach offers a comprehensive view of the cognitive and operational demands involved, supported by theoretical foundations, targeted interventions and case-based or empirical evidence.

The CAR approach ensures that the theoretical framework flows seamlessly into the solution space, reinforcing the central argument that resilient and safe autonomous maritime operations must be built on a foundation of human-centred design and cognitive compatibility.

To explore HSI and supervisory control, the Canadian ASV case study was examined through a qualitative analysis of operator interactions during structured field trials conducted in the designated Canadian marine autonomous

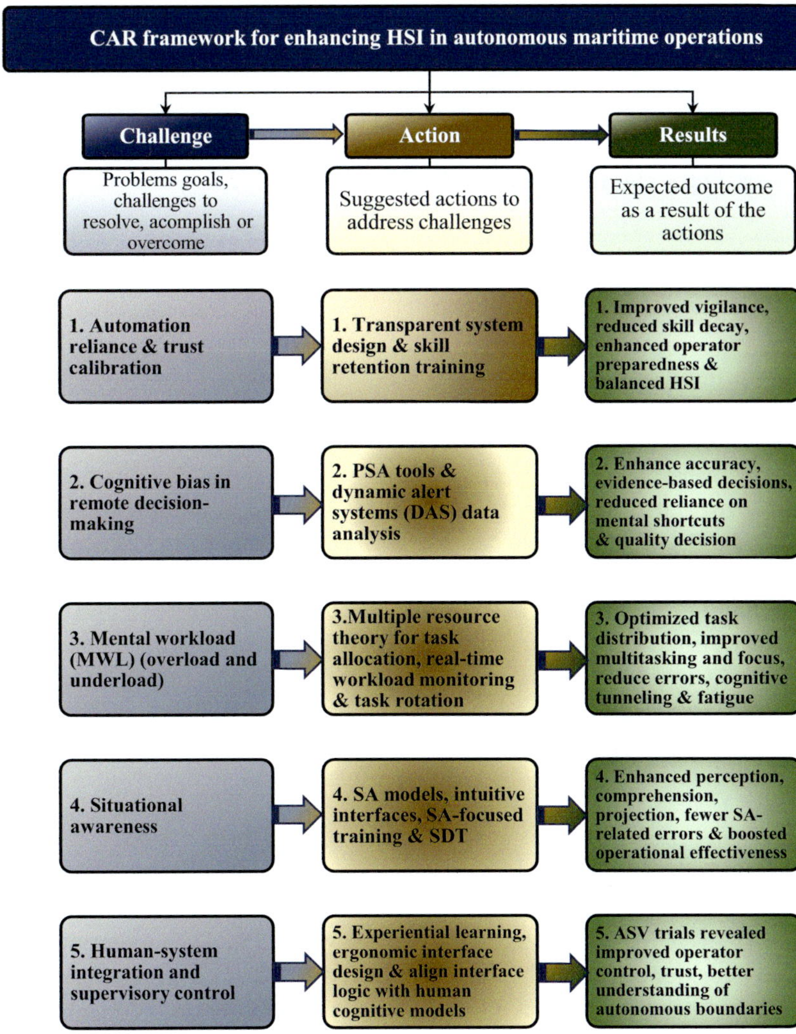

FIGURE 4.2 CAR framework analysis

test zone (MATZ). Data from observational field notes, post-trial debriefings, system performance logs and user feedback during training exercises and manual override scenarios were analysed to identify recurring patterns of cognitive strain, interface challenges and variations in SA and decision-making across different operational modes. Particular attention was given to moments of transition between autonomous and manual control, as well as to operator responses to ambiguous or degraded communication scenarios. Thematic coding was used to extract key HSI issues, focusing on supervisory control dynamics, cognitive workload, trust calibration and bias-related behaviours. The finalised codes were grouped into broader themes that capture meaningful patterns across the dataset, providing a structured framework for interpreting human-system interaction trends. Findings were then synthesised to inform HSI recommendations aimed at enhancing operator engagement, system transparency and resilience in remote maritime operations.

5 Automation Challenges and Cognitive Impacts

5.1 Trust in Automation

Trust in autonomous systems is a key factor in effective human-technology collaboration. Under-reliance on automation may lead to excessive manual intervention, while over-reliance can reduce operator vigilance and increase the risk of oversight errors. Proper training and system transparency help calibrate trust, ensuring that operators understand automation limitations (Wickens et al., 2004). In 2022, Mallam et al. emphasised the positive impact of empathy on the design, organisation and operations of complex systems, highlighting its role as an entry point for user-centred approaches, while advocating proactive training to develop empathic skills. This raises the question of whether the maritime community is ready to put its trust in automated shipboard systems. Alberg et al. (2024) concluded that the evolution of trust from scepticism to reliance on automated systems is contingent on alignment with professional standards rooted in the seafarers' identity.

5.1.1 Under-Reliance on Automation

Under-reliance on automation occurs when operators fail to utilise automated systems effectively, leading to excessive manual intervention and increased workload. This phenomenon can degrade performance, reduce efficiency and heighten the risk of human error (Dixon et al., 2007). Hence, the effectiveness of automated systems depends on how well humans interact with them. While much research focuses on over-reliance on automation, under-reliance, where users do not sufficiently engage with automated systems, can be equally detrimental.

A key factor contributing to under-reliance is a persistent lack of trust in automated systems. Operators may develop scepticism based on previous system failures or inconsistencies, reinforcing perceptions of unreliability (Lee & See, 2004). This distrust is further exacerbated when automation lacks transparency. If system behaviour is opaque or its decision-making logic is not communicated clearly, operators may hesitate to defer to it (Endsley, 2017). Such uncertainty can limit operators' willingness to allow automation to function independently.

Compounding these challenges is the issue of insufficient training. When users are not adequately prepared to understand or interact with automated systems, confidence in automation diminishes (Parasuraman & Riley, 1997). Negative experiences, particularly those involving system failures, can further entrench automation bias, whereby operators generalise past problems to future interactions, leading to avoidance behaviour (Cummings, 2017). In some cases, operators may also prefer manual control, not because of distrust, but due to a desire for active engagement or a belief that manual operation helps preserve essential maritime skills (Kaber, 1996).

The consequences of under-reliance extend beyond individual operator performance. Cognitive overload becomes more likely as operators assume tasks that automation could manage, leading to slower response times and an increased potential for human error (Wickens, 2008). Operational efficiency also suffers, with decision-making processes delayed or degraded due to the bypassing of automated support systems (Hoff & Bashir, 2015). In complex or time-critical situations, this hesitation can create bottlenecks, placing undue strain on the human operator and compromising overall system performance (Bainbridge, 1983).

To mitigate under-reliance, the literature emphasises several interdependent action strategies aimed at reinforcing operator trust, improving system usability and promoting healthy human-automation collaboration. Enhancing the reliability and transparency of automation systems is a foundational step. When operators are informed about what the system is doing and why, they are more likely to trust its functionality (Hoff & Bashir, 2015). Supported by user-centred design practices and intuitive, standardised interfaces, automated systems can reduce cognitive friction and promote consistent operator engagement (Mallam, 2023).

Equally important is the role of comprehensive training and familiarisation with the new systems, as emphasised by Driskell and Salas (1991), who found that training can reduce stress and improve trust in decision aids. Training programmes that focus on system capabilities, limitations and appropriate use cases can build user confidence and reduce hesitation (Parasuraman et al., 2000). Adaptive automation offers another avenue for improvement, allowing systems to adjust their level of support based on user behaviour and contextual demands, thereby aligning system actions with operator expectations (Kaber, 1996). Feedback mechanisms also play a pivotal role. Providing timely and informative feedback during system use not only supports decision-making but also reinforces correct usage patterns, encouraging appropriate reliance (Lee & See, 2004).

Ultimately, overcoming under-reliance on automation in remote maritime environments requires a multifaceted approach, one that integrates technical improvements, human factors principles and organisational support. Future research should continue to explore how these elements interact to shape operator behaviour, with the goal of enabling automation to serve as a true extension of human capability, neither ignored nor blindly trusted, but thoughtfully and appropriately engaged.

5.1.2 Over-Reliance on Automation

The growing reliance on automated systems across safety-critical domains, including autonomous shipping, has drawn attention to their impact on human cognitive performance, particularly SA. Over-reliance on automation poses serious risks by dulling operators' vigilance, eroding critical thinking and diminishing the ability to respond swiftly during manual interventions (Parasuraman & Riley, 1997). As operators increasingly delegate decision-making responsibilities to automation, a false sense of system infallibility can emerge. This often results in complacency, whereby the operator assumes the system is always correct and refrains from actively monitoring or questioning automated outputs. Over time, this excessive dependence can lead to skill decay, weakening operational readiness and reducing performance in situations that demand rapid, high-stakes decision-making.

Addressing these issues requires a multifaceted set of action strategies, beginning with reinforcing operators' manual control competencies. Regularly scheduled manual override drills, accompanied by situational awareness training, are vital in keeping operators cognitively engaged (Baum-Talmor & Kitada, 2022). These exercises not only reduce cognitive overload through practice but also counteract the natural decline of unused skills. Research suggests that many critical skills deteriorate within six months if not actively maintained, highlighting the importance of multi-day, hands-on training programmes specifically targeting rarely used but essential capabilities. In this context, reinforcing operator preparedness directly supports SA and improves skill retention and decision-making resilience under pressure (Sanli & Carnahan, 2018; Wulf et al., 2010; Kantak & Winstein, 2012).

To further enhance cognitive engagement and prevent passive monitoring, the implementation of a dynamic alert system (DAS) can prove invaluable. DAS frameworks are designed to support timely and accurate responses to emerging hazards without overwhelming the operator's cognitive capacity. By incorporating auditory cues or visual prompts, the DAS actively encourages manual system assessments, interrupting patterns of blind trust and stimulating deliberate cognitive involvement. These systems enhance vigilance and promote more thoughtful interactions with automation. Within this context, SDT operates as a foundational mechanism underpinning DAS effectiveness. As an applied framework, it guides the calibration of alert thresholds to differentiate between true threats and irrelevant stimuli. This reduces false alarms and alarm fatigue while ensuring that critical warnings are not overlooked, thereby preserving operator attention and decision quality (Schmidt et al., 2023; Stone et al., 2018).

A crucial component in mitigating over-reliance is the design of the human-machine interface (HMI) itself. Interfaces that prioritise essential operational information while allowing access to deeper system data through layered displays can significantly reduce information overload. Such structuring supports more efficient cognitive processing, particularly during time-critical scenarios. By simplifying how information is presented and accessed, layered HMI design not only improves usability but also minimises the risk of human error. Importantly, effective HMI encourages operators to remain actively engaged by facilitating manual cross-checking and discouraging automatic acceptance of system outputs, thereby reinforcing a critical layer of human oversight (Mallam, 2023; Stone et al., 2018).

Lastly, the integration of real-time performance feedback mechanisms during both training and operations plays a powerful role in refining operator behaviour. These systems provide immediate alerts when lapses in monitoring or errors in judgement occur, offering operators the opportunity to self-correct in real time. Such feedback enhances pattern recognition, strengthens problem-solving skills and reinforces the operator's understanding of both the capabilities and limits of automation. More importantly, it encourages adaptive learning, allowing users to proactively adjust their behaviour and improve preparedness for future tasks. The combination of experiential feedback and dynamic learning cycles supports operational readiness and reduces long-term risks associated with over-reliance on automation (Stone et al., 2018; Sanli & Carnahan, 2018; Kantak & Winstein, 2012).

Together, these mitigation strategies emphasise the need for an integrated, human-centred approach to automation in remote maritime operations. They highlight the importance of balancing technological sophistication with operator engagement, ensuring that human cognitive capabilities are neither sidelined by automation nor overwhelmed by it. By promoting vigilance, transparency and hands-on familiarity, such strategies support more resilient and adaptive HSI.

5.2 Cognitive Biases in Decision-Making

As remote autonomous operations increasingly place critical decision-making responsibilities on human operators, it becomes essential to scrutinise the cognitive shortcuts, heuristics that underpin decision-making under uncertainty. While heuristics can be adaptive in time-pressured environments, they often lead to systematic errors or cognitive biases, which may undermine safety, efficiency and operator trust in autonomous systems (Kahneman et al., 1982; Stone et al., 2018). In contrast to rational actor models that presume optimal choice-making, cognitive psychology highlights that decisions are frequently shaped by bounded rationality, in which limitations in time, attention and memory lead to simplified judgements (Simon, 1957). While some scholars argue that such heuristics reflect efficient adaptations to complex tasks (Gigerenzer & Gaissmaier, 2011), others contend that biases are persistent vulnerabilities that must be actively mitigated through interface design and decision support (Parasuraman & Manzey, 2010). The maritime context, characterised by time-critical, uncertain and data-saturated environments, renders such biases particularly consequential. Moreover, understanding how individuals make decisions, the factors that influence their choices and the tools that can support better decision-making is essential for improving performance in high-stakes environments (Hansen et al., 2024).

5.2.1 Confirmation Bias

Confirmation bias is the tendency to favour information that supports pre-existing beliefs while disregarding contradictory evidence. It is a well-established cognitive bias that can significantly impair decision-making. In high-stakes settings such as autonomous maritime navigation, this bias increases safety risks, as operators under pressure may unconsciously overlook critical cues that conflict with their expectations. To mitigate such risks, PSA tools can offer algorithmically generated forecasts based on real-time and historical data. These tools challenge operator assumptions and support more evidence-based decision-making (Parasuraman & Manzey, 2010; Stone et al., 2018; Sheela & Mannering, 2020; Howard & Borenstein, 2019). However, while these tools reduce bias, they do not eliminate it entirely, particularly if operators place greater trust in AI-generated outputs than in their own situational perception, potentially creating new blind spots.

For instance, in scenarios involving limited visibility, such as navigating through dense fog, PSA systems can provide timely and detailed information about nearby vessel trajectories and evolving environmental conditions. These insights reduce the likelihood of an operator relying solely on partial or biased data and instead support a more balanced and accurate situational assessment. The Canadian ASV combines multiple sensors with intelligent software to provide a comprehensive understanding of a vessel's surroundings. This system is particularly beneficial in poor weather conditions, congested waters or during night operations, enhancing SA for onshore operators.

5.2.2 Availability Bias

Availability heuristic/bias refers to the cognitive tendency to overestimate the likelihood of events based on how easily similar instances come to mind, particularly when they are recent, emotionally charged, or memorable. In high-pressure environments such as autonomous maritime operations, this bias can distort risk assessments, leading operators to prioritise recent experiences, such as a recent mechanical failure, over less obvious but potentially more critical threats. As a result, safety protocols may be compromised by reactive rather than proactive decision-making or under-preparedness for less salient yet more statistically probable threats (Parasuraman & Manzey, 2010; Stone et al., 2018; Tversky et al., 2009; Siegrist, 2021).

To mitigate this bias, PSA tools can integrate historical data with real-time sensor input to identify patterns that may not be immediately apparent to human operators. By expanding the informational frame beyond recent or salient events, PSA enhances risk assessments and reduces the influence of availability bias. For example, predictive maintenance systems use long-term performance data to anticipate rare or hidden failure trends, supporting more proactive and effective decision-making. However, the challenge lies in ensuring that cognitive aids do not themselves become sources of saliency bias, where more visually striking alerts are overprioritised irrespective of actual urgency.

5.2.3 Anchoring Bias

Anchoring bias refers to the cognitive tendency to rely too heavily on the first piece of information encountered, often called the "**anchor**", when making decisions. Even when new or contradictory information becomes available, individuals tend to adjust insufficiently from this initial reference point (Stone et al., 2018; Endsley, 2015).

In autonomous maritime operations, where conditions can change rapidly, such as due to unexpected weather or traffic congestion, anchoring bias can compromise safety by causing operators to rigidly adhere to initial plans despite evolving hazards. PSA tools provide a critical countermeasure by continuously processing real-time sensor and environmental data to generate dynamic models and forecasts, thereby preventing operators from remaining anchored to outdated plans (Endsley, 1995; Parasuraman & Manzey, 2010; Sheridan, 2017). By integrating real-time environmental models, PSA tools can disrupt cognitive anchoring through ongoing risk reassessment. However, such systems must balance corrective feedback with operator autonomy, as excessive or contradictory updates may confuse rather than support decision-making, emphasising the need for clear and consistent feedback mechanisms.

5.2.4 Overconfidence Bias

Overconfidence bias is a cognitive phenomenon in which individuals place excessive trust in their own judgements, often leading to an underestimation of risks and an overestimation of capabilities (Stone et al., 2018). In autonomous maritime operations, this bias can result in inadequate preparation, misjudgement of environmental conditions and failure to respond effectively to emerging threats, especially when operators rely too heavily on initial assessments. PSA tools provide a counterbalance by surfacing probabilistic models that reveal the uncertainties inherent in sensor inputs and forecasts. By continuously analysing real-time and historical data, these systems challenge initial assumptions and deliver dynamic updates that support more accurate decision-making. For example, while an operator may initially project optimal fuel usage, PSA tools monitor changing sea conditions and currents to update forecasts, ensuring more realistic planning and adaptive responses. Yet the reliance on automation can also amplify overconfidence if operators misinterpret system outputs as definitive rather than probabilistic. Hence, interface design must communicate confidence intervals or likelihood ratings to ground operator expectations in calibrated realism (Endsley & Jones, 2012; Sheridan, 2017; Mallam et al., 2019b, 2020; Endsley, 1990).

5.3 Mental Workload Challenges

SA plays a pivotal role in the safe and efficient operation of autonomous ships (Endsley, 1995). It enables operators to perceive, interpret and anticipate changes in the maritime environment. However, maintaining high levels of SA is often compromised by MWL challenges, especially in high-stakes and dynamic scenarios. As automation increases in maritime operations, understanding the cognitive demands placed on remote operators becomes essential.

In high-demand environments such as remote vessel operation, operators frequently experience cognitive overload, which impairs their ability to process information efficiently and leads to increased errors and delayed decision-making. This deterioration in cognitive performance has a direct impact on SA and overall safety (Endsley, 1995). Task prioritisation and automation-assisted decision support systems play a crucial role in mitigating cognitive overload, thereby supporting efficient and safe operations (Wickens et al., 2004; Stanton et al., 2013).

Additionally, adaptive automation can alleviate operators' workload by taking over routine or non-critical tasks while leaving key decisions to the human operator (Parasuraman et al., 2000). For instance, automating data logging during a collision avoidance scenario allows operators to focus their attention on navigation and manoeuvring. Conversely, operators engaged in continuous monitoring tasks often face cognitive underload. This state of under-stimulation can result in boredom, reduced vigilance and slower reaction times, increasing the likelihood of missing critical environmental cues (Young & Stanton, 2002).

Real-time workload monitoring combined with adaptive task allocation plays a vital role in maintaining operator engagement and preventing cognitive underload. Introducing dynamic, low-priority tasks during periods of reduced activity has been shown to sustain mental stimulation and responsiveness (Hancock & Warm, 1989). However, workload challenges are not solely a matter of task quantity; interface complexity also significantly affects MWL. Poorly designed or cluttered interfaces can obscure essential information, increasing cognitive strain and reducing the operator's ability to maintain SA (Wickens, 2008). To address this, redesigning interfaces with intuitive layouts and incorporating multimodal feedback, such as visual and auditory alerts, can enhance cognitive efficiency and reduce mental fatigue, enabling faster recognition and response to anomalies (Wickens et al., 2021).

Beyond interface design, the balance of task distribution between automation and human operators is equally critical. When automation is not optimally assigned, it can result in either cognitive overload or disengagement (Parasuraman & Riley, 1997). A more strategic task allocation, such as automating routine updates, for example weather data, while reserving complex navigational decisions for human control, can help maintain cognitive balance and support effective SA (Stanton et al., 2013). Additionally, external environmental stressors, including noise, poor lighting and frequent interruptions, can impair cognitive performance by reducing accuracy and slowing reaction times (Galy et al., 2017). Enhancing the physical workspace through better lighting, soundproofing and tools such as noise-canceling headsets can mitigate these stressors, helping to preserve focus and reduce cognitive fatigue (Szalma et al., 2011).

6 Signal Detection Theory

Cognitive challenges in human-technology interaction underscore the need for tools that promote active and informed operator engagement. One such tool is SDT, a modelling framework designed to enhance decision-making in complex environments. SDT offers a structured approach for distinguishing between true signals, such as navigational hazards, marine life or environmental anomalies, and noise, that is, irrelevant or background data, under uncertainty (Stone et al., 2018; Schmidt et al., 2023; Laming, 1968). By balancing the detection of real threats (hits) against the minimisation of false alarms and missed detections, SDT supports more accurate and timely responses.

In maritime contexts, this approach ensures that operators are neither overwhelmed by irrelevant information nor lulled into complacency by automation. When integrated into PSA tools, SDT principles help maintain vigilance, improve risk assessment and optimise operational safety (Masalonis & Parasuraman, 2003), thereby reinforcing the broader goal of resilient human-machine collaboration.

Autonomous maritime systems, which depend heavily on sensor arrays and remote decision-making infrastructure, benefit significantly from SDT principles that enhance system performance and reliability in dynamic environments (Stone et al., 2018). One of the primary contributions of SDT lies in its capacity to improve hazard detection by calibrating sensor thresholds to distinguish between genuine threats, such as debris (Tuzlukov, 2001), submerged obstacles, or adverse weather conditions and innocuous environmental variations, like small waves or floating matter. For instance, sonar systems guided by SDT can be fine-tuned to differentiate between a submerged buoy and harmless surface clutter, thereby reducing noise in threat assessment. Furthermore, SDT informs decision-making frameworks used by both remote operation centres (ROCs) and onboard systems by supporting the prioritisation of critical alerts. Rather than generating indiscriminate notifications, SDT enables systems to filter and elevate alerts that require immediate attention, thereby facilitating focused and effective operator responses (Stone et al., 2018). A central feature of SDT is its systematic handling of the trade-off between misses, where a genuine hazard goes undetected, and false alarms, where unnecessary interventions are triggered. By optimising this balance, SDT contributes to maintaining both safety and operational efficiency, ensuring that neither is compromised by an over- or under-reactive system (Kantak & Winstein, 2012).

The practical applications of SDT are particularly evident in the calibration and operational logic of sensor systems used in autonomous maritime platforms. Technologies such as LIDAR, sonar and optical cameras benefit substantially from SDT-guided tuning, which enhances their ability to perform real-time environmental monitoring with high fidelity. Through precise threshold setting, SDT enables these systems to accurately distinguish between relevant hazards and benign environmental features. For example, SDT allows sonar systems to identify submerged obstructions that pose a navigational risk while effectively filtering out acoustic signatures from marine life or surface wave interference, thereby minimising unnecessary alarms and maintaining system efficiency.

SDT also shapes the logic of navigation and collision avoidance systems by structuring the interpretation of sensor data through four detection outcomes: hits, misses, false alarms and correct rejections. A "**hit**" occurs when the system correctly detects a genuine hazard, such as an underwater obstruction, reef or fishing net, prompting an alert to the ROC and enabling timely intervention. Conversely, a "**miss**" represents a failure to identify a true threat, such as an undetected approaching vessel, which could lead to potential collisions. **False alarms** arise when harmless objects, like seaweed or driftwood, are misclassified as threats, leading to unnecessary evasive manoeuvres that can disrupt operations. Meanwhile, "**correct rejections**" occur when the system accurately dismisses non-threatening inputs, such as sonar fluctuations caused by small fish or minor wave reflections. By optimising these detection outcomes, SDT ensures that autonomous systems strike a balance between sensitivity and specificity, ultimately promoting navigational safety without compromising operational fluidity (McClure et al., 2010).

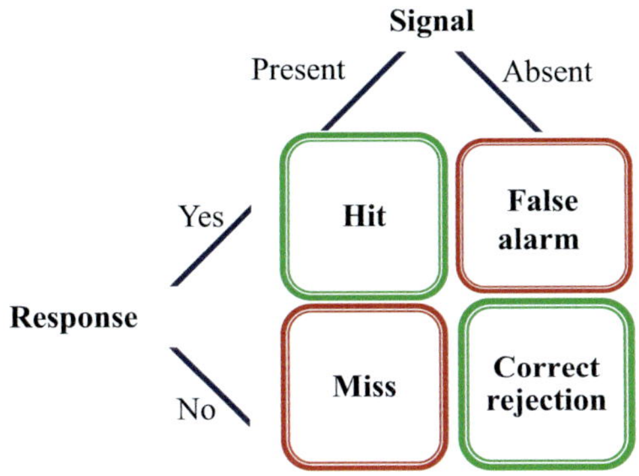

FIGURE 4.3 The four categories of responses from signal detection theory (McClure et al., 2010)

An essential aspect of SDT in remote operations is its ability to adapt sensitivity thresholds to changing environmental conditions. Threshold calibration is dynamic – in dense traffic zones, lower thresholds heighten responsiveness to fast-moving vessels that could pose sudden navigational risks. Conversely, in open sea conditions, where the likelihood of encountering threats is reduced, higher thresholds help filter out benign stimuli and minimise unnecessary alerts. Under poor visibility conditions, SDT-guided configurations may favour a reduced reliance on camera-based systems, whose visual accuracy may be compromised, and instead increase input weighting from LIDAR or sonar to maintain hazard detection accuracy. These adaptive calibrations underscore SDT's capacity to manage the trade-off between early hazard detection and the risk of generating an excessive number of false alarms that could impair operator performance or system trust.

The integration of SDT also has profound implications for human factors in supervisory control. By ensuring that system-generated alerts are clear, relevant and actionable, SDT contributes to reducing cognitive overload among operators, particularly during high-stress or time-sensitive decision-making scenarios (Schmidt et al., 2019; Scherer, 2019). This alignment enhances the quality of human-system interaction by allowing operators to focus on critical threats without the distraction of frequent or ambiguous notifications. Furthermore, regular system calibration informs targeted training programmes that help operators interpret alerts effectively and respond to emergencies with greater readiness (Sanli et al., 2018).

Precision in detection systems, driven by SDT, reduces the likelihood of human errors such as misidentifying threats or failing to act on critical information (Stone et al., 2018). Importantly, it helps reduce slips and lapses, errors of execution that occur when actions are unintentionally triggered or incorrectly omitted due to cognitive fatigue or contextual distractions. SDT-driven alert systems, when designed to be unambiguous and context sensitive, can significantly lower the incidence of such unintentional deviations from protocol. Finally, SDT's emphasis on continuous threshold adjustment and reliability testing promotes consistent system behaviour across diverse maritime scenarios, enhancing both trust and safety (Kantak & Winstein, 2012).

7 Future Directions in Human-System Integration: Canadian ASV Case Study

As maritime operations evolve towards autonomous operations, maintaining effective Human-System collaboration remains critical to ensuring safety, resilience and operational efficiency. The Canadian ASV case study provides a compelling example of the challenges and opportunities in this domain. Operating in Canada's complex coastal and offshore environments, which are characterised by unpredictable weather, maritime traffic and ecologically sensitive areas, the case study highlights the demanding conditions faced by both autonomous systems and their human supervisors. Designed to operate for up to 14 days in a row in waves reaching four metres and near gale-force winds, the 8-metres ASV is governed by a robust safety management system (SMS) protocol that ensures standardised mission planning, risk assessment,

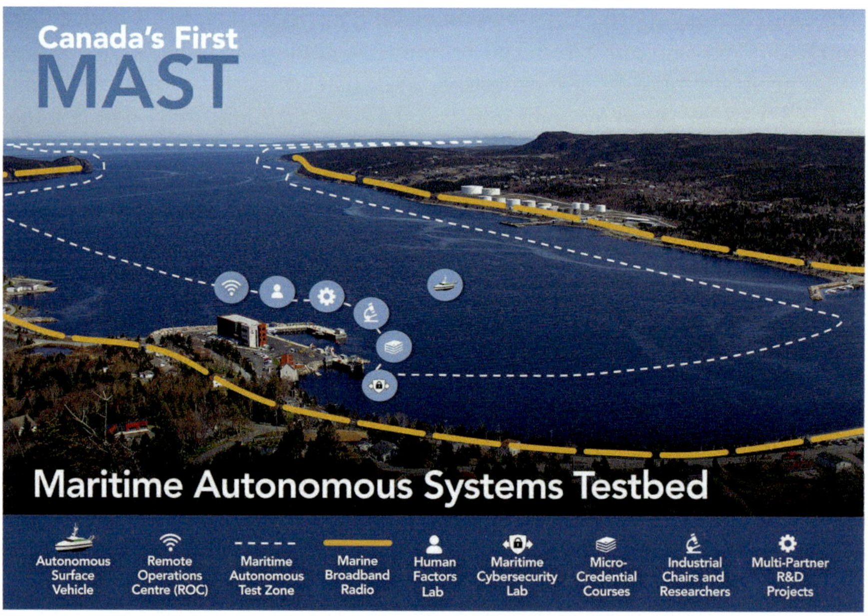

FIGURE 4.4 Marine autonomous systems testbed (MAST) – the Launch – Image courtesy of Fisheries and Marine Institute of Memorial University of Newfoundland

emergency response procedures and environmental protection, in compliance with Transport Canada regulations.

The SMS testing protocol within the MATZ mandates real-time coordination among personnel, including a master vehicle operator, a chaperone or support vessel and a designated person ashore (DPA). Each operation follows structured briefings, checklists, safety checks and launch-to-recovery procedures, integrating key safety elements such as cybersecurity, emergency response, visual identification and environmental protection.

The cognitive challenges outlined in this chapter, including MWL, SA, trust calibration and decision-making biases, have direct implications for the design and operation of remote operations centres (ROCs) and the roles of remote operators. In ROC settings, where operators are responsible for overseeing high-risk environments, SA is heavily reliant on system feedback, interface design and the interpretation of real-time data. Addressing these challenges requires the integration of SDT to optimise alert sensitivity and minimise false alarms, as well as the development of adaptive HMIs that respond dynamically to changing workload and urgency levels. These approaches, in combination with PSA tools and bias-mitigation training, form the foundation of a more resilient human-system collaboration model. The Canadian ASV project offers a unique opportunity to examine HSI challenges and strategies within the context of real-world autonomous maritime operations. Unlike simulated settings, the ASV trials take place under operational conditions that reveal the full complexity of remote supervision, manual override and adaptive autonomy.

Unlike simulated settings, the Canadian ASV trials take place in operational conditions that expose the full complexity of remote supervision, manual override and adaptive autonomy. This allows for a more authentic observation and assessment of how interface ergonomics and automation transparency influence operators' cognitive demands, decision-making processes, workload and trust.

Serving as a live testbed, the ASV case study contributes valuable insights into HSI strategies for enhancing SA, mitigating cognitive bias and fostering effective human-system collaboration. Lessons learned from the field trials offer critical guidance on supervisory control, trust calibration and the human factors essential to the safe and efficient deployment of autonomous maritime technologies.

7.1 Human-System Integration and Cognitive Challenges in the Canadian ASV Operations

7.1.1 Supervisory Control and Over-Reliance on Automation

While autonomous systems offer significant operational advantages, they have also been associated with a decline in operator skills and reduced readiness

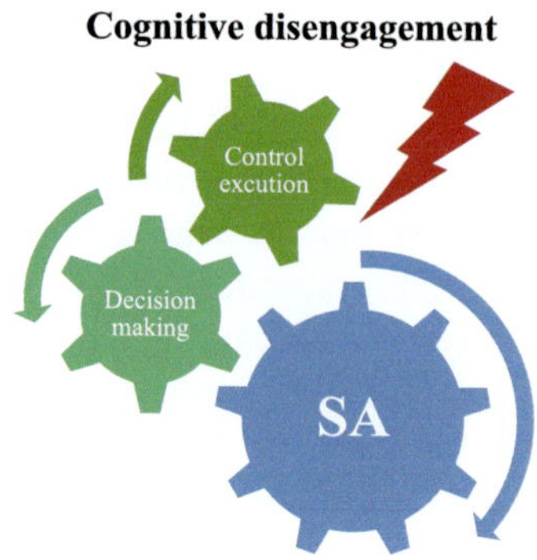

FIGURE 4.5 Cognitive disengagement in human system interaction

Source: Endsley, 2025.

to intervene during critical events (Endsley, 2017; Parasuraman et al., 2000). This is often attributed to "out-of-the-loop" performance problems, where prolonged monitoring of automated processes leads to diminished situational awareness, reduced vigilance and lower cognitive engagement. Operators may retain access to relevant information but fail to process or act upon it deeply due to passive involvement. Empirical evidence suggests that manual skills deteriorate over time when users are not actively engaged in task execution, resulting in weaker comprehension and slower response times (Wickens et al., 2021). These challenges are observed not only in real-time control tasks, such as piloting or remote navigation, but also in decision-support contexts, where over-reliance on automated outputs can lead to superficial assessments and a failure to grasp underlying system dynamics.

These concerns are reflected in Canadian ASV operations, where human operators are tasked with mission planning, monitoring system health and making critical decisions during unexpected events. Their role is predominantly supervisory, involving intermittent but high-stakes interventions. For training and educational purposes, however, operators are also given opportunities to manually control the vessel via a remote controller. To maintain situational awareness, they rely on a suite of technologies including radar, LIDAR, AIS, sonar and GPS. A key challenge lies in deciding which functions should be automated and which require human oversight. Poorly calibrated automation can exacerbate out-of-the-loop issues, compromising SA and limiting the operator's ability to respond effectively, particularly during system malfunctions or novel scenarios. In ASV trials, this was evident when operators struggled to quickly reorient themselves in off-nominal conditions due to complex or ambiguous situations such as loss of communication, intermittent GPS signal degradation, and frozen or delayed video feeds.

7.1.2 AI and Machine Learning in Autonomous Decision-Making

The ASV's current navigation and obstacle-avoidance systems do not yet employ advanced AI algorithms. Instead, the vessel primarily relies on GPS for waypoint navigation, radar and AIS for communication and situational awareness, and LIDAR as a backup failsafe for close-range obstacle detection.

As of now, machine vision and video-based perception, key enablers of AI in autonomous vehicles, are not actively integrated into the ASV's decision-making process. The camera feeds are used solely by human operators, emphasising a clear opportunity for further automation through ML-based image recognition for obstacle detection and improved environmental awareness.

Some operators have reported challenges in assessing vessel motion and interpreting navigational feedback. As one operator noted: "We had to watch the wake . . . otherwise we didn't really have an indication of if the vehicle was purposefully moving forward." As a result, they relied on visual cues such as the camera wake-up time (the camera starts recording a few seconds after detecting motion) to determine whether the vessel was moving as planned. This reliance on subjective interpretation underscores the potential value of an **AI-enhanced feedback system**. By incorporating machine learning to analyse sensor fusion data (e.g. GPS, video, radar), such a system could provide automated, real-time performance assessments, for example, indicating propulsion status or course deviations. This would help reduce the cognitive workload of operators during monitoring and increase trust in autonomous systems by offering clear, objective feedback on vessel behaviour, without the need to rely on indirect visual indicators.

7.1.3 Situation Awareness

During the demo trials, the ASV initially operated autonomously as expected, demonstrating predictable system behaviour. Following this, users were given the opportunity to control the vessel manually using a remote controller. This hands-on exercise revealed a gap between theoretical supervision and practical control. The purpose was not only to evaluate system response but also to expose users to the challenges of direct remote operation. This case highlights that even in predominantly autonomous contexts, understanding manual control dynamics is essential for effective supervisory roles. It reinforced the importance of experiential learning in developing user appreciation for control complexity, especially when transitions between autonomy and manual override are required. The controller was always mapped relative to the bow of the boat, but when the vessel moved towards the user, directional inputs became cognitively reversed. This led to observable behaviour changes, such as participants physically turning around to align their perspective with that of the vessel. This embodied coping strategy points to a mismatch between control logic and intuitive spatial reasoning, especially for users with limited spatial awareness. The incident underscores the importance of designing interfaces that support cognitive alignment and reduce the mental translation required during operation, particularly when directional perception is reversed.

Another challenge related to maintaining SA emerged from reliance on 2D video feeds, which lacked immersive depth cues. Users reported that visual judgement was impaired compared to real-world perspective and that the numeric-based interface was cognitively demanding, with remarks like "You don't get a true depth as you would if you were actually sitting on the real core . . . you've got to get used to that," referring to the difficulty in spatial judgement via screens. Others said, "I would really like a more graphical representation . . . not just the numbers". These examples underscore the value of human-centred design and immersive interfaces that align with natural spatial reasoning and reduce perceptual strain.

Together, these situations highlight how low-fidelity interfaces can impair operators' ability to maintain accurate SA, a critical capability in remote maritime operations. They emphasise the importance of human-centred interface design and the integration of intuitive, immersive feedback systems that support spatial cognition and reduce perceptual strain.

7.1.4 Trust in the Autonomous System

Trust plays a central role in determining how operators interact with autonomous operations. In the ASV case, inconsistencies in system behaviour, particularly during obstacle avoidance or rule-of-the-road navigation, can create hesitation among operators to rely fully on automated processes. Some operators intervened unnecessarily while others delayed action due to overreliance. This finding highlights the mismatch between system transparency and operator expectations, emphasising the need for clear, predictable behaviour and reliable feedback mechanisms within the HMI.

The ASV demo trial sessions offered valuable insights into how trust is developed and disrupted. While the ASV's consistent autonomous performance helped establish initial confidence, the challenges of manual control such as disorienting interface ergonomics and spatial confusion revealed how quickly trust can erode. This highlights that trust depends not only on system reliability but also on perceived controllability, both of which are strongly influenced by interface design and user experience.

Although the ASV used GPS, radar and AIS for navigation and potential future collision avoidance, camera feeds were often not integrated into machine decision-making. Some users confirmed that they relied on video feeds during remote operation while the system algorithms did not, highlighting a disconnect between human trust in visual data and automation's reliance on abstracted data. This gap can lead to situations where humans override or mistrust automated systems, especially when outcomes appear inconsistent with visual evidence, increasing the chance of automation bias and manual intervention.

7.1.5 Cognitive Workload

Piloting the ASV, especially remotely via cameras, imposed a high mental load on operators. Some users explained their experience of hyper-focus on the video feed during figure-eight manoeuvres around a buoy, making it difficult to monitor other data like heading or battery level at the same time. This reflects **cognitive tunnelling**, where excessive attention to one source (video feed) detracts from broader situational monitoring.

One operator said, "I had to focus entirely on the video feeds . . . when someone asked, 'What's your heading?' I had to quickly glance away."

This also underscores the need for effective **interface design** that better supports multitasking and information prioritising.

7.1.6 Cognitive Bias

A practical illustration of **availability bias** emerged during one of the Canadian ASV collision-avoidance test scenarios. The test team had meticulously prepared in alignment with Transport Canada guidelines, including implementation of the COLREGs Storyboard, deployment of an onshore operator, an onboard safety representative for emergency interventions and the use of a chaperone vessel. However, when a communication issue arose during final preparations, the team initially interpreted it as a technical malfunction, drawing from similar past experiences. Upon further investigation, it was revealed that the actual cause was an expired RADAR licence, an oversight not immediately considered due to the unavailability of such a case in recent memory.

This incident underscores the critical role of cognitive framing in operational environments. Because the vessel's RADAR system could not legally or functionally operate without a valid licence, the test had to be postponed. Without RADAR, the remote operator could not fulfil the visual lookout requirement stipulated under COLREGs Rule 5, even with the support of AI and alternative sensors. RADAR is fundamental not only for detecting other vessels but also for identifying landmasses and navigational hazards. The team's initial response, shaped by **availability bias**, delayed the correct diagnosis and resolution of the issue.

Another example of cognitive bias occurred during a Canadian ASV demonstration. In this case, users were asked to manually control the vessel using a handheld remote after observing its autonomous navigation performance. Many users, anchored to their prior assumption that manual control would mirror video game-like responsiveness, underestimated the complexity of real-time maritime navigation. This mental anchor led to overconfidence in handling, despite delays in command execution caused by latency and environmental factors such as wind and current. As a result, several users initially made incorrect directional inputs, particularly when the vessel was approaching them, and control orientation became reversed. This example illustrates how prior expectations, formed from familiar but unrelated contexts, can **anchor user perception** and impair performance in high-stakes remote maritime operations. It highlights the importance of training that helps operators recalibrate their expectations when transitioning between familiar control paradigms and real-world autonomous vessel systems.

7.2 The Application of SDT to the Canadian ASV

SDT involves a systematic process to enhance navigation and SA. First, sensors like LIDAR, sonar and cameras are calibrated to detect true hazards while minimising false alarms by setting context-specific detection thresholds. Next, the ASV's decision-making systems are analysed to balance hits (accurate detections) and misses (undetected threats) while managing false alarms and correct rejections. Sensitivity adjustments are made dynamically based on environmental conditions, such as relying on sonar in low visibility. Human factors are integrated by designing clear, actionable alerts, training operators for effective interpretation of these alerts, and reducing cognitive load. Finally, outcomes are evaluated using SDT metrics, ensuring the ASV operates safely and efficiently in complex maritime environments.

The effectiveness of SDT is evaluated by examining key operational outcomes, including hit rates, misses, false alarms and correct rejections. Hit rates reflect the system's success in accurately detecting genuine hazards, while misses and false alarms represent errors that may compromise operational safety by either failing to identify real threats or triggering unnecessary responses. Correct rejections, on the other hand, demonstrate the system's ability to dismiss irrelevant or non-threatening inputs appropriately. This approach enables a structured assessment of how well the ASV responds to uncertain and dynamic maritime conditions.

8 Conclusion and Recommendations

Automation undoubtedly offers significant improvements in efficiency, safety and reliability; however, its successful integration hinges on striking a careful balance between machine autonomy and human oversight. Both over-reliance and under-reliance on automation introduce safety risks and operational inefficiencies. Therefore, adaptive system design, transparent AI and targeted training programmes are paramount in fostering trust, sustaining operator engagement and mitigating cognitive overload and underload.

The Canadian ASV environment can serve as a microcosm for the broader challenges facing HSI in autonomous maritime operations. Insights from this case study underscore the need for advanced HSI strategies as autonomy becomes more deeply embedded in maritime operations. It demonstrates that successful human-system collaboration will depend not only on technological advancements but also on thoughtful system design, continuous operator engagement, institutional rules and an adaptive operational mindset. Key insights include:

- **Human Factors and Training:** Real-world ASV scenarios emphasise the need for training programmes that address cognitive biases, support skill retention and reflect the complexities of remote decision-making.

FIGURE 4.6 The Canadian ASV. Image courtesy of Fisheries and Marine Institute of Memorial University of Newfoundland

- **SDT-Based Detection Systems:** The ASV project demonstrated the value of applying SDT to enhance hazard recognition while reducing false alarms, which is crucial for maintaining operator trust during long-duration remote operations.
- **Flexible Operational Frameworks:** Future models of autonomy should not rigidly adhere to pre-programmed protocols but instead allow flexible, human-guided adjustments based on emergent SA. The Canadian case highlights the value of hybrid decision-making models, in which human expertise and machine capabilities complement rather than replace one another.

Ultimately, the evolution of maritime operations must not merely be technological but also cognitive and ethical. Remote operators require not only advanced tools but also the training and decision-support systems necessary to maintain high performance in complex, high-stakes environments. A human-centred design philosophy and advancing regulatory, education and technical frameworks are essential for stakeholders to ensure that automation acts as an enabler, enhancing rather than diminishing human expertise.

To conclude, the future of autonomous maritime operations depends on continuous collaboration among relevant maritime stakeholders. As these systems become more intelligent and pervasive, there must also be a sustained commitment to understanding and supporting the cognitive capabilities of the humans who will operate alongside them.

References

Abugohar, M. A., & Yassin, B. (2020). Hands-on: Elevating the quality of classroom participation through challenge-action-result technique in English-medium instruction to medical Arab students. Universal Journal of Educational Research, 8(9), 4071–4079.

Alberg, A. L., Holen, S. M., Kongsvik, T., & Wahl, A. M. (2024). Does it do the same as we would? How trust in automated shipboard systems relates to seafarers' professional identity. Safety Science, 172, 106426. https://doi.org/10.1016/j.ssci.2024.106426.

Anderson, J. R., Reder, L. M., & Simon, H. A. (2000). Applications and misapplications of cognitive psychology to mathematics education. Texas Educational Review, 1(2), 29–49.

Bainbridge, L. (1983). Ironies of automation. In Analysis, design and evaluation of man–machine systems (pp. 129–135). Pergamon.

Baum-Talmor, P., & Kitada, M. (2022). Industry 4.0 in shipping: Implications to seafarers' skills and training. Transportation Research Interdisciplinary Perspectives, 13, 100542. https://doi.org/10.1016/j.trip.2022.100542

Bedny, G., & Meister, D. (1999). Theory of activity and situation awareness. International Journal of Cognitive Ergonomics, 3(1), 63–72.

Bekker, H. L., Hewison, J., & Thornton, J. G. (2003). Understanding why decision aids work: Linking process with outcome. Patient Education and Counseling, 50, 323–329.

Boehm-Davis, D. A., Durso, F. T., & Lee, J. D. (2015). APA handbook of human systems integration (pp. 277–292). American Psychological Association. https://doi.org/10.1037/14528-018
Bolstad, C. A., & Endsley, M. R. (2000). The effect of task load and shared displays on team situation awareness. In Proceedings of the human factors and ergonomics society annual meeting (Vol. 44, No. 1, pp. 189–192). SAGE Publications.
Brown-Schmidt, S., Cho, S.-J., Boeck, P. D. (2023). Incorporating functional response time effects into a signal detection theory model. Psychometrika 88, 1056–1086. https://doi.org/10.1007/s11336-023-09906-9
Chen, T. L. & Pritchett, A. R. (2001). Development and evaluation of a cockpit decision-aid for emergency trajectory generation. Journal of Aircraft, 38, 935–943.
Cummings, M. L. (2017). Automation bias in intelligent time-critical decision support systems. Journal of Cognitive Engineering and Decision Making, 11(1), 58–72.
Dixon, S. R., Wickens, C. D., & McCarley, J. S. (2007). On the independence of compliance and reliance: Are automation false alarms worse than misses? Human Factors, 49(4), 564–572. https://doi.org/10.1518/001872007X215656
Driskell, J. E., & Salas, E. (1991). Training decision makers: The role of training in decision making. In D. G. Houghton & J. A. Morelli (Eds.), Cognitive processing in decision making (pp. 1–26). Academic Press.
Durso, F. T., Hackworth, C. A., Truitt, T. R., Crutchfield, J., Nikolic, D., & Manning, C. A. (1998). Situation awareness as a predictor of performance in en route air traffic controllers (DOT/FAA/AM-99/3). Federal Aviation Administration Office of Aviation Medicine. https://www.faa.gov/sites/faa.gov/files/data_research/research/med_humanfacs/oamtechreports/AM99-03.pdf
Endsley, M. R. (1990). Predictive utility of an objective measure of situation awareness. In Proceedings of the human factors society annual meeting (Vol. 34, No. 1, pp. 41–45). SAGE Publications.
Endsley, M. R. (1995). Toward a theory of situation awareness in dynamic systems. Human Factors, 37(1), 32–64. https://doi.org/10.1518/001872095779049543
Endsley, M. R. (2015). Situation awareness misconceptions and misunderstandings. Journal of Cognitive Engineering and Decision Making, 9(1), 4–32. https://doi.org/10.1177/1555343415572631
Endsley, M. R. (2017). From here to autonomy: Lessons learned from human–automation research. Human Factors, 59(1), 5–27. https://doi.org/10.1177/0018720816681350
Endsley, M. R. (2021). A systematic review and meta-analysis of direct objective measures of situation awareness: A comparison of SAGAT and SPAM. Human Factors, 63(1), 124–150. https://doi.org/10.1177/0018720819875376
Endsley, M. R. (May 2025). Building user centered AI for safety critical industries. Presentation to human factors and AI: Opportunities & risks for safety critical industries for human factors in control (HFC), Canada.
Endsley, M. R., & Jones, D. G. (2012). Designing for situation awareness: An approach to user-centered design. CRC Press.
Endsley, M. R., Tartaglia, R., Bagnara, S., Albolino, S., Fujita, Y., & Alexander, T. (2018). Situation awareness in future autonomous vehicles: Beware of the unexpected. In Proceedings of the 20th congress of the international ergonomics association (IEA 2018) (Vol. 824, pp. 303–309). Springer International Publishing AG. https://doi.org/10.1007/978-3-319-96071-5_32
Fossen, T. I. (2011). Handbook of marine craft hydrodynamics and motion control, Vademecum de navioum motu contra aquas et de motu gubernando. John Wiley & Sons.
Gaba, D. M., & Howard, S. K. (1995). Situation awareness in anesthesiology. Human Factors, 37(1), 20–31.

Galy, E., Paxion, J., & Berthelon, C. (2017). Measuring mental workload with the NASA-TLX needs to examine each dimension rather than relying on the global score: An example with driving. Ergonomics, 61(4), 517–527. https://doi.org/10.1080/00140139.2017.1369583.

Gigerenzer, G., & Gaissmaier, W. (2011). Heuristic decision making. Annual Review of Psychology, 62(1), 451–482. https://doi.org/10.1146/annurev-psych-120709-145346

Gilson, R. D. (1995). Situation awareness, special issue preface. Human Factors, 37 (1), 3–4.

Goerlandt, F. (2020). Maritime autonomous surface ships from a risk governance perspective: Interpretation and implications. Safety Science, 128, 104758. https://doi.org/10.1016/j.ssci.2020.104758

Goodall, N. J., Beiker, S., & Meyer, G. (2014). Machine ethics and automated vehicles. In Road vehicle automation (pp. 93–102). Springer International Publishing AG. https://doi.org/10.1007/978-3-319-05990-7_9

Hancock, P. A., & Warm, J. S. (1989). A dynamic model of stress and sustained attention. Human Factors, 31(5), 519–537. https://doi.org/10.1177/001872088903100503.

Hansen, M., Nazir, S., Harris, D., & Li, W.-C. (2024). Situational awareness and decision-making in maritime operations: A cognitive perspective. In Engineering psychology and cognitive ergonomics (Vol. 14692, pp. 165–189). Springer. https://doi.org/10.1007/978-3-031-60728-8_14

Hoff, K. A., & Bashir, M. (2015). Trust in automation: Integrating empirical evidence on factors that influence trust. Human Factors, 57(3), 407–434. https://doi.org/10.1177/0018720814547570

Howard, A., & Borenstein, J. (2019). Trust and bias in robots. American Scientist, 107(2), 86–89. https://doi.org/10.1511/2019.107.2.86

Janis, I. L., & Mann, L. (1977). Decision making: A psychological analysis of conflict, choice, and commitment. Free Press.

Jaskólski, K., Felski, A., & Piskur, P. (2019). The compass error comparison of an onboard standard gyrocompass, fiber-optic gyrocompass (FOG) and satellite compass. Sensors, 19(8). https://doi.org.qe2a-proxy.mun.ca/10.3390/s19081942

Jones, D. G., & Endsley, M. R. (1996). Sources of situation awareness errors in aviation. Aviation, Space, and Environmental Medicine, 67(6), 507–512. https://doi.org/10.3357/asem.3735.2006

Kabashkin, I., & Susanin, V. (2024). Unified ecosystem for data sharing and AI-driven predictive maintenance in aviation. Computers (Basel), 13(12), 318. https://doi.org/10.3390/computers13120318

Kaber, D. B. (1996). The effect of level of automation and adaptive automation on performance in dynamic control environments. Texas Tech University.

Kahneman, D., Slovic, P., & Tversky, A. (1982). Judgment under uncertainty: Heuristics and biases (1st edition). Cambridge University Press. https://doi.org/10.1017/CBO9780511809477

Kantak, S. S., & Winstein, C. J. (2012). Learning–performance distinction and memory processes for motor skills: A focused review and perspective. Behavioural Brain Research, 228(1), 219–231.

Kim, Te., Mallam, S. C. (2020). A delphi-AHP study on STCW leadership competence in the age of autonomous maritime operations. WMU Journal of Maritime Affairs, 19, 163–181. https://doi.org/10.1007/s13437-020-00203-1

Klein, G. (1998). Sources of power: How people make decision. Massachusetts Institute of Technology.

Klein, G., Orasanu, J., Calderwood, R., & Zsambok, C. E. (Eds.). (1993). Decision making in action: Models and methods. Ablex.

Laming, D. R. J. (1968). Information theory of choice-reaction times. Academic Press.

Lee, J. D., & See, K. A. (2004). Trust in automation: Designing for appropriate reliance. Human Factors, 46(1), 50–80. https://doi.org/10.1518/hfes.46.1.50_30392

Mallam, S. C. (2023). Developing user interface standards for energy conscious and safe maritime operations. Journal of Ocean Technology, 18(4), vi–viii.

Mallam, S. C., Nazir, S., & Renganayagalu, S. K. (2019b). Rethinking maritime education, training, and operations in the digital era: Applications for emerging immersive technologies. Journal of Marine Science and Engineering, 7(12), 428. https://doi.org/10.3390/jmse7120428

Mallam, S. C., Nazir, S., & Sharma, A. (2019a). The human element in future maritime operations – perceived impact of autonomous shipping. Ergonomics, 63(3), 334–345. https://doi.org/10.1080/00140139.2019.1659995

Mallam, S. C., Nordby, K., Johnsen, S. O., & Bjørneseth, F. B. (2020). The digitalization of navigation: Examining the accident and aftermath of US Navy Destroyer John S. McCain. Proceedings of the royal institution of naval architects damaged ship V, 55–63.

Mallam, S. C., Nordby, K., van de Merwe, K., Veitch, E., Nazir, S., & Veitch, B. (2022). Empathy from afar? Towards empathy for future maritime designers and remote operators. Proceedings of the Human Factors and Ergonomics Society Annual Meeting, 66(1), 508–512. https://doi.org/10.1177/1071181322661062

Marine Autonomous Systems Testbed (MAST) – the Launch – Fisheries and Marine Institute of Memorial University of Newfoundland. (2023). www.thelaunch.mi.mun.ca/project/marine-autonomous-systems-testbed-mast/. Accessed 29 Apr. 2025.

Masalonis, A., & Parasuraman, R. (2003). Fuzzy signal detection theory: Analysis of human and machine performance in air traffic control, and analytic considerations. Ergonomics, 46(11), 1045–1074. https://doi.org/10.1080/0014013031000121986

McClure, M. J., Lydon, J. E., Baccus, J. R., & Baldwin, M. W. (2010). A signal detection analysis of chronic attachment anxiety at speed dating: Being unpopular is only the first part of the problem. Personality and Social Psychology Bulletin, 36(8), 1024–1036. https://doi.org/10.1177/0146167210374238

Neisser, U. (1976). Cognition and reality: Principles and implications of cognitive psychology. W. H. Freeman.

Norman, D. A. (1991). The problem with automation. Philosophical Transactions of the Royal Society, 327, 585–593.

Parasuraman, R., & Manzey, D. H. (2010). Complacency and bias in human use of automation: An attentional integration. Human Factors, 52(3), 381–410. https://doi.org/10.1177/0018720810376055

Parasuraman, R., & Riley, V. (1997). Humans and automation: Use, misuse, disuse, abuse. Human Factors, 39(2), 230–253. https://doi.org/10.1518/001872097778543886

Parasuraman, R., Sheridan, T. B., & Wickens, C. D. (2000). A model for types and levels of human interaction with automation. IEEE Transactions on Systems, Man and Cybernetics. Part A, Systems and Humans, 30(3), 286–297. https://doi.org/10.1109/3468.844354.

Payne, J. W. (1976). Task complexity and contingent processing in decision making. An information search and protocol analysis. Organization Behavior and Human Performance, 16, 366–387.

Payne, J. W., Bettman, J. R., & Johnson, E. J. (1988). Adaptive strategy selection in decision making. Journal of Experimental Psychology: Learning, Memory and Cognition, 14(3), 534–552.

Porathe, T., Hoem, Å. S., Rødseth, Ø. J., Fjørtoft, K. E., & Johnsen, S. O. (2018). At least as safe as manned shipping? Autonomous shipping, safety and "human error". In T. Aven & J. E. Vinnem (Eds.), Safety and reliability – Safe societies in a changing world (Vol. 1, pp. 417–425). CRC Press.

Porathe, T., Prison, J., & Man, Y. (2014). Situation awareness in remote control centres for unmanned ships. In Proceedings of Human Factors in Ship Design & Operation, 26–27 February 2014, London, UK (p. 93). https://doi.org/10.3940/rina.hf.2014.12

Prison, J., Dahlman, J., & Lundh, M. (2013). Ship sense, striving for harmony in ship manoeuvring. WMU Journal of Maritime Affairs, 12(1), 115–127. https://doi.org/10.1007/s13437-013-0038-5

Ringbom, H. (2019). Regulating autonomous ships concepts, challenges and precedents. Ocean Development & International Law, 50(2–3), 141–169.

Sanli, E. A., & Carnahan, H. (2018). Long-term retention of skills in multi-day training contexts: A review of the literature. International Journal of Industrial Ergonomics, 66, 10–17.

Sanli, E. A., Ennis, K. A., Brown, R., & Carnahan, H. (2018). The development and validation of key performance indicators for two tasks related to marine emergency duties training. International Journal of Training Research, 16(2), 145–154.

Scherer, K. R. (2019). Towards a prediction and data driven computational process model of emotion. IEEE Transactions on Affective Computing, 12(2), 279–292.

Schmidt, P., Reiss, A., Dürichen, R., & Van Laerhoven, K. (2019). Wearable-based affect recognition. A review. Sensors, 19(19), 4079.

Schmidt, R. A., Lee, T. D., Winstein, C., Wulf, G., & Zelaznik, H. N. (2018). Motor control and learning: A behavioral emphasis (Chapter 3 Human Information Processing). Human Kinetics.

Sharma, A., Nazir, S., & Ernstsen, J. (2019). Situation awareness information requirements for maritime navigation: A goal directed task analysis. Safety Science, 120, 745–752.

Sheela, P. V., & Mannering, F. (2020). The effect of information on changing opinions toward autonomous vehicle adoption: An exploratory analysis. International Journal of Sustainable Transportation, 14(6), 475–487. https://doi.org/10.1080/15568318.2019.1573389

Sheridan, T. B. (2017). Modeling human-system interaction: Philosophical and methodological considerations, with examples. Wiley.

Siegrist, M. (2021). Trust and risk perception: A critical review of the literature. Risk Analysis, 41(3), 480–490. https://doi.org/10.1111/risa.13325

Simion, D., Postolache, F., Fleacă, B., & Fleacă, E. (2024). AI-driven predictive maintenance in modern maritime transport – Enhancing operational efficiency and reliability. Applied Sciences, 14(20), 9439. https://doi.org/10.3390/app14209439

Simon, H. A. (1957). Models of man, social and rational. Wiley.

Skrobonja, A., Jurdana, I., Panic, I., & Wakabayashi, N. (2020). Marine fiber optic and spinning mass gyrocompasses. 2020 43rd International Convention on Information, Communication and Electronic Technology (MIPRO), 1899–1903. https://doi.org/10.23919/MIPRO48935.2020.9245348

Stanton, N. A., Chambers, P. R. G., & Piggott, J. (2001). Situational awareness and safety. Safety Science, 39(3), 189–204.

Stanton, N. A., Salmon, P. M., Rafferty, L. A., Walker, G. H., Baber, C., & Jenkins, D. P. (2013). Human factors methods: A practical guide for engineering and design (2nd edition.). Ashgate Publishing Ltd. https://doi.org/10.1201/9781315587394

Stone, N. J., Chaparro, A., Keebler, J. R., Chaparro, B. S., & McConnell, D. S. (2018). Introduction to human factors: Applying psychology to design. CRC Press.

Szalma, J. L., Hancock, P. A., & Hinshaw, S. P. (2011). Noise effects on human performance: A meta-analytic synthesis. Psychological Bulletin, 137(4), 682–707. https://doi.org/10.1037/a0023987.

Tuzlukov, V. P. (2001). Signal detection theory (1st edition.). Birkhäuser Boston. https://doi.org/10.1007/978-1-4612-0187-8

Tversky, A., Kahneman, D., & Chater, N. (2009). Availability: A heuristic for judging frequency and probability. In Judgement and decision making (Vol. 4, pp. III3–III3). SAGE Publications Ltd. https://doi.org/10.1016/0010-0285(73)90033–9
Wang, Y., Chen, X., Wu, Y., Zhao, J., Postolache, O., & Liu, S. (2024). Visual navigation systems for maritime smart ships: A survey. Journal of Marine Science and Engineering, 12(10), 1781. https://doi.org/10.3390/jmse12101781
Wickens, C. D. (2008). Multiple resources and mental workload. Human Factors, 50(3), 449–455. https://doi.org/10.1518/001872008X288394.2012
Wickens, C. D. (2014). Effort in human factors performance and decision making. Human Factors, 56(8), 1329–1336. https://doi.org/10.1177/0018720814558419
Wickens, C. D., Gordon, S. E., Liu, Y., & Lee, J. (2004). An introduction to human factors engineering. Pearson Prentice Hall.
Wickens, C. D., Helton, W. S., Hollands, J. G., & Banbury, S. (2021). Engineering psychology and human performance (5th edition). Routledge. https://doi.org/10.4324/9781003177616
Woods, D., Dekker, S., Cook, R., Johannesen, L., & Sarter, N. (2017). Behind human error. CRC Press.
Wright, R. G. (2020). Unmanned and autonomous ships: An overview of mass. CRC Press LLC.
Wulf, G., Shea, C., & Lewthwaite, R. (2010). Motor skill learning and performance: A review of influential factors. Medical Education, 44(1), 75–84.
Young, M. S., & Stanton, N. A. (2002). Malleable attentional resources theory: A new explanation for the effects of mental underload on performance. Human Factors, 44(3), 365–375. https://doi.org/10.1518/0018720024497709

5

THE ROC ARCHITECTURE FRAMEWORK FOR REMOTE SHIP OPERATIONS

Etienne Gernez, Steven C. Mallam, Kjetil Nordby, Jon Erling Fauske, Bijan Johansen, Borgar Kløve Sandnes, Sunniva Lislevand Wildhagen, and Hanne Lockertsen

1 Introduction

As remote and autonomous ship operations become a reality, with several maritime autonomous surface ships (MASS) already in operation, there is a need to design and build remote operation centres (ROC) with differing functionalities and operations. The MASS segment is expected to continue growing (DNV, n.d.), so there is a need to establish design guidelines for ROC as a new type of workplace in the maritime industry.

However, there are currently limited design guidelines for ROC development. Design guidelines that may apply to ROC design include guidelines for the ergonomics of human-system interaction (ISO 9241), the ISO standard 11064 on the ergonomic design of control centres and, to some extent, the MASS Code developed by IMO. Design precedence is also limited, as the design of the ROCs that are currently in operation is proprietary and typically not made public. Further, the first generation of ROC equipment has predominantly involved the installation of traditional maritime equipment and interfaces found onboard ship bridges (e.g. conning, ECDIS, RADAR, engine data and so on), typically augmented with increased CCTV for live feeds of the surrounding bridge or ship environment. This is now evolving towards more tailored functionalities for the control and monitoring of remote structures in ROCs, moving away from typical onboard GUIs. As a result, the need for open design guidelines and accessible design precedence tailored for remote and autonomous operations, and not simply traditional onboard ship equipment and interfaces, is urgent, and poor ROC design may lead to suboptimal or even unsafe operations.

DOI: 10.4324/9781003586883-5

FIGURE 5.1 Example of a single-operator ROC workstation design based on the ROC architecture framework. Visual by Ocean Industries Concept Lab

To address this challenge, we have developed the ROC architecture framework (Figure 5.1). The framework covers four central aspects of ROC design: (1) the physical design of ROC workstations, (2) their integration with digital user interfaces, (3) support for remote collaboration between land- and ship-based operators, and (4) enhanced situational awareness through augmented video feeds. In practical terms, the ROC architecture framework consists of a design guideline and a design material library of physical and digital user interfaces. It is designed to support ROC designs that can be adapted and scaled to a wide variety of MASS operations.

The framework builds on the design system OpenBridge (OpenBridge, 2025). This design system is already in use in several commercial maritime systems, including for MASS operations and ROC design. OpenBridge benefits from over a decade of research in industrial and interaction design for distributed, multivendor maritime workplaces and provides a bottom-up standard for harmonised and consistent workplace design (Nordby et al., 2018, 2019a, 2019b).

2 The ROC Architecture Framework

When developing an architecture framework for the design of a workplace like ROCs, we define "workplace" as the physical and digital environments where users engage in tasks required to enable MASS operation. We define "architecture" as the assembly and integration of physical and digital user interfaces that support users in the execution of these tasks. In our research, "workplace architecture" therefore concerns the design and orchestration of physical and digital user interfaces, with the goal of enabling operators to perform their job safely and efficiently.

Our ambition is to progressively develop a set of design frameworks that address current and future user interface design requirements for physical and digital user interfaces of the ROC for MASS operation. The ROC architecture framework initially focuses on the functions traditionally executed by the navigational officers and the machinery officers – that is, the AROS-NAV and AROS-ENG functions, following the terminology of the DNV autonomous and remotely operated ships (AROS) class notation (DNV, n.d.). Following the same terminology, we are interested in user interfaces that support all four modes of operation (remote control, decision support, supervised autonomy and full autonomy) and all the combinations of control location (onboard, off-ship or hybrid).

The ROC architecture framework is being developed through the OpenAR and OpenRemote (Norwegian Research Council, n.d.) research projects, in collaboration with a network of international academic and industrial partners (OICL, n.d.). The development process follows an iterative, case-based methodology rooted in design research and human factors. Design cases are proposed by individual project partners, and the findings of each case are shared with all project partners. The methodology varies from case to case – we present the main approach below, across all the design cases.

To capture user and use-context requirements, we employed a range of complementary methods. These include an online survey, design-driven field studies with maritime operators (Lurås & Nordby, 2014; Gernez & Nordby, 2020; van den Oever et al., 2025), VR-reconstructed operational scenarios (VRROS) (Frydenberg et al., 2021; Frydenberg & Nordby, 2022; Aylward et al., 2021; Gernez et al., 2024), layered-scenario mapping (Lurås, 2016) and expert workshops with domain specialists. In terms of maritime and common user interface regulations, we applied the IEC regulation on iconography (IEC, 2014) and, later, the Web Content Accessibility Guidelines (WCAG) 2.1 (W3C, n.d.).

To generate design proposals, we used rapid prototyping with paper during field studies, and we worked in 2D using the design tool Figma, leveraging the OpenBridge design material both in the lab and during field work. We explored the integration of the 2D sketches into a 3D environment using the VRROS approach in the lab and using demonstrators during field work.

To evaluate the designs, we combined a mixed-methods approach of qualitative and quantitative methods. Qualitative approaches included collaborative critique sessions with designers from the lab and with domain experts, as well as think-aloud protocols during VRROS sessions. Quantitative methods included user testing with ship crew or maritime students, measuring situation awareness (SA) using a modified situation awareness global assessment technique (SAGAT) and SA-SWORD to compare scenario preferences (Houweling et al., 2024), along with usability assessments using the system usability scale (SUS) (van den Oever et al., 2023).

In the following sections, we present the individual components of the current version of the ROC architecture framework.

2.1 The ROC Workstation Framework

The ROC workstation framework is concerned with the physical user interfaces and the physical layout of ROC operator workstations. It was developed to lay the foundation for researching how physical and digital user interfaces can be coordinated and integrated in ROC environments. As such, this framework served as the initial step towards the development of the workplace integration framework described in the next section.

To develop the ROC workstation framework, we made the assumption that future ROCs will need to accommodate a wide variety of MASS operations, varying in the number and types of vessels to manage, degrees of autonomy and operational profiles. Consequently, the main goal was to develop a ROC workstation framework with the ability to scale and adapt. In its current form, it consists of a modular design proposal for a single ROC operator workstation that can be expanded into multi-operator workstations and supplemented with additional features, such as a corner workstation. The framework is intended as an example that illustrates how such workstations could be structured and what capabilities they should support.

2.1.1 Generic ROC Workstation Components

We break down the workstation into:

Basic components

- Desk area
- Chair
- Screens
- Lights
- Microphone
- Surround speakers
- Cup holder

Input controllers

- Mouse
- Keyboard
- Num pad
- Joystick

- Levers
- Alert buttons
- Maneuvering dials and buttons
- Command controls
- Dimming controls

Supporting hardware

- Microphone
- Surround speakers
- Eye tracking
- MR headset
- Operator's personal devices (laptop, phone)
- AC and ventilation

The workstation framework includes initial design guidelines for the design of physical buttons for the controls of, for example, dimming, speaker and microphone volume (Figures 5.2 to 5.4).

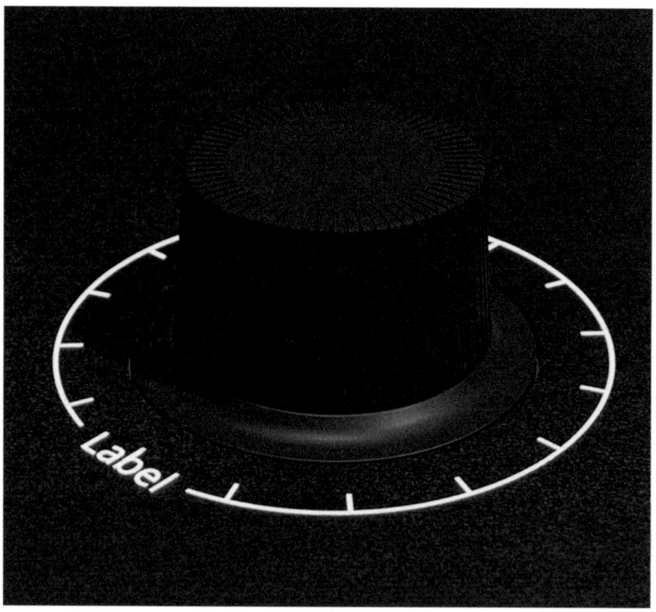

FIGURE 5.2 Physical button – infinite range. Visual by Ocean Industries Concept Lab

FIGURE 5.3 Physical button – range amount. Visual by Ocean Industries Concept Lab

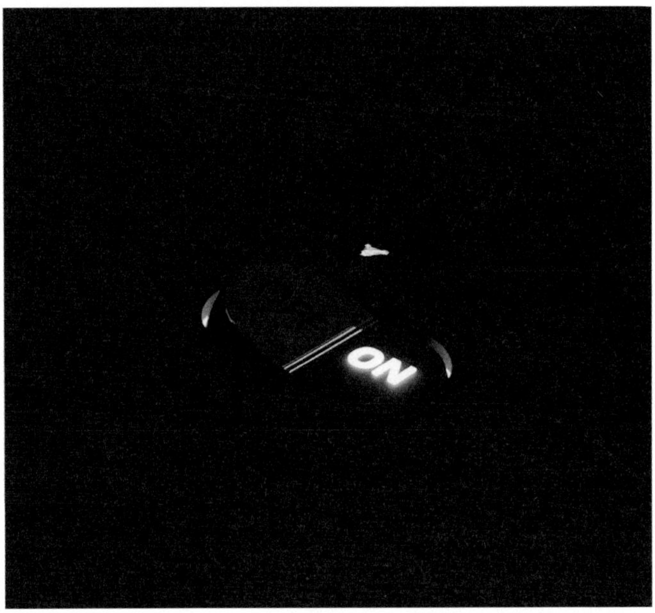

FIGURE 5.4 Physical button – toggle switch. Visual by Ocean Industries Concept Lab

2.1.2 Single-Operator Workstation

The single-operator version is illustrated in Figures 5.5 to 5.8, with variations in desk area, screen types and arrangement. Interestingly, the same framework was also used to redesign a dynamic positioning operator station (Figure 5.9), as it follows similar constraints. This shows the versatility of the framework and how it can maintain a consistent design result across various designs.

FIGURE 5.5 Single-operator workstation with two small screens and one wide screen. Visual by Ocean Industries Concept Lab

FIGURE 5.6 Single-operator workstation with three small screens and three large screens. Visual by Ocean Industries Concept Lab

FIGURE 5.7 Short single-operator workstation with two small screens and one wide screen. Visual by Ocean Industries Concept Lab

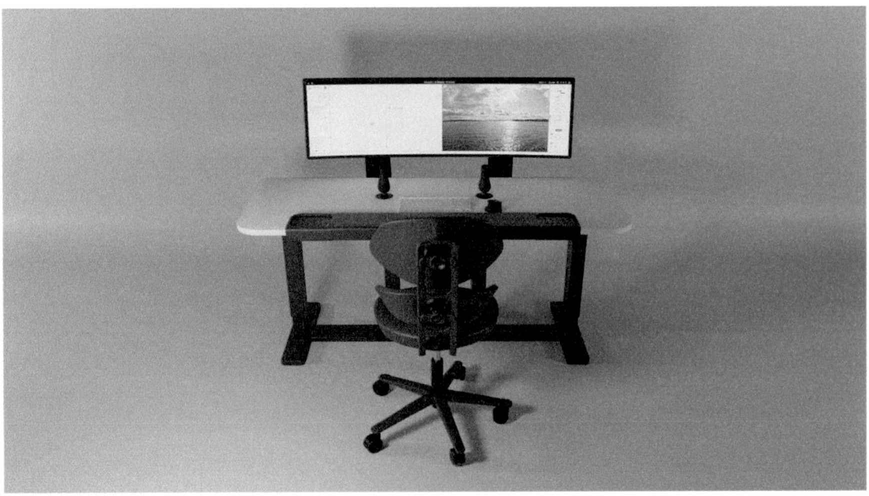

FIGURE 5.8 Shorter single-operator workstation with one wide screen. Visual by Ocean Industries Concept Lab

2.1.3 Multi-Operator Workstation and Corner Table

The multi-operator version is illustrated in Figure 5.10. A corner table was also designed to act as a divider and create a well-defined work zone around the ROC operator (Figures 5.11 and 5.12). The zone limits distractions

FIGURE 5.9 Dynamic positioning operator workstation based on the ROC workstation design framework. Visual by Ocean Industries Concept Lab

FIGURE 5.10 Workstation for two operators, three small screens and two wide screens. Visual by Ocean Industries Concept Lab

around the operator, while the corner table provides the additional function of storage for the operator and a standing height desk for discussions outside the work zone, with a clear view of what is happening inside the zone.

FIGURE 5.11 Workstation with corner table. Visual by Ocean Industries Concept Lab

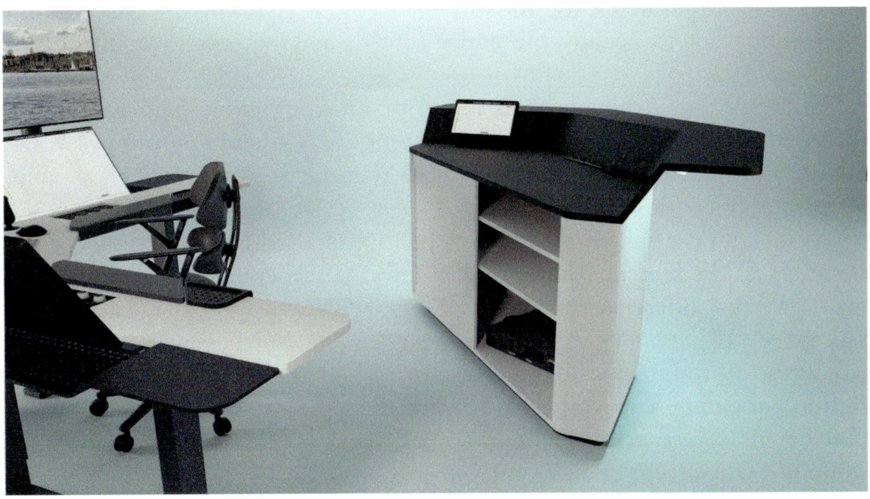

FIGURE 5.12 Detail of corner table. Visual by Ocean Industries Concept Lab

2.2 The Workplace Integration Framework

The workplace integration framework is concerned with the ROC digital user interfaces. It is an overarching framework that supports various applications and is tailored to support multi-vendor systems. In the framework, overarching functionalities such as fleet control, key information and application

FIGURE 5.13 The three main components of the integration framework: integration bar, main content area and application bar. Visual by Ocean Industries Concept Lab

selection are accessible through a scalable UI framed around each individual application. The framework is especially suitable for applications built on scaling principles associated with responsive design from the web tradition, where applications adapt to the available screen estate. This approach allows applications not to occupy the entire screen, making room for integration functionality.

The integration framework consists of an integration bar that can be anchored to any edge of the screen, content areas where applications reside and an optional application selection bar that enables single-click switching between applications (Figure 5.13).

The integration system also allows for optional widgets positioned along the edges of the screen, where smaller information components can display key data from different applications. These widgets apply the cluster button concept – clicking on a card opens a large temporary window in which users can access more information or interact with available functions. The integration bar can be applied across all screens in the workplace.

In a multi-screen display, the integration and application bars will be the same on each screen, and the content area will be different on each screen. Both the integration and application bars can be made to disappear when not in use and can reappear by hovering over the top and bottom parts of the screen (Figure 5.14).

2.2.1 Integration Bar

It includes the following functionalities (Figures 5.15–5.20):

- Status indication: monitoring or controlling a vessel
- Fleet and vessel control: visualising the information and controls of several or individual vessels

FIGURE 5.14 Example of the use of the integration framework with applications distributed over three small screens and one large screen. Visual by Ocean Industries Concept Lab

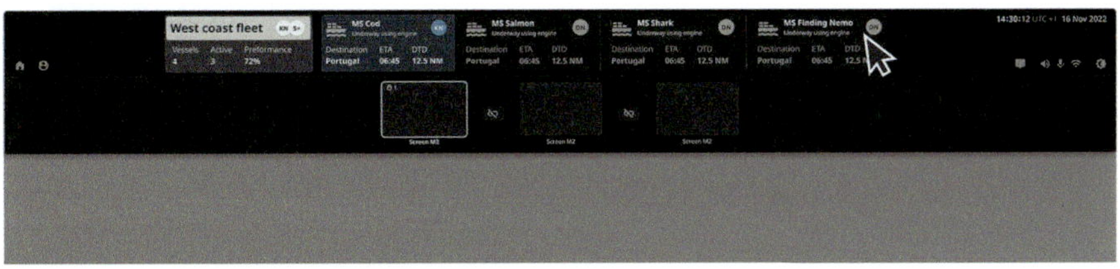

FIGURE 5.15 Integration bar – fleet and vessel control. Visual by Ocean Industries Concept Lab

- User control: who the user currently in charge is, access to log in, personalised settings
- Notification: view, acknowledge, expand notifications
- Settings: internet and network connectivity, microphone and loudspeaker sound control
- Screen control: individual controls for each screen, screen arrangement
- Display control: brightness levels, day/night palette

The integration bar can also be used as a sidebar. It can be exposed or hidden.

2.2.2 Application Bar

The application bar allows quick access to currently running applications and the ability to search for applications not currently running. As such, it is deliberately inspired by the application bar in Windows and Mac computer

FIGURE 5.16 Integration bar – user control. Visual by Ocean Industries Concept Lab

FIGURE 5.17 Integration bar – notifications control. Visual by Ocean Industries Concept Lab

FIGURE 5.18 Integration bar – settings control. Visual by Ocean Industries Concept Lab

operating systems (Figures 5.21–5.24). The bar also includes a quick-view selection, with predefined screen splits. For small screens, the application bar is removed and presented in the form of a widget instead.

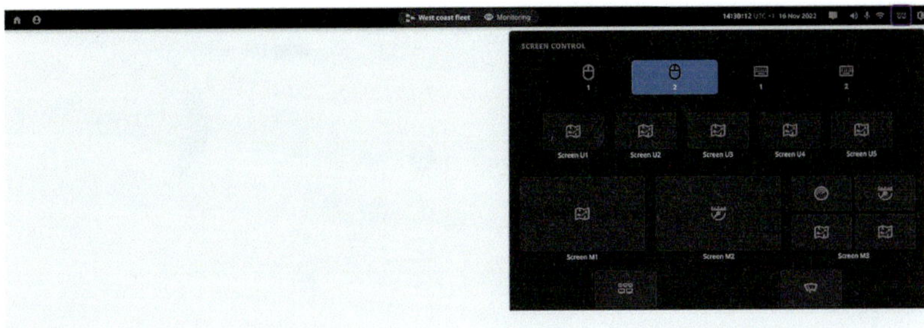

FIGURE 5.19 Integration bar – screen control. Visual by Ocean Industries Concept Lab

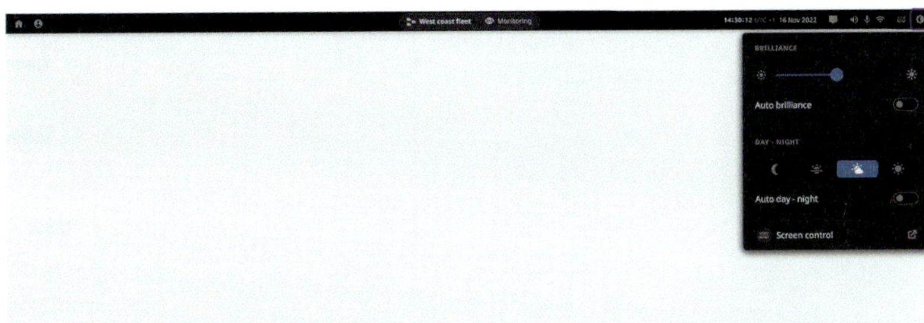

FIGURE 5.20 Integration bar – display control. Visual by Ocean Industries Concept Lab

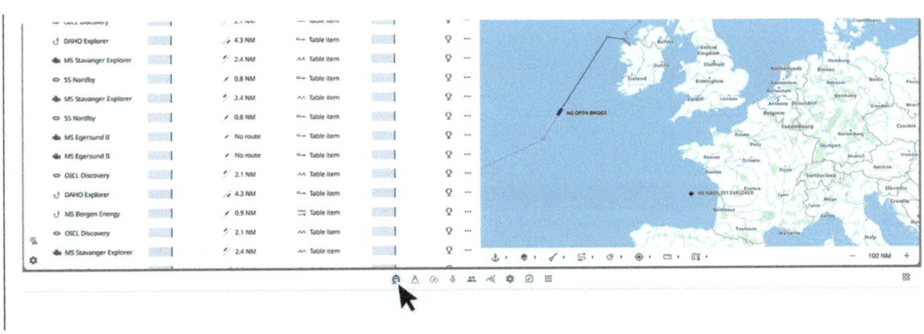

FIGURE 5.21 Application bar – quick access. Visual by Ocean Industries Concept Lab

2.2.3 *Content Area*

In between the top and bottom bars, the content area is dedicated to applications (Figures 5.25–5.27). All the OpenBridge applications can be displayed – Radar, ECDIS, route planner, Conning and so on. The content area

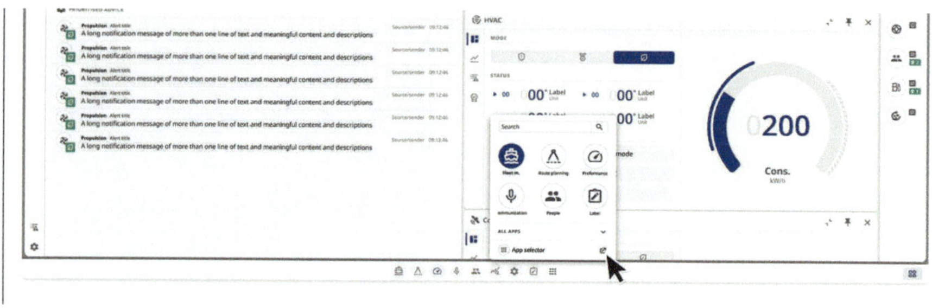

FIGURE 5.22 Application bar – app access. Visual by Ocean Industries Concept Lab

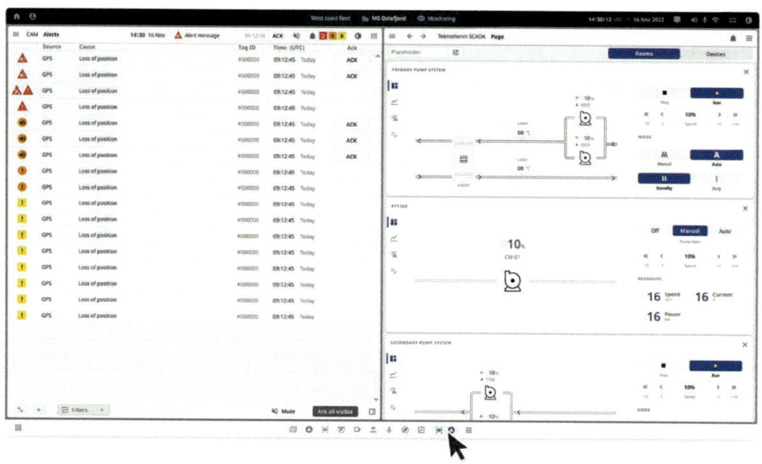

FIGURE 5.23 Application bar – predefined split-screen selection. Visual by Ocean Industries Concept Lab

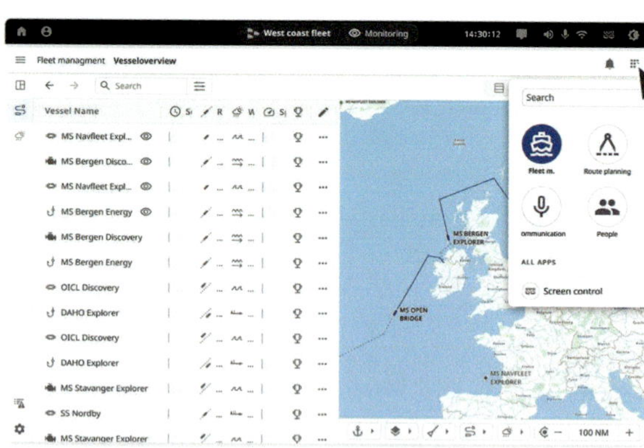

FIGURE 5.24 Application bar – small-screen version. Visual by Ocean Industries Concept Lab

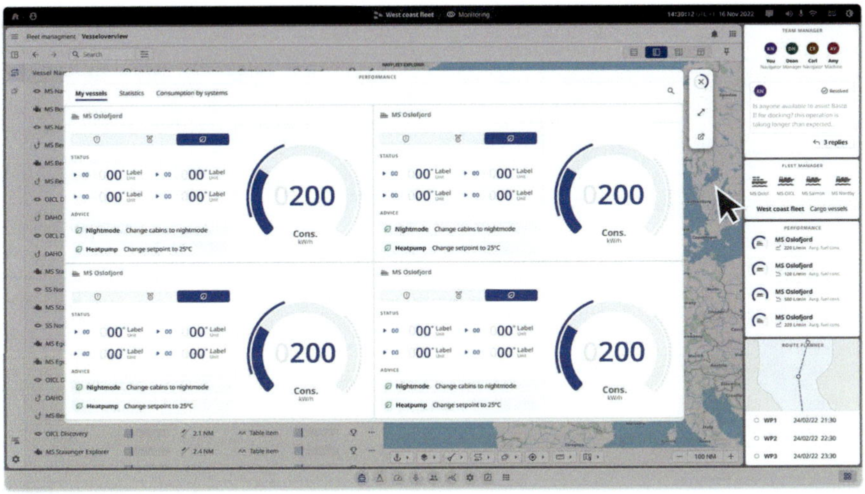

FIGURE 5.25 Content area – overlay and widgets. Visual by Ocean Industries Concept Lab

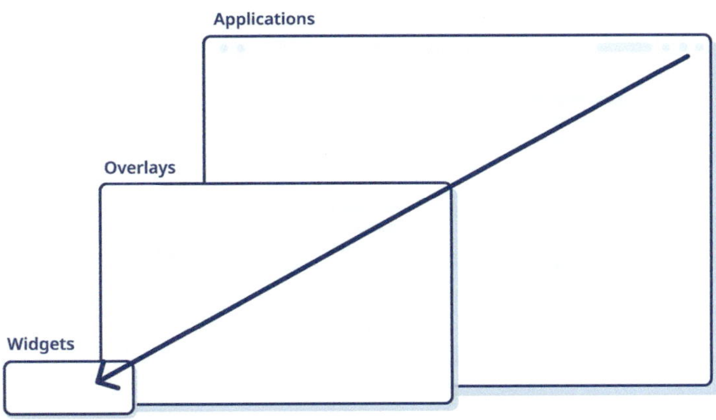

FIGURE 5.26 Content area – scalability. Visual by Ocean Industries Concept Lab

can be split by the user into several parts. When there is not enough space to display a full application, a widget will be displayed instead. In addition, overlays can be added to running applications. When hovering over a widget, a temporary small application will be laid over an opened application. This enables viewing the content of a widget in a larger format without needing to open a full application window or change the current screen split between opened applications (Nordby & Fauske, 2024).

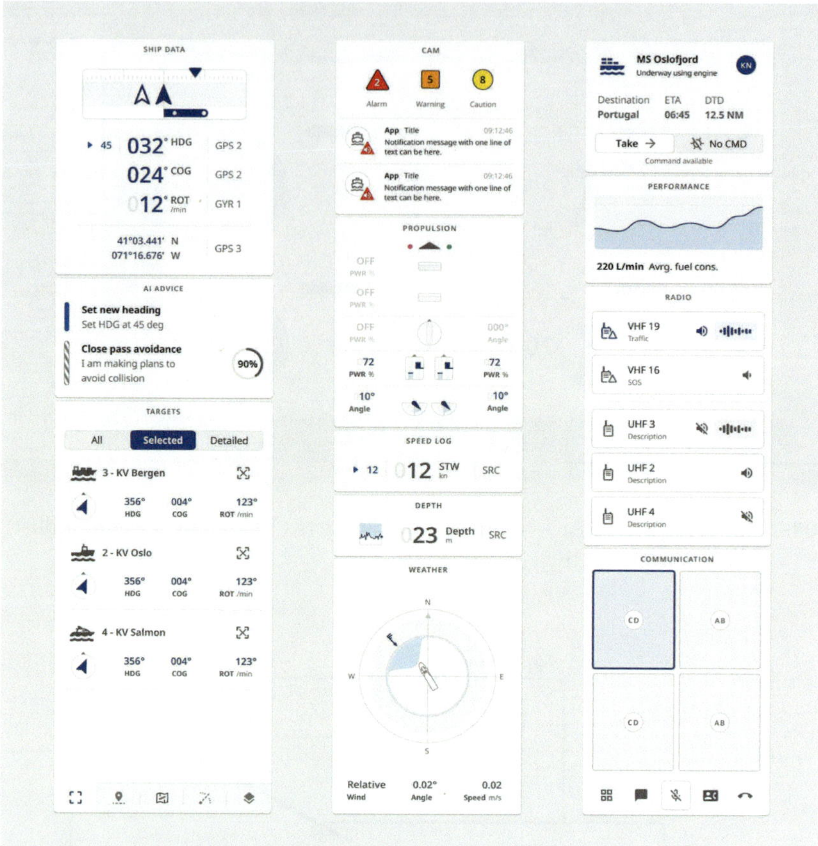

FIGURE 5.27 Content area – widget panels. Visual by Ocean Industries Concept Lab

2.3 The Remote Collaboration and Multi-User Environment Framework

This framework is in an early, exploratory phase of development. It is based on the premise that MASS operations are collaborative along two dimensions. In the human-to-human dimension, collaboration takes place between ROC-based and ship-based personnel, and ROC-based personnel may be located in different ROCs. In the human-to-automation dimension, ROC operators interact with autonomous systems. In these two dimensions, there is a need to make clear who the users involved in the MASS operation are, who is in command, who may take over and what information and level of command are available to whom.

FIGURE 5.28 Colour palette for multi-user. Visual by Ocean Industries Concept Lab

This initial iteration of the framework draws inspiration from collaborative online tools used in our own research and design processes. The initial goals for the framework development were

1 to facilitate shared understanding through common data access,
2 to enable users to work on tasks simultaneously and transparently, and
3 to support remote assistance, supervision and training, regardless of the operator's location.

To address these goals, we proposed the following initial multi-user features:

- Cursor sharing: display other users' cursor movements and clicks
- Shared views: all users can see the same interface
- Spotlight mode: follow the activity of one specific user
- Command transfer: hand over cursor control between users when needed
- Annotations: mark up and comment directly in the interface

Figures 5.28–5.32 show these features in more detail.

2.4 The Video Overlay Framework

This framework originated in research on the use of augmented reality to support navigation tasks (Nordby et al., 2020; Frydenberg et al., 2021). The primary focus was the display of information and data related to specific objects of attention in the environment surrounding a ship, also called "points of interest" (POI) (Nordby et al., 2024). The framework is compatible with

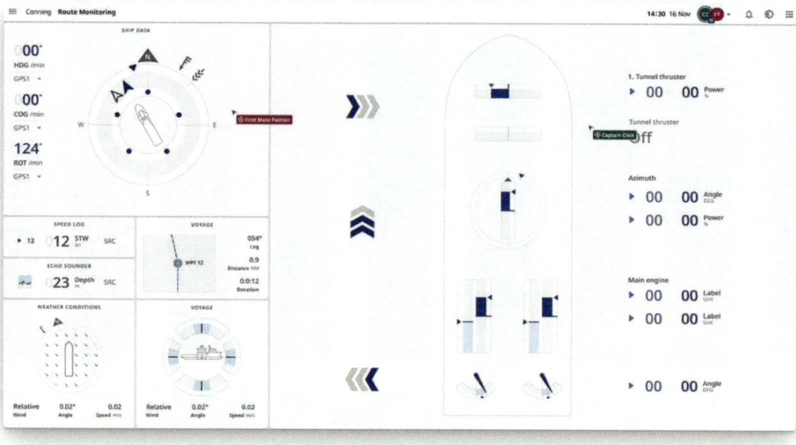

FIGURE 5.29 Cursor sharing. Visual by Ocean Industries Concept Lab

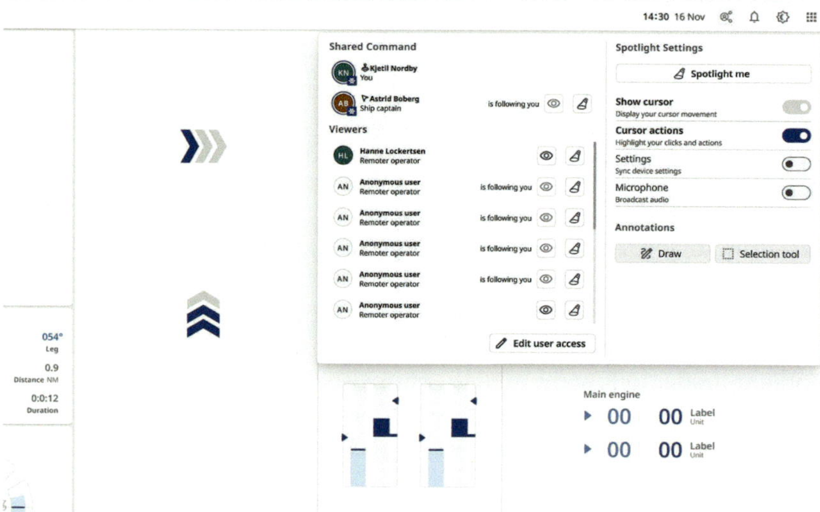

FIGURE 5.30 Multi-user hub. Visual by Ocean Industries Concept Lab

goggles that can be worn by operators (head-mounted display – HMD), displays that follow the gaze of operators (heads-up display – HUD), and overlays of information and data on video feeds on screens, such as CCTV feeds, for example. This last case is a central part of ROC solutions.

The framework is built on rules that define (1) the locations where information and data may be overlaid on reality or a video feed and (2) within

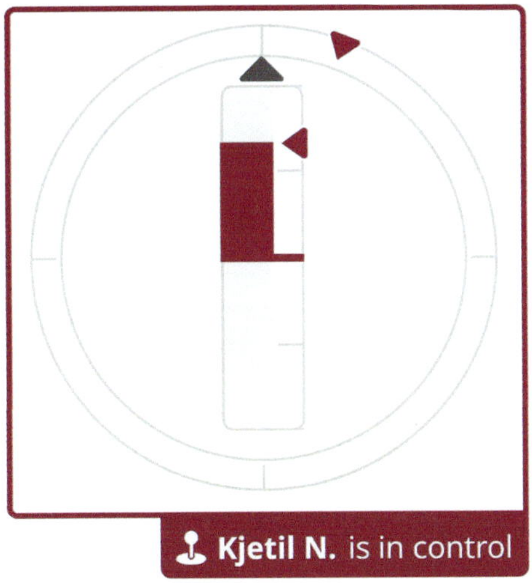

FIGURE 5.31 User in control. Visual by Ocean Industries Concept Lab

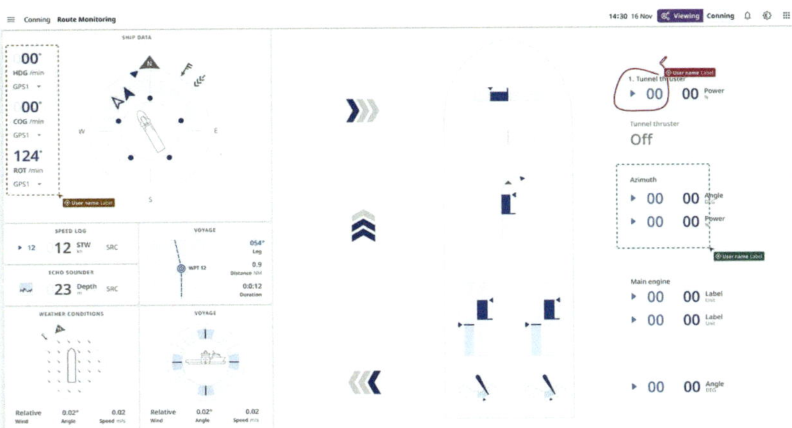

FIGURE 5.32 Annotation. Visual by Ocean Industries Concept Lab

these defined locations, how a specific type of information and data may be displayed and interacted with. The locations consist of the ocean surface and the horizon band (Figure 5.33). Currently, the information and data that may be overlaid consist of POIs and vessel path prediction. POIs are typically displayed on the horizon band, and path prediction on the ocean surface. In the next sections, we describe how POIs and path prediction are handled in the design framework, and we show how this applies when augmenting a CCTV video feed.

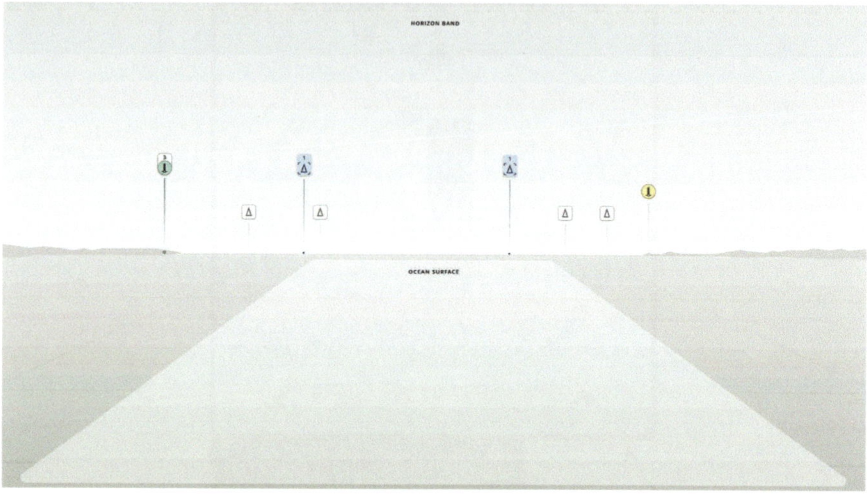

FIGURE 5.33 The two zones where information or data can be overlaid: horizon band and ocean surface. Visual by Ocean Industries Concept Lab

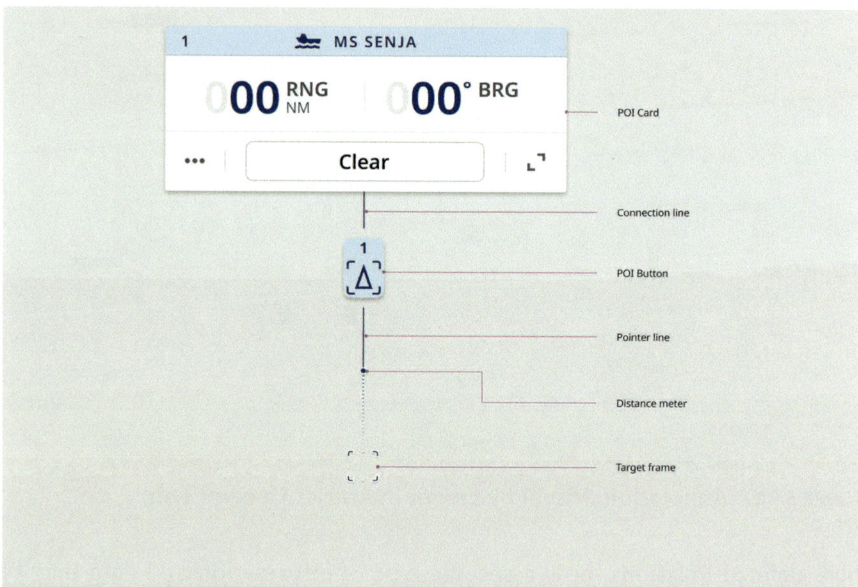

FIGURE 5.34 Base POI component. Visual by Ocean Industries Concept Lab

2.4.1 Points of Interest

The base component for POI display and interaction is a "POI card" that connects with a "target" highlighting a real object in the environment. The POI card gives the operator additional information about the real object (Figure 5.34).

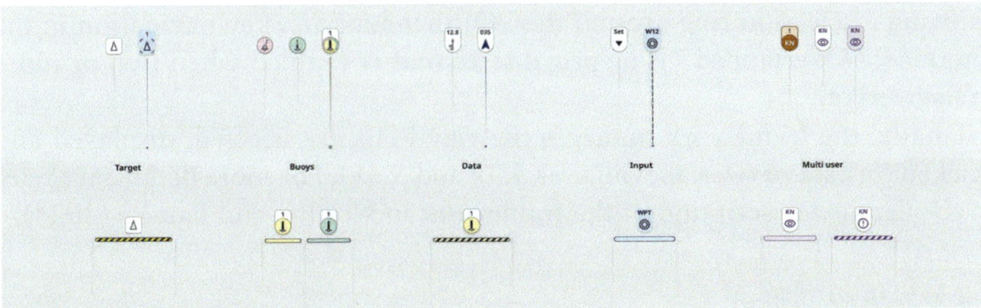

FIGURE 5.35 POI types. Visual by Ocean Industries Concept Lab

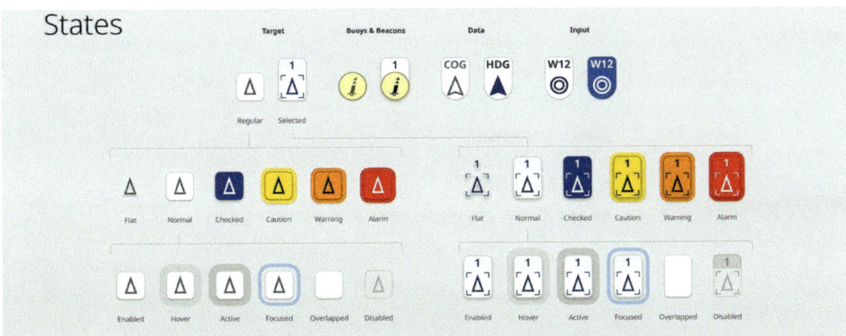

FIGURE 5.36 POI states. Visual by Ocean Industries Concept Lab

The base component is available in different colours and shapes to cover a wide variety of POIs (Figure 5.35):

- Target: a ship target that the operator may want to highlight and/or gain more information about
- Buoys: buoys, beacons, landmarks, as specified in the ECDIS charts
- Data: data from a sensor or any other type of data
- Input: input created by the operator, such as a waypoint
- Multi user: POIs that other operators are currently interacting with

The base component has different states, which are defined for each type of POI (Figure 5.36). The selected state is used to highlight a POI by "selecting" it. This follows current practices in Radar and ECDIS interfaces, where a target can be selected and highlighted in the interface. A POI that is not selected is in a "regular" state. The "component value" can indicate whether the POI is interactive or not. They can also show alert states such as warning, caution and alarm in line with IEC 62288 (IEC, 2014). When the component is interactive, the standard button states show its interaction status. This includes "enabled, hover, active, and disabled". "Focused" is a special state showing a selection ring around the POI that supports key navigation in the interface. "Overlapped" is a special state that is enabled when two or more POIs overlap.

Finally, the framework manages the way POIs are selected, displayed and stacked (in case of overlap) (Figures 5.37 and 5.38). For more details, we refer to the detailed description of the framework in Nordby and Fauske (2024).

2.4.2 Path Prediction

This part of the framework originates from research on the use of augmented reality in manoeuvring operations. In this research, we developed visual

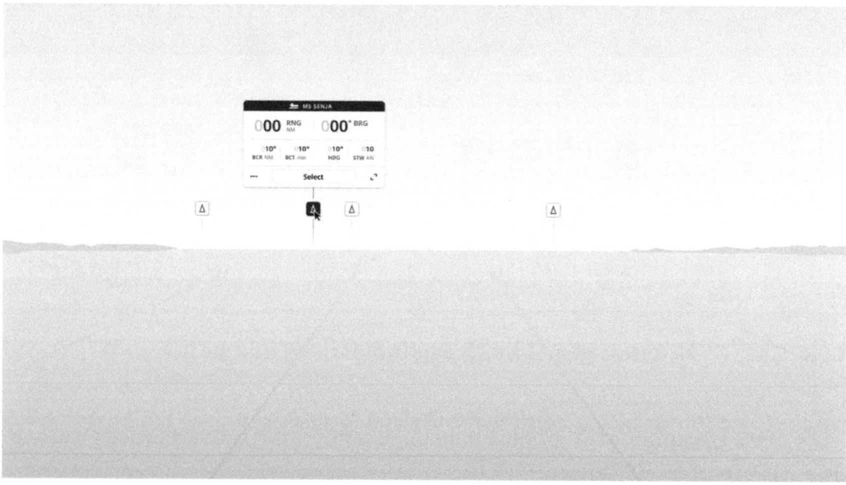

FIGURE 5.37 POI selection. Visual by Ocean Industries Concept Lab

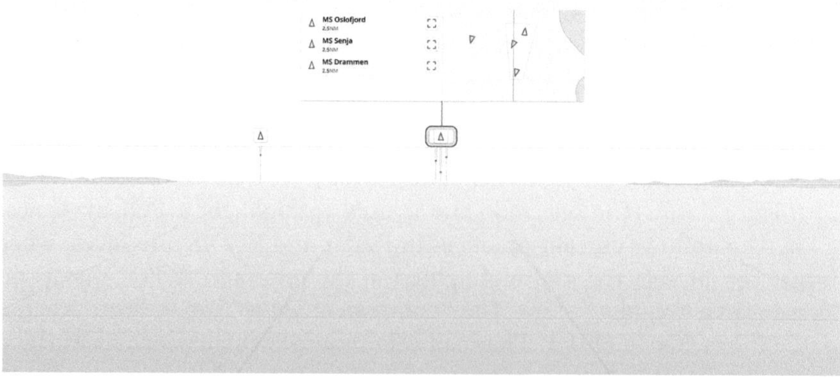

FIGURE 5.38 POI overlap. Visual by Ocean Industries Concept Lab

components that indicate the predicted path of a ship in the short term. These components are meant to be overlaid on the ocean surface part of the environment (see Figure 5.33). They enable to the indication of the future contour of the ship on the ocean (Figure 5.39 – *left*), the predicted path of the ship (Figure 5.39, *middle*) and the targeted docking position of a ship during docking operations (Figure 5.39, *right*).

2.4.3 Video Overlay in Applications

Finally, we show how the framework is used in applications. We start with a dedicated video feed application called "SA Cam" for situational awareness cameras (Figure 5.40).

SA Cam uses the POI system, the OpenBridge topbar, a compass component displayed as a bar just under the topbar, and widgets in the top left and right corners. Figure 5.41 shows the use of a compass widget, with an advice feature that displays a range into which the operator is advised not to head. This advice range is also displayed in the compass bar at the top of the screen.

Figure 5.42 shows the use of a map widget and how it can expand (Figure 5.43).

Figure 5.44 shows controls for the CCTV camera, with widgets for tilt, pan and zoom.

Finally, Figure 5.45 shows how the widgets can be organised on the left side of the screen, including a list of currently active ship targets.

We also show an example of using a video overlay in a conning application (Figure 5.46).

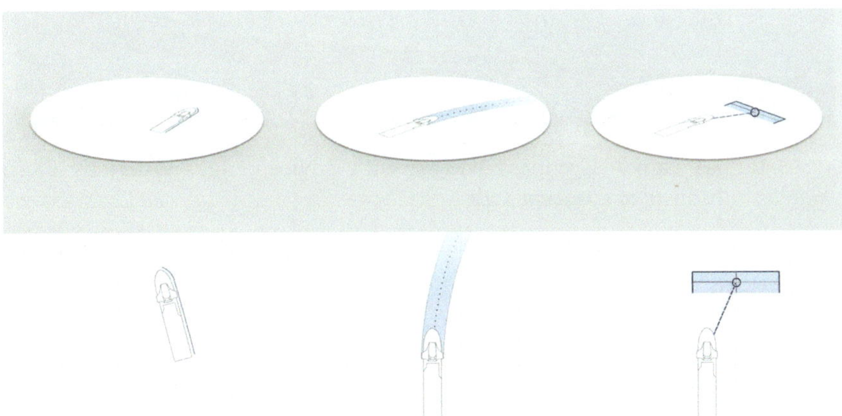

FIGURE 5.39 Path prediction. Visual by Ocean Industries Concept Lab

FIGURE 5.40 Use of the video overlay framework in an application. Visual by Ocean Industries Concept Lab

FIGURE 5.41 SA cam – Compass widget with advice range. Visual by Ocean Industries Concept Lab

3 Discussion

3.1 The Importance of Structured Design Guidelines for ROC Development

The design and development of ROCs for MASS operations require a structured, systems-level approach to interface design. A key challenge is ensuring consistency and coherence across physical and digital interfaces, which are developed by different vendors and deployed in diverse operational contexts.

FIGURE 5.42 SA cam – map widget. Visual by Ocean Industries Concept Lab

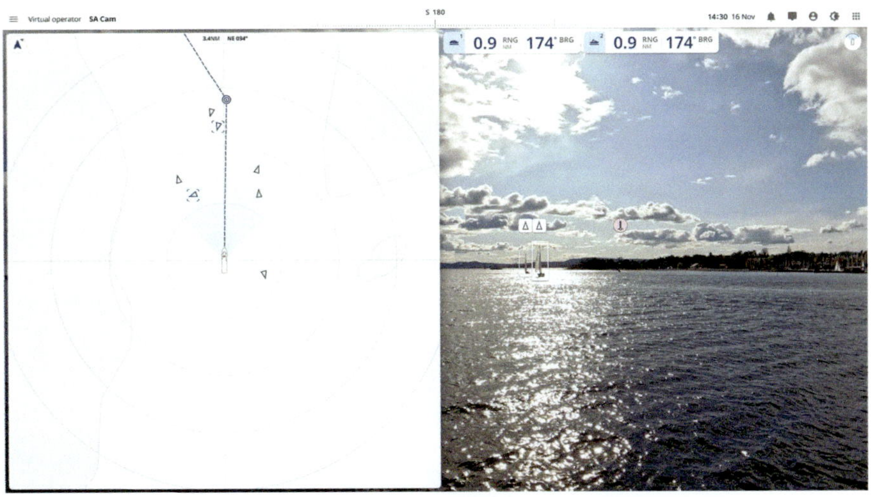

FIGURE 5.43 SA cam – map widget, large. Visual by Ocean Industries Concept Lab

Without clear design guidelines, ROCs risk becoming fragmented, with inconsistent user experiences, poor integration between systems and diminished operator situational awareness.

In the development of the ROC architecture framework, the OpenBridge design system has served as a foundation for addressing this challenge. OpenBridge supports the development of consistent, modular and scalable UIs that can integrate diverse applications into cohesive workplace environments. This is particularly important in the early stages of ROC evolution,

FIGURE 5.44 SA cam – tilt, pan and zoom control of CCTV camera. Visual by Ocean Industries Concept Lab

FIGURE 5.45 SA Cam – widget with targets. Visual by Ocean Industries Concept Lab

where the operational roles and capabilities of future MASS vessels may still evolve significantly, potentially imposing new needs and constraints on future ROC design configurations. There is a need to "future-proof" current ROC designs, allowing them to evolve in tandem with the technologies, tasks and operations they will ultimately need to support.

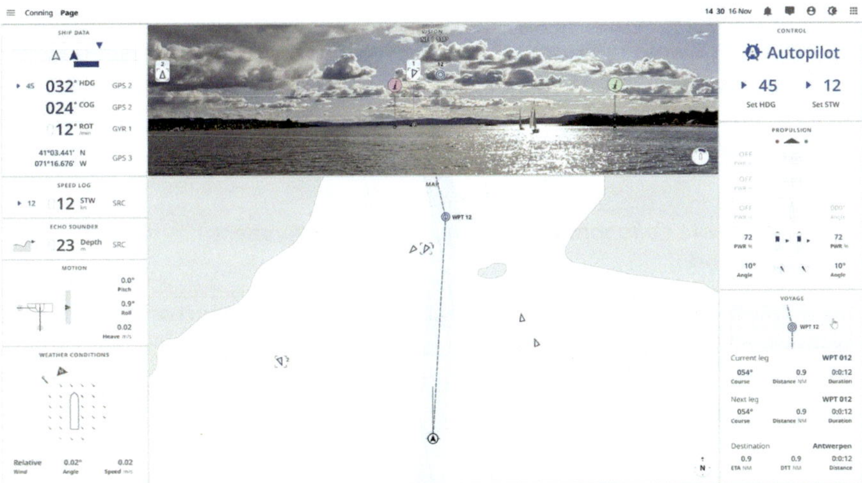

FIGURE 5.46 Example of the use of a video overlay in a conning application. Visual by Ocean Industries Concept Lab

3.2 Reflections on the Frameworks

3.2.1 The ROC Workstation Framework

The workstation framework addresses the foundational layout and physical interface of the ROC environment. Its importance lies in establishing a modular, ergonomic baseline that accommodates both current operator needs and future configurations. In any of these configurations, the framework's ambition is to support consistent placement of controls and displays, which is critical for reducing cognitive load and supporting operational safety.

In line with the future-proofing challenges of designing for MASS operations, a key challenge for the ROC workstation framework is to support modular workstation set-ups that can be adapted or reconfigured based on operational needs. To support the growth of MASS in terms of operator competence development, there is also a need to design hybrid spaces supporting both supervision and training.

3.2.2 The Workplace Integration Framework

The integration framework plays a central role in unifying digital interfaces across different applications and screen configurations. Its purpose is to enable a seamless and holistic user experience across multiple workstations and ROCs, making it possible to operate multi-vendor, multi-system environments without sacrificing usability or consistency.

It is particularly important in multi-vessel operations and distributed control scenarios, where operators may need to switch rapidly between different views, roles or vessels. The same integration challenges apply to scenarios where control is shared or distributed between automation systems and human operators.

3.2.3 The Remote Collaboration and Multi-User Environment Framework

This exploratory framework addresses collaboration across human and non-human actors in shared and distributed control scenarios. Its importance lies in formalising how multiple operators – whether co-located or remote, whether human or automated – can share control, information and awareness.

The framework introduces features such as shared views, cursor tracking, spotlighting and command transfer, inspired by modern collaborative digital tools. These tools aim to support transparent, cooperative work while ensuring clarity in roles, authority and control. Designing for command transfer, in particular, is a very important and complex challenge.

3.2.4 The Video Overlay Framework

The video overlay framework explores how augmented reality elements can be layered onto video feeds to enhance operator situational awareness. A central area of application is when operators lack physical proximity to the vessel and rely solely on indirect views of the environment.

As video-based systems evolve, the framework must integrate additional types of sensor data and increased use of sensor data. In the long term, the use of overlays may also expand to immersive environments (e.g. VR control spaces), requiring extensions to spatial interaction design and multimodal inputs.

3.3 Future Research Directions for ROC Design

We refer to the DNV AROS class notation to review the future needs for research in ROC design (DNV, n.d.). Currently, the ROC architecture framework covers the majority of the functions for AROS-NAV and AROS-ENG, but it does not cover the AROS-SAFE and AROS-OPS functions, for example, fire detection and firefighting, ballasting, cargo handling, passenger handling and payload operations.

In addition to these specific functions, future critical needs for ROC design are topics related to emerging technologies and the transition towards higher degrees of autonomy and automation (supervised autonomy and full autonomy in the AROS notation). This includes, for example, requirements related to cybersecurity, AI and automation transparency, and multimodal interaction (e.g. haptic feedback, voice control, natural language understanding). At a more fundamental level, there is a need to test different ROC workstation layouts, for instance the distance between ROC workstations, and between ROC workstations and screens.

4 Conclusion

In this chapter, we introduced the ROC architecture framework, a design framework for ROC as a workplace, enabling MASS operations. The framework addresses four critical dimensions of ROC design. The workstation framework provides a scalable foundation for designing operator consoles and physical workstations. The workplace integration framework supports the seamless integration of physical and digital user interfaces across multi-screen and multi-vessel settings. The remote collaboration and multi-user environment framework is an initial exploration of UI features that help to facilitate distributed collaboration – both between humans and between humans and automation. Finally, the video overlay framework explores the integration of real-time data overlays into situational awareness tools.

Together, these frameworks demonstrate the necessity of a structured, consistent, human-centred approach to UI design in remote ship operations. Poorly integrated or ad hoc design solutions may compromise operational safety, efficiency and user performance. We argue that our methodology, based on a design system that follows ergonomic standards and interaction design principles, is critical to meeting the technological challenges of MASS operation and their impact on the user experience of ROC operators.

As such, the OpenBridge design system is a central research infrastructure in our work. OpenBridge enables rapid prototyping, expert feedback and a consistent integration strategy across varied design cases. Its community of users and open-source access support knowledge transfer and industry adoption beyond the scope of the OpenRemote project. Future developments will continue to expand on the ROC architecture framework using OpenBridge and will include requirements for emerging technologies such as AI transparency, multimodal interfaces and cybersecurity. Our ambition is that, by expanding our approach, ROC design remains adaptable and ready to meet the future challenges of MASS operation.

CRediT Author Statement

Etienne Gernez: Writing – original draft preparation
Steven C. Mallam: Writing – reviewing and editing
Kjetil Nordby: Conceptualisation, supervision, software, writing – reviewing and editing
Jon Erling Fauske: Software, visualisation
Bijan Johansen: Software, visualisation

Hanne Lockertsen: Software, visualisation
Sunniva Lislevand Wildhagen: Software, visualisation
Borgar Kløve Sandnes: Software, visualisation

Acknowledgements

The authors would like to thank the OpenAR and OpenRemote project partners, the OpenBridge community and the Norwegian Research Council for funding (OpenAR project grant 320247, OpenRemote project grant 336398).

References

Aylward, K., Dahlman, J., Nordby, K., Lundh, M., 2021. Using operational scenarios in a virtual reality enhanced design process. *Education Sciences* 11, 448.

DNV, n.d. Autonomous and remotely operated ships – AROS class notation. Available at: https://www.dnv.com/news/new-aros-class-notation-for-autonomous-and-remotely-operated-ships-229425 (Accessed 23 Apr. 2025).

DNV, n.d. Available at: https://www.dnv.com/maritime/autonomous-remotely-operated-ships/ (Accessed 10 June 2025).

Frydenberg, S.G., Aylward, K., Nordby, K., Eikenes, J.O.H., 2021. Development of an augmented reality concept for icebreaker assistance and convoy operations. *Journal of Marine Science and Engineering* 9, 996. https://doi.org/10.3390/jmse9090996

Frydenberg, S.G., Nordby, K., 2022. Virtual fieldwork on a ship's bridge: Virtual reality-reconstructed operation scenarios as contextual substitutes for fieldwork in design education. *Virtual Reality*. https://doi.org/10.1007/s10055-022-00655-1

Gernez, E., Fauske, J.E., Nordby, K., Strange, E., 2024. An online, real-time, collaborative, immersive tool for early- phase, operation-centric maritime design. *Presented at the RINA Human Factors Conference, Wageningen, The Netherlands.*

Gernez, E., Nordby, K., 2020. A 10-day course to plan and execute field studies for maritime design processes. *Presented at the RINA International Conference on Marine Design, The Royal Institute of Naval Architects, Cadiz, Spain*, pp. 135–146.

Houweling, K.P., Mallam, S.C., van de Merwe, K., Nordby, K., 2024. The effects of augmented reality on operator situation awareness and head-down time. *Applied Ergonomics* 116, 104213. https://doi.org/10.1016/j.apergo.2023.104213

IEC, 2014. *Maritime navigation and radio communication equipment and systems.* International Electrotechnical Commission: Geneva, Switzerland, 2014.

Lurås, S., 2016. Layered scenario mapping: A multidimensional mapping technique for collaborative design. *CoDesign* 12, 133–150. https://doi.org/10.1080/15710882.2015.1072221

Lurås, S., Nordby, K., 2014. Field studies informing ship's bridge design. *Presented at the International Conference on Human Factors in Ship Design and Operation, 26–27 February 2014, London, UK.* https://doi.org/10.3940/rina.hf.2014.05

Nordby, K., Fauske, J.E., 2024. Realizing larger click surfaces for maritime user interfaces using function grouping. *Presented at the Human Factors 2024, The Royal Institution of Naval Architects, Wageningen, The Netherlands.*

Nordby, K., Fauske, J.E., Gernez, E., Mallam, S. C., 2024. A user interface design framework for augmented-reality-supported maritime navigation. *Journal of Marine Science and Engineering* 12, 505. https://doi.org/10.3390/jmse12030505

Nordby, K., Frydenberg, S., Fauske, J., 2018. Demonstrating a maritime design system for realising consistent design of multi-vendor ship's bridges. *Presented at the Human Factors Conference, London, UK.*

Nordby, K., Gernez, E., Frydenberg, S., Eikenes, J.O., 2020. Augmenting OpenBridge: An open user interface architecture for augmented reality applications on ship bridges. *Proceedings of COMPIT 2020 19th International Conference on Computer and IT Applications in the Maritime Industries. Presented at the 18th International Conference on Computer and IT Applications in the Maritime Industries, Pontignano, Italy*, pp. 180–195. https://doi.org/10.13140/RG.2.2.15067.13607

Nordby, K., Gernez, E., Mallam, S. C., 2019b. OpenBridge: Designing for consistency across user interfaces in multi-vendor ship bridges, in: Ergoship 2019. *Presented at the Ergoship 2019 Conference, Haugesund, Norway.*

Nordby, K., Mallam, S.C., Lützhöft, M., 2019a. Open user interface architecture for digital multivendor ship bridge systems. *WMU Journal of Maritime Affairs* 1–22.

Norwegian Research Council, n.d. *OpenAR – Framework for augmented reality in advanced maritime operations – Prosjektbanken [WWW Document]*. Prosjektbanken – Forskningsrådet. Available at: https://prosjektbanken.forskningsradet.no/project/FORISS/320247 (Accessed 6 Nov. 2025a).

Norwegian Research Council, n.d. *OpenRemote – Harmonising design of remote connected maritime workstations – Prosjektbanken [WWW Document]*. Prosjektbanken – Forskningsrådet. Available at: https://prosjektbanken.forskningsradet.no/project/FORISS/336398 (Accessed 6 Nov. 2025b).

Ocean Industries Concept Lab, n.d. *Projects [WWW Document]*. Available at: https://www.oicl.no/projects (Accessed 6 Nov. 2025).

OpenBridge, 2025. *OpenBridge design system*. https://www.openbridge.no (Accessed 16 Apr. 2025).

van den Oever, F., Fjeld, M., Orthmann, B., Nordby, K., Sætrevik, B., 2025. A field study of multi-user augmented reality to facilitate collaborative ship navigation. *IISE Transactions on Occupational Ergonomics and Human Factors* 1–13. https://doi.org/10.1080/24725838.2025.2477234

van den Oever, F., Sætrevik, B., Fjeld, M., Nordby, K., 2023. *A virtual reality experiment shows that augmented reality can improve collaboration in ship navigation*. https://doi.org/10.31234/osf.io/ts5wx

W3C, n.d. *Web Content Accessibility Guidelines (WCAG) 2.1 [WWW Document]*. Available at: https://www.w3.org/TR/WCAG21/ (Accessed 6 Nov. 2025).

6

A SYSTEMATIC ANALYSIS OF MEASUREMENT METHODS FOR HUMAN FACTORS IN REMOTE SHIPPING

Robert Grundmann, Arbresh Ujkani and Pascal Hohnrath

1 Introduction

Remote ship operation represents a significant technological advancement in maritime transportation, offering potential benefits in operational efficiency, crew welfare and resource allocation. *Remote operations* in shipping are also seen as one of the most promising use cases within the autonomous shipping market, according to a recent survey of more than 50 European maritime industry actors, thus representing an important emerging technology (Burmeister et al. 2024). However, the transition from conventional on-board navigation to remote operation introduces distinct challenges for human operators that must be systematically addressed (Wróbel, Gil and Chae 2021).

Traditional human factors research in maritime operations has primarily focused on on-site navigation scenarios, where operators benefit from direct sensory feedback and physical presence. These established research approaches cannot be directly applied to remote operations due to fundamental differences in the operator's perception, interaction capabilities and situational context. More on that will be discussed in Section 1.5.

The safety and efficiency of remote ship operation depend critically on the operator's ability to maintain appropriate situation awareness (SA) despite these constraints. SA includes the perception of environmental elements, comprehension of their meaning and projection of their status in the near future – all essential capabilities for effective navigation (Endsley 1995). However, the remote context fundamentally alters how operators develop and maintain this awareness.

This requires the development of adapted measurement methods and standardised assessment procedures specifically designed for remote maritime operations. Such methods must account for the unique characteristics

DOI: 10.4324/9781003586883-6

of remote-control environments while providing reliable metrics for comparing performance with conventional navigation. Without robust evaluation frameworks, the success and safety implications of remote ship operations cannot be suitably assessed.

While the maritime industry faces unique challenges in implementing remote operations, valuable insights can be drawn from non-maritime industries where remote operation is more established. Shore-based remote crane operations have demonstrated considerable maturity in addressing situational awareness challenges (Martin and Irani 2024). The crane industry's progression from fully manual to semi-autonomous remote operations provides a relevant developmental roadmap and offers tested methodologies for situational awareness assessment that may be applicable to the maritime context with appropriate modifications.

This research addresses this methodological gap by analysing existing measurement approaches, identifying relevant performance indicators and examining test environments that can realistically reproduce the challenges of remote ship operation. The goal is to establish evidence-based guidelines for standardised testing that can support the safe and effective implementation of remote maritime operations.

2 Relevant Human Factors in Navigation

Multiple human factors are critical for the effective execution and optimisation of remote operations (Kari and Steinert 2021). In addition to the more traditional aspects such as attentiveness, decision-making behaviour, communication and teamwork (Salmon et al. 2009), other factors are also relevant in the context of remote operations.

The key parameters include trust in automated systems (Lee and See 2004) and the stability of the technical infrastructure. In addition, SA and vigilance (without triggers from the real environment, such as environmental influences, smells, direct human interaction, or discreet acoustic alarms and signals) must be reassessed. The operator of a remote station must have sufficient confidence in the system to be able to hand over routine tasks to it. Vigilance should be maintained in the meantime to be able to intervene directly in the event of alarms. Other factors, such as fatigue and monotony, can lead to a decline in performance over time. This is particularly the case during prolonged monitoring without events, such as during long passages with minimal manoeuvring (Wahlström et al. 2015).

In detailed analysis, many different factors are crucial. The literature, however, emphasises two factors. Operator SA and workload are among the more important human factors that influence the safe and effective operation of remote operations (Man et al. 2015). These factors have a significant impact on the operator's performance, especially in dedicated high-stress tasks such as recognising critical events, maintaining control and intervening in time. The exact extent of the influence of these factors varies in different operational situations. The existing literature highlights SA and workload as particularly relevant constructs in the context of remotely piloted maritime operations (Man et al. 2015; Yan et al. 2022; Grundmann et al. 2023).

In the systematic literature review, the objective was to focus on available research methods in the maritime context with a view to human factors and remote operations. This was intended to map the state of research at precisely this interface.

A search for literature related to the topic was carried out in the Web of Science to achieve this.

Besides the criteria of publication year (2000–2025), type of publication (articles and conference papers) and language (English), primary attention was paid to a clear orientation of the query. The terms currently used are still not very standardised; therefore, the query had to be adapted accordingly. The aim was to focus on available research methods in the maritime context, with an emphasis on human factors and remote operations.

The search query used in Web of Science was:

((human factor* AND "workload" AND "situational awareness" OR "situation awareness" OR "SA") AND (maritim* AND "vessel" OR "ship") AND ("testbed" OR "trial" OR "field study" OR simulat* OR "experiment" OR "test" OR "performance") AND (maritim* AND remote* OR teleoperat* OR "shore-based" OR "unmanned"))

The asterisk "*" is a wildcard that replaces any number of characters to include all word endings.

The result was an output of 58 publications, three of which were excluded as not suitable for the research question. From the 55 publications that remained, the keywords were analysed and transferred into suitable clusters for standardisation. The central clusters include *remote operation*, *human factors*, *situation awareness*, *simulation*, *metrics & assessment* and *trust in automation*. UAV, USV and MASS were explicitly considered separately to better visualise their significance in the literature and their interconnectedness with other subject areas. It is certainly arguable that each of these transportation concepts has some form of remote monitoring or control. However, combining these clusters with remote operation would cloud the picture here. The result can be seen in Figure 6.1.

The analysis reveals several key findings:

1 SA, maritime navigation and sensor fusion and perception are important nodes, demonstrating the dominant role of holistic user perception, advanced sensor technologies and foresight techniques in the maritime context (Wang, Prasad Perera and Batalden 2024).

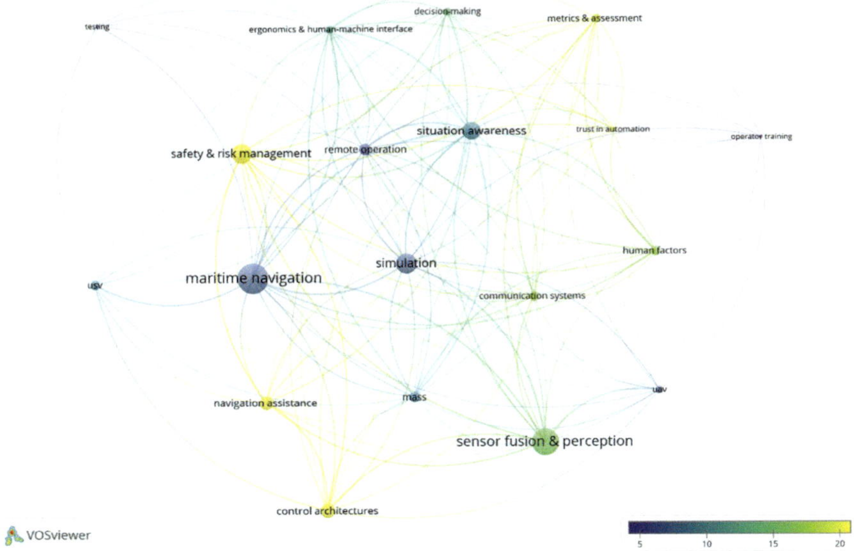

FIGURE 6.1 Overlay visualisation of co-occurrence of keywords by cluster (right below avg. citations)

2 Simulation is an essential component of the literature reviewed; however, the link to methodology is too broad.
3 Remote operation has clearly arrived thematically in the maritime context and is positioned between autonomy, maritime navigation and navigation support.

Several research gaps are also apparent:

1 Trust in automation and operator training are clearly underrepresented. A lack of techniques and models to capture trust-building in this subject area is therefore evident (Hoff and Bashir 2015).
2 Metric & assessment and testing show a lower network density compared to ergonomics & human-machine interface (HMI). There is a lack of concrete approaches to measuring the human factor in modern control and monitoring concepts.

Overall, the analysis shows a high scientific relevance of human-centered research in the field of remote control and remote assistance in the maritime domain.

The literature analysis in Figure 6.1 directly informed the selection of measurement methods for this study. The identified research gap in "metrics & assessment" and "testing" (showing lower network density) highlighted the need for robust, validated measurement approaches in maritime remote operations. Given that SA emerged as a dominant node in the literature, SAGAT was selected as the primary objective measure to address this gap. Similarly, the underrepresentation of workload assessment methods in the maritime remote operations literature justified the inclusion of NASA-TLX as a complementary subjective measure.

2.1 Situation Awareness

The operator's understanding of the current situation, also known as the "situation picture", is referred to as SA. SA consists of three stages (Endsley 1995):

1 perception of the relevant elements in the environment,
2 understanding of their significance and
3 projection of their possible future development.

On board a ship, SA arises from the multitude of sensory impressions and direct observations; for example, the view from the bridge windows, direct observation of navigational instruments and equipment, alarms, interaction within the bridge team and movements of the ship. In the remote operation centre (ROC), these are partially missing or have been replaced. Interactions, observations and possible interpretations of movements can only be obtained by monitoring sensor data. The spatial distance and media disruptions limit the maintenance of a high level of situational awareness. In the literature, there is mention of the loss of "ship sense", the feeling that experienced navigators have for the ship and its surroundings, when switching from shipboard to shore-based operations (Porathe, Prison and Man 2014).

The remote operator must assemble his situation picture from fragmented sources of information (Kawashima et al. 2023). Within this changed requirement profile, the mental model of the situation can be incomplete due to the incorrect interpretation or oversight of critical signals. Maintaining adequate SA for remote operators is therefore a central research concern. Studies are investigating the design of displays and interfaces to provide the user with comprehensive SA in a timely manner (Man, Lundh and Porathe 2014).

To address these human-centred challenges in remote ship operations, the International Maritime Organization (IMO) has issued guidelines on Software Quality Assurance and Human-Centred Design for e-Navigation (IMO 2015). These guidelines emphasise that maritime systems, especially those enabling remote or autonomous navigation, must be developed with explicit attention to user needs, cognitive limitations and operational contexts. By applying HCD principles, such as iterative usability testing and participatory design, systems can better support the formation and maintenance of SA, even when traditional sensory input and interaction are reduced. In particular, the guidelines advocate interface and information design that enables accurate perception, understanding and projection, aligning directly with Endsley's model of SA.

2.2 Other Human Factors in Ship Bridge Navigation

While SA represents a primary focus in ship navigation, several other human factors significantly impact performance and safety in both conventional and remote operation contexts. These additional factors interact with and influence SA, creating a complex web of human performance considerations.

2.2.1 Workload

Workload is a critical factor in remote navigation operations, particularly mental workload, as physical tasks are largely absent. Remote operators primarily engage in monitoring, planning and intervention. These tasks are characterised by long phases of low workload, punctuated by sudden peaks during alarms or unexpected events. Such workload variability can cause underload-related inattention or overload-related stress and increased error rates. Veitch et al. demonstrated that increasing the number of vessels supervised and reducing decision-making time windows significantly raises the likelihood of errors (2024). Conversely, prolonged low-stimulus monitoring, despite causing boredom, resulted in only minor performance drops. The distinction between short- and long-term boredom effects is crucial but understudied – chronic understimulation over extended deployments may produce fundamentally different performance degradation patterns than the brief monitoring periods typically examined in laboratory settings. Importantly, workload and SA are closely connected. Excessive workload can impair SA, while strong SA can mitigate cognitive strain by enhancing orientation and perceived control (Endsley 1995).

2.2.2 Human-Machine Interaction

Interface design significantly influences navigation performance. Key usability factors, including information accessibility, design consistency and error-prevention mechanisms, have been identified (Danielsen 2023). In remote operations, these factors become even more critical, as operators rely entirely on technology-mediated information presentation.

2.2.3 Fatigue and Vigilance

Extended watchkeeping periods and monitoring requirements contribute to fatigue and vigilance decrements. Fatigue has been implicated in a significant proportion of maritime incidents involving human error. For example, fatigue-related accidents have been linked to non-compliance with rest period requirements, particularly among crews on long-haul voyages (Chukwuemeka 2024).

2.2.4 Communication and Teamwork

Effective communication among team members is essential for safe navigation. Remote operations require more structured communication protocols to compensate for the lack of non-verbal cues and shared physical context. Studies have shown that communication dynamics, including clarity and coordination, are critical in both standard and emergency scenarios (Lochner et al. 2018).

2.2.5 Decision-Making Process

Navigators employ both analytical and intuitive decision-making approaches. In remote operations, decision-making is influenced by factors such as technological interfaces and situational awareness. Research indicates that human factors, including stress and memory limitations, can disturpt decision-making processes in remote ship operations (Kari and Steinert 2021).

2.2.6 Competency and Training

Remote operations require specialised skills combining traditional navigation knowledge with technology management competencies. Training programmes must address the unique challenges of remote operations, including the development of decision-making capabilities and the management of complex human-machine interactions.

2.2.7 Measurement Environments

The context in which human factors are measured significantly impacts data validity and applicability. Maritime human factors research employs various testing environments, each with distinct advantages and limitations. Table-top simulations offer a cost-effective initial assessment but have limited ecological validity. Ship handling simulators (SHS) provide more realistic navigation experiences with standardised scenarios and comprehensive data collection capabilities. Connected ship handling simulators enable the testing of distributed teams and multi-vessel interactions. Real bridge environments offer the highest ecological validity but present challenges in experimental control and data collection. ROCs represent the newest environment specific to remote navigation, allowing assessment of human factors within the actual technological context in which operators will function. The choice of measurement environment must align with specific research questions, balancing fidelity requirements against practical constraints.

3 Measurement Methods

A variety of methods exist to measure human factors, each offering unique advantages and limitations depending on the specific aspect of human performance being assessed. The selection of an appropriate measurement method is contingent on the factor under investigation and the context in which the measurement occurs. Broadly, these methods can be categorised into subjective and objective measures.

Subjective Measurement Methods:

- NASA task load index (NASA-TLX)
- Situation awareness rating technique (SART)

Objective Measurement Methods:

- Electroencephalography (EEG)
- Eye tracking
- Heart-rate monitoring
- Situation awareness global assessment technique (SAGAT)

Subjective measures rely on individuals' self-reports, often obtained through structured questionnaires, rating scales, interviews or debriefing sessions. Instruments such as the NASA task load index (NASA-TLX) (Hart and Staveland 1988), which assesses perceived mental, physical and temporal demands, and the situation awareness rating technique (SART) (Taç and Tavacıoğlu 2019), which gauges an operator's perceived level of SA during task execution, are commonly employed in human factors research. Subjective methods are particularly valued for their capacity to capture internal states and personal experiences, which are often inaccessible through purely observational or physiological means. Additionally, they are relatively simple to implement in both experimental and operational settings, making them resource-efficient. However, subjective measures are prone to inherent limitations, such as biases arising from social desirability effects, memory distortions, and variability in individual self-perception or interpretation of scales. To enhance the reliability and validity of findings, subjective data are often triangulated with objective measures, facilitating a more holistic and accurate understanding of human performance and system interactions. In maritime contexts, subjective measures play a critical role in evaluating decision-making processes and responses to high-stress or high-workload situations, in which individual perception significantly influences operational outcomes.

Objective measures, in contrast, yield quantifiable data that can be directly observed, recorded and analysed. These measures encompass a variety of performance metrics, such as task completion times, error rates, reaction times and decision-making accuracy, which serve to evaluate an operator's ability to perform tasks effectively under both routine and emergency conditions.

The SAGAT method is a well-known method for measuring SA (Endsley 1995). In this method, a simulation is paused at unpredictable moments for the test person, and questions are asked about the current situation. All displays are hidden. The accuracy of the answers – that is, how many questions are answered correctly – serves as a quantitative measure of the user's SA. High SAGAT scores indicate that the navigator has perceived, correctly interpreted and monitored the relevant objects and factors in the situation.

A subcategory of objective measures is behavioural measures, which focus on the direct observation and documentation of human actions during task execution. These measures are particularly useful in maritime environments, where operators' actions – such as responses to navigational challenges or adherence to safety protocols – are observed during both simulator-based exercises and real-world operational trials. Behavioral measures provide valuable insights into human performance, including the effectiveness of task execution, decision-making under stress, and interactions with navigational systems and team members. By recording specific behaviours, these methods can pinpoint areas for improvement, such as deficiencies in operator skills or flaws in system design. However, behavioural measures are limited in that they often capture only the outcomes of actions, such as errors or reaction times, without explaining the cognitive processes or emotional states that underpin those behaviours. Consequently, while behavioural data are essential for assessing task performance, they may not provide a complete understanding of the cognitive mechanisms, such as attention or decision-making strategies, involved in human performance.

Another subcategory of objective measures is physiological measures, which assess human responses to stress, cognitive load and environmental factors by monitoring physiological indicators such as heart rate, brain activity and skin conductance. These measures are instrumental in providing real-time insights into an operator's physical and psychological state, which may not be readily apparent through subjective reports or behavioural observations. In maritime contexts, physiological data can be invaluable for understanding the impact of long shifts, high workload or complex navigation tasks on crew members (Orlandi and Brooks 2018). Techniques such as heart rate monitoring, electroencephalography (EEG) and eye-tracking provide critical data on factors like stress, fatigue and cognitive overload (Kari,

Gausdal and Steinert 2022). However, while physiological measures offer objective and quantifiable data, they come with limitations, including high cost, technical complexity and potential participant discomfort. Additionally, interpreting physiological data in the context of specific tasks can be challenging, as individual physiological responses to stress or cognitive load can vary significantly.

For the current maritime navigation study, several measurement methods were deliberately excluded despite their utility in other domains. Methods such as dual-task paradigms, commonly used in cognitive load assessment, were deemed inappropriate due to their potential interference with primary navigation tasks, where safety is paramount. Similarly, while galvanic skin response (GSR) provides reliable stress indicators, the maritime environment's humidity and temperature variations compromise sensor reliability. Think-aloud protocols, though valuable for understanding decision-making processes, were rejected as they fundamentally alter the naturalistic work environment and could mask communication patterns critical to bridge operations. The selected combination of SAGAT, NASA-TLX and behavioural observation was chosen specifically because these methods can capture SA and workload without compromising operational realism or introducing artificial task demands.

4 The BEYOND Method

Standardised test procedures for measuring and evaluating SA regarding nautical systems and HMIs have been lacking so far. The BEYOND research project, Building an Experience to Yield Optimal Nautical Displays, provides a structured, simulation-based test methodology for the evaluation of maritime HMIs, including the SA achieved by users (Schwarze et al. 2024). BEYOND uses the SAGAT method to make SA measurable. SAGAT is used across domains to objectively measure SA. It enables comparisons between different scenarios and systems.

The freeze-probe method provides an objective assessment of the operators' SA. This means that they do not have to think out loud during the journey or be questioned afterwards.

The BEYOND method itself was implemented in a full-mission ship-handling simulation (Mahadevan et al. 2025). The test subjects (experts and novices) went through several complex scenarios using navigation systems such as radar and electronic chart display and information system (ECDIS), as well as the view from the bridge.

A key feature of the BEYOND method is its reproducibility. By using simulators, questionnaires and interfaces (DIS protocol (IEEE 1995)), the tests can be repeated as often as required under the same conditions. The DIS protocol also allows scenarios to be started, paused and reloaded.

The simulation data can also be made available to other processes in this way (e.g. evaluation software such as MATLAB for statistical analysis, Python-based machine learning frameworks for pattern recognition or specialised maritime simulation analysis tools like DNV GL's Sesam).

The BEYOND methodology was tested in an extensive user study. The results of the study proved the validity of the approach. In addition to the objective SA score, various questionnaires were used in the BEYOND project to record the subjective feedback of the test subjects. Collaborating directly with nautical experts, 55 key questions were developed. These cover various aspects of the maritime situation picture. They are divided into four main categories: hazards, own ship, target ships and environment, with subcategories for more specific aspects of information. It was important to cover all three SA levels: perception (e.g. "What objects are in your vicinity?"), understanding significance (e.g. "What is the next navigational obstacle on your course?") and Projection (e.g. "Where will a particular vessel be in 10 minutes?").

The resulting BEYOND toolbox, consisting of standardised questionnaires and scenarios, simulation control tools, evaluation mechanisms and survey tools, has developed a holistic method that provides a comprehensive picture of a navigator's performance and the suitability of a navigation system. The methodology's key advantage lies in its standardised, reproducible framework that enables objective comparison of maritime systems.

5 Challenges in Measuring Human Factors in Remote Operations Versus On-Site Operations

Remote ship operation introduces unique measurement challenges compared to traditional on-site navigation. While conventional navigation assessment benefits from established methodologies and direct observation, remote operation requires new approaches that account for the technological mediation of maritime tasks. This section examines the key challenges in measuring human factors across these different operational contexts.

5.1 Specific Challenges in Remote Operations

Remote ship operations present several human factors challenges, including *information overload* and the absence of *physical feedback*, which can affect operator decision-making (Wahlström et al. 2015). These concerns highlight the critical need for designing shore control centres that directly address such issues to support operator performance and safety.

Additionally, *time delays* in data transmission present a significant challenge in remote navigation tasks. Studies have demonstrated that even small latencies can significantly affect operator performance, particularly during high-stakes manoeuvres requiring precise timing (Khasawneh et al. 2019). In another study, it was noted that time delays of less than a second are acceptable for dynamic manoeuvres (Burmeister, Grundmann and Schulte, situational awareness in AR/VR during remote manoeuvring with MASS: The Tug Case, 2020). These findings suggest that human factors measurements must account for the temporal aspects of information flow in remote systems.

Visual distortion is another critical challenge, particularly when camera-based views replace direct line-of-sight observation. Research highlights that maritime video-based object detection faces numerous difficulties, including camera motion on floating platforms, dynamic water backgrounds, the absence of static reference cues, the presence of small objects in distant backgrounds and varying illumination effects (Prasad et al. 2016). These factors can impair effective SA and object tracking, underscoring the importance of optimising camera systems and display interfaces to support accurate visual perception in remote-control environments.

Given these specific human factors challenges in remote ship operations, it becomes crucial to assess operator performance and system interactions carefully. However, measuring human factors in remote contexts presents its own unique methodological difficulties, as explored below.

5.2 Human Factors Measurement in Remote Operations

While the fundamental methods for measuring human factors in remote operations are largely the same as those employed in on-site (i.e. on-bridge) operations, the application of these methods to the remote context introduces unique challenges. All general advantages and limitations associated with subjective, behavioural and physiological measures apply equally to the assessment of remote operators. However, specific pitfalls must be carefully considered when planning human factors evaluations in remote-control scenarios.

Human factors assessments are typically conducted under highly controlled conditions to ensure reproducibility. As outlined in Section 4 ship-handling simulators (SHS) are commonly used to replicate the environment of a ship's bridge as realistically as possible.

However, transferring findings from SHS-based trials to real-world remote operations presents significant challenges. SHS environments are optimised to simulate traditional bridge operations, not remote-control settings. Thus, results obtained from simulator studies may not accurately reflect the conditions, constraints and cognitive demands faced by remote operators.

Trust in the system is particularly difficult to assess accurately in the context of remote operations. In a SHS, participants interact with a system that provides consistent, non-contradictory information. In real-world remote-control scenarios, however, information consistency cannot be taken for granted. Operators often face incomplete, delayed or ambiguous sensor data and camera feeds.

Moreover, navigators on a ship's bridge have access to an external "ground truth" through direct visual observation of the environment. In contrast, remote operators must rely entirely on mediated information, without the possibility of direct sensory verification. This fundamental difference significantly influences trust dynamics and makes it difficult to replicate real-world trust-calibration processes within a simulator setting. Consequently, trust measurements conducted in conventional simulators may either overestimate or underestimate the trust experienced during actual remote operations.

Another significant factor influencing human factors measurement is the physical and cognitive environment in which operators work. SHSs are typically designed to closely resemble conventional bridge layouts. By contrast, remote operator stations can vary substantially, ranging from minimalistic computer workstations to highly integrated, multi-screen control rooms.

This discrepancy in the working environment may affect not only operator performance but also cognitive processes such as attention allocation, situational awareness and decision-making strategies. Therefore, to ensure ecological validity, it is essential either to adapt simulators to closely match the design of remote-operation workstations or to introduce simulated data directly into the remote-control environments during trials.

To summarise the text, these are the core areas that define the unique landscape of remote maritime operations and their associated measurement challenges, each requiring careful consideration in the development of effective remote ship control systems:

Primary Human Factors Challenges

- Information processing limitations (overload, absence of feedback)
- Communication delays
- Visual perception issues
- Environmental awareness constraints

Core Measurement Challenges

- Simulation-to-reality transfer gaps
- Trust-assessment complications
- Mediated versus direct information processing
- Workspace design variations

6 Opportunities for Improving Human Factor Measurement in Remote Operations

The shift to remote ship operations introduces new possibilities for advancing human factors technologies. Several areas offer particular potential:

6.1 Advanced Simulation Environments

The integration of virtual reality (VR) and augmented reality (AR) technologies offers significant potential to bridge the gap between traditional ship bridge simulations and remote operation environments. By recreating the physical and perceptual context of ship operations in immersive environments (for example, see Figure 6.2), VR/AR can restore elements of sensory richness and spatial awareness lost in remote-control scenarios (Tittle, Roesler and Woods 2002). Advanced simulation can improve the measurement of SA, trust and cognitive load under realistic and reproducible conditions.

6.2 Adaptation of Measurement Methods

Existing subjective and objective measurement tools require adaptation to remote-specific contexts. Traditional SA assessments, such as SAGAT, may need to be extended with questions that account for multiple-vessel monitoring, sensor fusion and mediated perception. Similarly, workload measures like NASA-TLX could be adjusted to emphasise information management, remote interface complexity and communication dynamics specific to shore-based operation centres.

6.3 Sensor Fusion and Multimodal Pipelines

A multimodal approach to data collection, combining behavioural performance metrics (e.g. error rates, reaction times) with physiological measures (e.g. heart rate variability, eye tracking, EEG), allows for a more comprehensive understanding of operator state. Sensor fusion enables the detection

FIGURE 6.2 Augmented reality in a SHS

of latent factors, such as hidden stress or cognitive fatigue, that may not manifest in performance outcomes alone, thereby supporting more proactive operator support strategies.

6.4 Digital Twins for Predictive Modelling

The emerging concept of digital twins – virtual models that replicate the behaviour of real-world ships and operators – offers novel possibilities for human factors research. By modelling operator interaction patterns, workload trajectories and SA development over time, digital twins can be used to predict performance degradations or trust breakdowns before they manifest operationally. This predictive capability can inform training programmes, interface design improvements and adaptive system support mechanisms.

In summary, technological advancements and methodological adaptations present significant opportunities to enhance the measurement of human factors in remote shipping operations. These innovations are essential for ensuring that remote operation systems are designed, evaluated and operated with a human-centred focus that supports safety, efficiency and reliability.

7 The Adapted BEYOND Method

With the growing and already existing use cases of new control concepts for seagoing and inland vessels, it is recommended to bring the existing BEYOND method from the ship's bridge to the remote centres and to the operators ashore. Its objective should be to record the situational awareness of shore-based operators just as accurately as that of officers on board.

Due to the diverse and non-standardised set-ups of existing remote operation workstations, the most obvious solution is to supply the necessary data for measuring SA to the existing set-ups as part of the test set-up. The simulation infrastructure of the ship-handling simulators would serve as the foundation for this. The movement data of the ships would continue to be generated via the ship simulator and then sent to the adapted workstations using the DIS protocol. Some points are very different in the remote operator's workplace compared to the workplace on board. In addition to the latency and the lack of presence on board, the data supplied also has its pitfalls.

A major barrier is the provision of realistic-looking video data, as decisions in the context of remote operation are primarily made through verification with an external view. In this context, an important point to note is that the digital environments in current ship-handling simulators do not present the real world, either in terms of shore and sea or the vessels, in an appealing way. Participants can clearly see that they are in an artificial environment. Recent developments, especially in the field of immersive technology, have brought significant improvements. Nevertheless, the standard simulators are equipped with low graphic quality in the external view and are utilised as the main tool for training and further education. In the context of providing visualisations of the external view and the ships for tests in remote operation, predefined live recordings or highly realistic graphical representations could help to keep the simulation more realistic and the findings and measurements more valid. In addition, a realistic presentation could open another topic of interest, which is spatial awareness (Tittle, Roesler and Woods 2002).

The adaptation also focuses on scenario design for shore-based settings. Here, unlike on a ship's bridge, remote operators must reconstruct their situation entirely from imaging data and sensor messages. Further adjustments to the design of the scenarios consider the fact that a shore operator sometimes must focus distributed attention on several objects or even several vessels. In the future, not just one vessel, but multiple vessels will be served by one operator. The SA questions must be expanded accordingly to cover the special features of the remote setting.

In addition, the scenario should include realistic remote conditions, such as slight transmission delays or limited sensor availability, to reflect the challenges of real remote operation.

In the classic BEYOND set-up, mobile eye trackers were used. In the extended remote set-up, stationary systems could increase the quality of the recorded data. This is only possible because the remote operator has an assigned workstation, and the navigator changes position on the bridge or in the simulator. Eye tracking makes it possible to understand where the operator directs their visual attention and thus indirectly what information they perceive or overlook.

The adaptation of the BEYOND method in the context of remote operation in the maritime sector requires further holistic development on several levels. However, it is a journey that is extremely rewarding, not only for the objective measures but also in the context of maritime training, further education and development, and the testing of new human-machine interfaces in modern control centres such as the ROC.

8 Outlook and Future Research Directions

The remote operation of ships presents significant opportunities for advancing human-centred design and evaluation methodologies in the maritime domain. However, several critical challenges remain that must be addressed through comprehensive future research initiatives:

- Cross-validation of assessment methods between conventional and remote contexts
- Development of standardised testing protocols and regulatory frameworks

- Integration with OpenBridge design systems and established frameworks
- Extended studies examining operator adaptation and skill maintenance
- Creation of shared testbeds and benchmarks for consistent evaluation

First, cross-validation of methods represents a fundamental requirement, as measurement techniques for SA and cognitive workload must be rigorously validated across both remote and conventional maritime operational contexts to ensure scientific comparability and operational reliability. Such validation establishes whether existing assessment tools maintain their utility and accuracy when transferred to remote settings.

Second, the development of standardised test procedures is essential, as there is a pressing need for robust regulatory frameworks and thoroughly defined testing protocols specifically tailored to remote operation environments. These frameworks would support certification processes, operational guidelines and training standards that account for the unique challenges of monitoring and controlling vessels from a distance. Recommendations for such standardised test procedures have been provided by the BEYOND project.

Third, integration with Open Bridge design systems would significantly enhance standardisation efforts. By building upon established open-source frameworks like OpenBridge (Open Bridge 2025) and similar initiatives, developers can leverage existing design guidelines, interface components and evaluation metrics that have already been validated in traditional maritime contexts. These open design systems provide a foundation that can be extended to accommodate the unique requirements of remote operations while maintaining consistency with familiar navigation paradigms, thereby reducing the learning curve.

Fourth, elongated studies are crucial to understanding the temporal dynamics of remote operations. Such research should systematically investigate how operator trust in automation, technical competence, decision-making strategies and error-recovery capabilities evolve over extended periods with prolonged exposure to remote monitoring and control systems. These studies would reveal adaptation patterns and potential skill-degradation issues that may not be apparent in short-term evaluations.

Finally, the creation of shared testbeds and open benchmarks would substantially advance the field. Establishing standardised simulation platforms, scenario databases and open datasets would facilitate experimental reproducibility, cross-institutional collaboration and more efficient knowledge transfer within the research community. Such resources would accelerate innovation while enabling direct comparisons of different interface designs, automation strategies and training methodologies.

By comprehensively addressing these interconnected research areas, future studies can establish a robust foundation for the safe, efficient and human-centred implementation of remote maritime operations that meet both commercial and regulatory expectations.

References

Burmeister, H. C., R. Grundmann, and B. Schulte. "Situational Awareness in AR/VR During Remote Maneuvering with MASS: The Tug Case." *Global Oceans 2020 Singapore*, – US. Gulf Coast, *1*, 2020: 217–222. https://doi.org/10.1109/IEEECONF38699.2020.9389455

Burmeister, H. C., J. Weisheit, J. Küchle, L. Franziska Bluhm, and M. Bergmann. "An Emerging Market? The European Maritime Industry's View on Autonomous Maritime Systems: A Survey." Journal of Physics: Conference Series, *2867*, 2024: 012017. https://doi.org/10.1088/1742-6596/2867/1/012017

Chukwuemeka, A. E. "Analysing the Impact of Human Factors on Marine Accidents." *International Journal of Research and Innovation in Applied Science (IJRIAS)*, *9*, 2024.

Danielsen, B.-E. *Usability in Ship Bridge Design – A Mission Impossible? A Qualitative Study of Maritime Stakeholders' Perspectives on Usability in Ship Bridge Design*. Trondheim: NTNU, 2023.

Endsley, M. R. "Measurement of Situation Awareness in Dynamic Systems." *Human Factors, 37(1)*, 1995: 65–84.

Grundmann, R., A. Ujkani, J. Weisheit, J. Seppänen, M. Salokorpi, and H. C. Burmeister. "Use Case Remote Pilotage – Technology Overview." *Journal of Physics: Conference Series*, *2618*, 2023: 012007. https://doi.org/10.1088/1742-6596/2618/1/012007

Hart, S. G., and L. E. Staveland. "Development of NASA-TLX (Task Load Index): Results of Empirical and Theoretical Research." *Advances in Psychology*, *52*, 1988: 139–183.

Hoff, K. A., and M. Bashir. "Trust in Automation: Integrating Empirical Evidence on Factors That Influence Trust." *Human Factors, 57(3)*, 2015: 407–434.

IEEE. *IEEE Standard for Distributed Interactive Simulation – Application Protocols*. New York, NY: Institute of Electrical and Electronics Engineers, 1995.

IMO. *Guideline on Software Quality Assurance and Human-Centred Design for E-Navigation*. London: International Maritime Organization, 2015.

Kari, R., A. H. Gausdal, and M. Steinert. "EEG Based Workload and Stress Assessment During Remote Ship Operations." *TransNav, the International Journal on Marine Navigation and Safety of Sea Transportation*, 2022: 295–305.

Kari, R., and M. Steinert. "Human Factor Issues in Remote Ship Operations: Lesson Learned by Studying Different Domains." *Journal of Marine Science and Engineering*, 2021: 385.

Kawashima, S., H. Itoh, Y. Kawamura, and H. Otsuka. "Analysis of the Situation Awareness of Remote Ship Operators in an Emergency: A Simulation-based Study for Small Ships." *Transactions of Navigation, 8(2)*, 2023: 45–55.

Khasawneh, A., H. Rogers, J. Bertrand, K. C. Madathil, and A. Gramopadhye. "Human Adaptation to Latency in Teleoperated Multi-Robot Human-Agent Search and Rescue Teams." *Automation in Construction*, *99*, 2019: 265–277.

Lee, J. D., and K. A. See. "Trust in Automation: Designing for Appropriate Reliance." *Human Factors, 46(1)*, 2004: 50–80.

Lochner, M., A. Duenser, M. Lützhöft, B. Brooks, and D. Rozado. "Analysis of maritime team workload and communication dynamics in standard and emergency scenarios." *Journal of Shipping and Trade Vol. 3*, 2018: 2364–4575.

Mahadevan, H. S., A. Kumar, R. Grundmann, and A. Schwarze. "Assessment of Situational Awareness in Relation to Advanced Navigation Systems Using Ship Handling Simulators." *Engineering Proceedings, 88(1)*, 2025: 36.

Man, Y., M. Lundh, and T. Porathe. "Seeking Harmony in Shore-Based Unmanned Ship Handling – From the Perspective of Human Factors, What is the Difference We Need to Focus on from Being Onboard to Onshore?" *5th International Conference on Applied Human Factors and Ergonomics and the Affiliated Conferences*, 2014: 5.

Man, Y., M. Lundh, T. Porathe, and S. N. Mackinnon. "From Desk to Field – Human Factor Issues in Remote Monitoring and Controlling of Autonomous Unmanned Vessels." *Procedia Manufacturing*, *3*, 2015: 2674–2681.

Martin, I. A., and R. A. Irani. "The Examination of Operator Performance When Controlling a Shipboard Crane Anti-Sway Control System Within a Virtual-Reality Simulator." *Ocean Engineering*, *298*, 2024: 117164. https://doi.org/10.1016/j.oceaneng.2024.117164

Open Bridge. *Open Bridge Design System 5.0*. 30. 04 2025. https://www.openbridge.no/2025.

Orlandi, L., and B. Brooks. "Measuring Mental Workload and Physiological Reactions in Marine Pilots: Building Bridges Towards Redlines of Performance." *Applied Ergonomics*, *69*, 2018: 74–92.

Porathe, T., J. Prison, and Y. Man. "Situation Awareness in Remote Control Centres for Unmanned Ships." *Human Factors in Ship Design & Operation*, 2014: 5.

Prasad, D. K., C. K. Prasath, D. Rajan, L. Rachmawati, E. Rajabally, and C. Quek. "Challenges in Video Based Object Detection in Maritime Scenario Using Computer Vision." *19th International Conference on Connected Vehicles, Zurich, Switzerland, 13–14 January 2016*, pp. 1–6.

Salmon, P., N. Stanton, G. Walker, and D. Jenkins. *Distributed Situation Awareness: Theory, Measurement and Application to Teamwork*. CRC Press, 2009.

Schwarze, A., S. Bhattacharya, R. Grundmann, H. Sundar Mahadevan, S. Hochgeschurz, and F. Motz. "BEYOND – Building an Experience to Yield Optimal Nautical Displays – Measuring Nautical Situation Awareness." *Journal of Physics: Conference Series*, 2024: 2867.

Taç, U., and L. Tavacıoğlu. "Subjective Evaluation of Seafarers' Situational Awareness on Collision Avoidance." *Indian Journal of Science and Technology, 12(5)*, 2019.

Tittle, J. S., A. Roesler, and D. D. Woods. "The Remote Perception Problem." *Human Factors and Ergonomics Society Annual Meeting*, *46(3)*, 2002a.

Veitch, E., O. A. Alsos, T. Cheng, K. Senderud, and I. Bouwer Utne. "Human Factor Influences on Supervisory Control of Remotely Operated and Autonomous Vessels." *Ocean Engineering*, *299*, 2024: 117257.

Wahlström, M., J. Hakulinen, H. Karvonen, and I. Lindborg. "Human Factors Challenges in Unmanned Ship Operations – Insights from Other Domains." *Procedia Manufacturing 3*, 2015: 1038–1045.

Wang, Y., L. Prasad Perera, and B.-M. Batalden. "Localized Advanced Ship Predictor for Maritime Situation Awareness with Ship Close Encounter." *Ocean Engineering*, *306*, 2024.

Wróbel, K., M. Gil, and C.-J. Chae. "On the Influence of Human Factors on Safety of Remotely-Controlled Merchant Vessels." *Applied Sciences, 11(3)*, 2021: 1145.

Yan, S., Y. Wei, F. Li, and C. C. Tran. "Develop a Comprehensive Method to Evaluate the Mental Workload of Ship Operators." *Journal of Marine Science and Engineering*, *10(8)*, 2022: 1133.

7

TEACHING AND RESEARCH INFRASTRUCTURE REQUIREMENTS TO TRAIN FUTURE MARITIME AUTONOMOUS SURFACE SHIP OPERATORS UNDER REMOTE OPERATION CENTERS

Muhammad Adnan and Lokukaluge Prasad Perera

1 Introduction

Maritime autonomous surface ships (MASSs) gained significant attention from multiple maritime stakeholders (shipping industry, search and rescue, law enforcement agencies) due to the following influential reasons: (i) operating in harsh ocean environments, (ii) possible operational cost reduction, (iii) considerable emission reduction and renewable energy harvesting, (iv) considerable increase in operational safety and (v) robust decision-making capabilities, that is, complex information processing within a shorter period, with AI-driven algorithms [1]. Due to rapid technological development, especially through the utilisation advanced AI techniques, the idea of remote operation centers (ROCs) has also gained considerable attention [2] in the shipping industry. Multiple R&D projects have started worldwide to turn the idea of autonomous ships into reality for better resource management, such as precision and energy consumption in the maritime sector [3]. The significant economic benefits of autonomous ships can include having no crew on board, which can be a solution to the human workforce shortage in the maritime sector [4][5]. Due to these factors, autonomous technology has substantially attracted the attention of shipping companies, including maritime authorities.

The utilisation of advanced automation and control-based systems in the maritime sector has resulted in a shift from local discrete control systems to centralised bridge-based controls, which are usually run by various automated systems with less interference from human influence [6][7]. These systems can reduce the number of possible safety-critical situations that can occur due to the negligence of human operators [8]. Implementing such

DOI: 10.4324/9781003586883-7

advanced automation technologies still requires additional modifications in the currently available technology and system versions from the perspective of navigation safety and security, the sea environment, and resources. In the design phase of the autonomous navigation systems that can be a part of the MASS, human and AI-based system interactions should be considered to reduce the risk of navigation errors and ensure safe ship operation [9].

Implementing autonomous navigation technology in the maritime sector will increase onshore job opportunities and decrease onboard human resource requirements. Overall, the number of onboard jobs will be reduced due to the heavy involvement of advanced automation and AI-based technology [10][11]. It is expected that this change may reduce the number of maritime accidents and increase safety as well [12]. In autonomous ships, various tasks still require ROC operators' help and monitoring to ensure safe ship operations. Depending on the autonomy level of ship operations, these remote operators can handle and supervise different operational functions. A low-level autonomous ship may need more supervision from ROC operators for its operational tasks than highly autonomous ships, which only require supervision of critical tasks, mainly in emergency situations [13].

One of the key expected benefits of utilising autonomous ships is to reduce the number of accidents caused by human operator negligence. Research identifies that accidents due to human error or negligence significantly contribute to maritime accidents, but finding the actual numbers or percentages may be associated with higher uncertainty [14]. Autonomous ships can potentially reduce the number of accidents caused by human operator errors [15]. However, autonomous ships still require supervision from ROC human operators in numerous tasks where the system fails to guarantee safe ship operations. In general, the ROC operators need the relevant information about the operating environment and the ship's systems to remotely supervise the ships. These dependencies on human ROC operators can still trigger accidents if there is a lack of experience or skills in remote ship operations.

The ship control interface shifts from a ship bridge to an ROC, bringing multiple new human factors such as information overload, situational awareness, skill degradation and boredom regarding possible human error and negligence [16][17]. According to e-Navigation system requirements, significant measures and R&D must be carried out in the autonomous ship domain to reduce the navigational error rate as much as possible [18]. Furthermore, additional research activities are needed to identify the required modifications in teaching and research infrastructure according to the expected skills of ROC operators [19].

The maritime sector is experiencing intensive technological changes, from high-level automation, such as autopilot systems, to autonomous navigation [20][21]. Training human operators according to modern technologies may be another challenge in the future of the marine industry. Hence, the

ROC operators' education and training programmes/materials may require significant modifications according to the implemented autonomous technology level [22]. Currently available navigator training material mainly covers the content of traditional seafarer training, even though the concept and operational handling will change significantly in ROCs in the future. The human factor element still exists even in autonomous ship operations, albeit in different forms or natures than in traditional ship operations. Autonomous technology, along with the human element aspect, should be considered during the design phase of these remote ROC operators' training courses at all levels of autonomous navigation [23].

The transfer of system operations from the ship bridge to the ROC required new skills and knowledge for the operators, such as IT knowledge, a basic understanding of AI, cybersecurity, system technology, communication, simulator training with sufficient hands-on experience and so on [24]. Simulator training is the key module for ROC operators to gain the required competency for ship operations. The latest technology can enable simulation training to be more robust using AR and VR technology [25][26]. Adopting such technologies during the training phase can enhance the education and training levels not only for future ROC operators but also for traditional operator training [27].

During the educational material design phase for ROC operators, international training standards codes such as COLREGs [28], STCW [29] under the MASS, and technical and non-technical competence requirements related to ROCs and autonomous ships should be considered [30][31]. The current maritime education and training competency is insufficient or not up to standard to meet the needs of autonomous ships and ROCs for future maritime operations. The available educational courses lack content related to autonomous systems, AI, information technology and so on, which are necessary to train these ROC operators [32].

The role of humans in advanced automated systems still needs to be investigated [33]. The currently available system demonstrates that intelligent automation can handle complex tasks [34], which demands different innovative skills for ROC operators to perform remote ship navigation. Hence, the functional requirements should be identified to build the supportive infrastructure, such as ROC for MASS operations [35]. Some studies have discussed the operational and navigational framework for MASS operations under ROC [36][37]. Researchers have also identified the role of ROCs and operators in remotely operated vessel operations [38].

This study aims to identify the required modifications in teaching and research infrastructure regarding autonomous and remote vessel operations through future ROC. Section 2 explains the teaching and research modifications needed to train future ROC operators and to conduct relevant research and development activities in this domain. Section 3 concludes the overall study.

2 Proposed Modification in Existing Teaching and Research Infrastructure

Some studies suggest the transition path for traditional ship navigators to become ROC operators by obtaining the required operator skills [39][40]. Based on the proposed framework, the infrastructure for remotely operated vessels should comprise two components: the pre-existing infrastructure of manned ships and the proposed modification. The pre-existing infrastructure is intended for training operators of manned vessels, while the modification is associated with the ROC aspect. Given the differences between remotely operated and conventional vessels, the teaching system for training ROC operators should be modified accordingly. This means basic skills that pre-exist in MET should also be part of the ROC operator curriculum, as described and regulated by the IMO [29]. Developing remotely operated vessels will also open new research directions in the maritime sector.

2.1 Proposed ROC Operator Teaching Competence Modification

The ROC operator is the key person responsible for operating autonomous ships in critical situations. The skills and knowledge of these operators are crucial to ensure the safety of vessel navigation, sea environments, cargo and other nearby operating ships. There is a lack of standard teaching and training methods, as well as the required infrastructure, to train future ROC operators. The teaching programme for ROC operators should cover different methods such as case studies, presentations, group work and dialogues, reading, simulator exercises, desktop exercises, e-learning and lab exercises related to remote ship operations. ROC trainees should complete both theoretical and practical training modules; that is, the training should focus on all aspects of ROC.

The traditional operator teaching material lacks content required to train ROC operators. The current study divides the ROC operator teaching and training materials into six major modules, as shown in Figure 7.1. In the proposed MET modules, two significant modules are added that relate to autonomous systems and technology. These added modules can help remote operators learn the basic skills required for remote operation and the handling of autonomous ships through ROC. Autonomous ships rely heavily on an automation system combining AI, data science and advanced sensor technology. The current study identifies the required modifications in ROC operator MET material at an abstract level, as described below in each module (Tables 7.1–7.7) concerning autonomous ship operations. The identified modifications are based on the literature review from various sources, such as articles, project reports and lessons learned from different research projects, as well as the onshore operation centre (OOC) project

TABLE 7.1 Maritime competencies

Operational competencies	*Detail*
1 Ensure the availability of essential operational resources	1.1 Can ensure that the power/energy resources are sufficient for the whole journey remotely. 1.2 Should be competent in remotely ensuring the working status of emergency operational functions. 1.3 The operator should be capable of remotely checking the working status of all required systems on board before departure.
2 Understand the functions related to cargo handling	2.1 Know the port terminal requirements for vessel operations handling according to the type of destination port. 2.2 The vessel should be managed according to the port mooring and release scheme through the ROC. 2.3 Understand types of cargo (dry and wet) and their behaviour during sea transport. 2.4 Be proficient in lashing, securing and storage techniques.
3 Cargo remote monitoring	3.1 ROC operators should be capable of remotely monitoring cargo handling through available monitoring systems, such as vision-based systems. 3.2 Detect any damage that may occur during cargo handling. 3.3 Familiar with cargo control system limitations concerning the operating ship types. 3.4 Ensure the safety of ships by following the cargo-handling standards procedure before departure from the port. 3.5 Should be competent in solving stability issues on the ship due to cargo weights, weather conditions, sea conditions and so on. 3.6 Capable of estimating the stability of ships based on predicted future operating conditions and able to take mitigation measures if necessary.
4 Communication b/w ship and ROC	4.1 ROC operators should understand the standard protocol related to communication functions. 4.2 ROC operators should have the competencies to manage and understand communication using a ROC-designed interface working scheme. 4.3 The ROC operator should be familiar with the limitations of the available communication functions and any alternative solutions if existing onboard.

(*Continued*)

TABLE 7.1 (Continued)

Operational competencies	*Detail*
5 The ability to manoeuvre the vessel remotely	5.1 Should be familiar with the limitations of the navigational system concerning remote control through ROC. 5.2 Capable of planning the (de-)berthing plan and monitoring the process. 5.3 The operator should be capable of performing safe manoeuvres by using the remote control.
6 Ship stability and ballast operations	6.1 In-depth knowledge of ship stability principles. 6.2 Competence in remote ballasting and de-ballasting operations in both port and open sea conditions.

TABLE 7.2 Maritime competencies

Navigational competencies	*Detail*
1 Determine traffic conditions	1.1 Capable of determining the operational environment using maps and checking traffic conditions before planning the route for sailing. 1.2 Should be able to use available tools and systems to predict future traffic conditions, which can be used for efficient route planning. 1.3 The operator should know how to operate the advanced vision-based monitoring system and understand its working scheme. For example, cameras can be used to get a true sense of the operating sea area. 1.4 The operator should be able to interpret the data and assess the reliability of signals received from the monitoring system. 1.5 The operator should be capable of taking correct actions based on all available information to ensure safe operation.
2 Understanding and perception of ROC systems	2.1 Must be familiar with the essential elements of ROC. 2.2 Must understand and learn the differences between onboard ship handling and remote handling. 2.3 Know the differences in communication delay factors for operational control between ROC and onboard vessels. 2.4 Understand the limitations of ROC control perception. 2.5 Must be capable of classifying normal and abnormal signals from the ship's system.

(*Continued*)

TABLE 7.2 (Continued)

Navigational competencies	*Detail*
3 Automation awareness	3.1 Understanding the psychological impact of advanced automation (e.g. "technostress"). 3.2 Emphasis on utilising the designed system interface through some training hours to better understand it and reduce operator error during real ship operations. 3.3 Training in interpreting and managing complex data from navigation systems.
4 Properly understand the human in ROC and ship control system interactions	4.1 Understand the flow of interaction between ROC and ship systems. 4.2 Operators must possess the required skills and experience to make correct decisions in remote operations.
5 Situational awareness in a remote location.	5.1 Must know how to utilise sensor information to enhance situational awareness onboard vessels and ROCs. 5.2 Getting a true sense of the navigation situation is essential for the right action. Must know the time delay between the remote-control system command and its execution. 5.3 Must be capable of using advanced radar and vision-based systems to understand the operating area.
6 Ability to operate modern navigation aids remotely	6.1 Must know how navigation equipment works and its capabilities, such as Doppler log, weather station/wind indicator, rate of turn, radar, electronic chart display and information system (ECDIS), cameras, VHF, AIS, GPS, engine control and so on. 6.2 Should have knowledge about the defined standards related to navigation equipment. 6.3 Due to remote operation, the ROC operator must be able to determine the effect of nearby passing ships on the controlled ship. 6.4 Must train the ROC operator to control the ship in narrow passages or high-traffic areas under all possible scenarios.
7 Remote manoeuvring of MASS	7.1 Use of VR bridge simulators and hybrid simulation environments. 7.2 Exposure to hydrodynamic effects and collision avoidance using scaled ship models and so on. 7.3 Understanding wave impact and attempting to avoid undesirable ship motions, that is, roll. 7.4 Ability to utilise software tools that predict and mitigate risks from synchronous and parametric resonance.

(*Continued*)

TABLE 7.2 (Continued)

Navigational competencies	*Detail*
8 Collision detection and avoidance capabilities	8.1 Must be familiar with the alarms and signals related to collision detection and avoidance. 8.2 Must be capable of interpreting the data available through sensors such as ECDIS, radar and cameras to take corrective action for collision avoidance. 8.3 The operator should have some experience in utilising advanced collision prediction tools. 8.4 The operator must understand the limitations and operational capability of the collision detection and avoidance system.

TABLE 7.3 Engineering

Engineering competencies	*Detail*
1 ROC operators must know the basics of mechanical, electrical, electronics and control engineering.	1.1 Must know the installed onboard mechanical apparatus, navigation apparatus, sensors and control systems. 1.2 Be familiar with the remote-operation functions linked to ROC operator actions for operational monitoring and control. 1.3 Must know the automation level implemented for various machinery controls and their reliability. 1.4 Must be familiar with the alert or alarm management system to take priority actions in multiple-event handling situations. 1.5 Must be familiar with the outcomes than an alarm can produce or be considered. 1.6 Must be familiar with standard errors that can occur during the operation of this equipment and know how to take corrective action to manage such errors. 1.7 Must know and follow the defined ROC protocol standards for error handling. 1.8 Should be capable of restoring and calibrating the ROC equipment functions from time to time. 1.9 Must be competent to interpret observations via visual and electronic control systems. 1.10 Should be capable of finding the root cause if a significant error occurs during operation. 1.11 Skills in mechatronics engineering, for example, the integration of mechanical, electronic and computing systems.

(*Continued*)

TABLE 7.3 (Continued)

Engineering competencies	*Detail*
2 Power management	2.1 Understanding of EEDI, SEEMP and EEOI frameworks. 2.2 Application of energy-efficiency principles in remote operations.
3 Sustainable propulsion systems	3.1 Familiarity with hydrogen fuel cells, battery systems, ammonia, biofuels and renewable energy sources (wind, wave, solar). 3.2 Must be familiar with the advantages and limitations of each fuel technology during operations.
4 Be familiar with machine and system interaction	4.1 The operator must be familiar with the system integration, its interoperability, working scheme and interaction.
5 Maintenance management	5.1 The operator should schedule routine maintenance. 5.2 The maintenance process should be monitored remotely through a vision-based monitoring system such as a camera. 5.3 The ROC operator should be able to provide remote guidance during the maintenance process whenever necessary. 5.4 Ensure the quality of repair work, follow standard procedures and record all maintenance work for tracking purposes.
6 Must be capable of predicting the operational risk	6.1 ROC operators should possess sufficient knowledge and experience to assess the potential risk factors associated with different levels of autonomy. 6.2 It should be capable of predicting the risks related to the current systems implemented in the remote ROC. 6.3 Ability to alter circumstances that impact the ROC operations. 6.4 Capable of performing safe operations remotely even with limited functionality available for operation. 6.5 Must know the available safety control functions onboard and in the ROC. 6.6 Should be capable of assessing emergency situations remotely based on available information.

TABLE 7.4 IT competencies

IT competencies	*Detail*
1 Be familiar with the operating systems installed in ROC and remote ships	1.1 Must be familiar with different operating systems, such as Linux, Windows, Unix and so on, at an abstract level. 1.2 Ability to handle the operating systems installed onboard and in ROC.
2 Knowledge about computer systems operation and integration	2.1 Familiar with installed computing infrastructure. 2.2 Understand the system information flow. 2.3 Familiar with system integration.
3 Ability to safely manage software updates in both ROC and ship systems.	3.1 Predict the potential risks of software updates that may disturb the current running system. 3.2 Be aware of available remedies in case software updates cause errors or malfunctions.
4 Knowledge about networking devices used in ship and ROC	4.1 Must be familiar with available devices and their functions. 4.2 Be familiar with backup options in case operation failure occurs. 4.3 Should have some abstract knowledge about Wi-Fi, 3G, 4G, 5G, 6G LAN, WAN, MAN and so on.
5 Sensors Data Management	5.1 Understand the installed sensors' data management plan and scheme.
6 Cyber-security Basics	6.1 Knowledge about spam and viruses. 6.2 Ability to use cyber-security protection tools such as firewalls, anti-virus software and so on. 6.3 ROC operator should understand the cybersecurity requirements and ensure that any new equipment installed or changed onboard meets these standards.
7 Automation system troubleshooting	7.1 Skills in diagnosing and resolving automation system faults.

TABLE 7.5 Autonomous competencies

Autonomous competencies	*Detail*
1 Understanding the basics of AI and data science	1.1 Should understand the basic terminology of AI and data science. 1.2 Should have a basic operational understanding of the utilised AI/DS tool.
2 Data infrastructure	2.1 Understanding about maritime data space and secure data exchange.

(*Continued*)

TABLE 7.5 (Continued)

Autonomous competencies	*Detail*
3 Big data and AI integration	3.1 Processing and integrating data from multiple sources. 3.2 Use of enhanced fusion and sensor data (EFSD) system to enhance situational awareness. 3.3 Application of AI, neural networks and machine learning for predictive analytics and feedback.
4 Immersive technologies	4.1 Use of VR/AR for realistic training. 4.2 How human-computer interaction (HCI) and brain-computer interface (BCI) work for intuitive system control. 4.3 3D immersive scenarios for decision-making training.
5 Intelligent system design	5.1 Must be familiar with the design limitations of the system.
6 System decision process	6.1 Must be familiar with the decision process and the system working scheme.
7 System-generated data analysis	7.1 Must be capable of understanding the reliability of system-generated results. 7.2 Able to identify outliers in AI-generated results. 7.3 Able to interpret the meaning of data, such as graphs or figures generated by the system.

TABLE 7.6 Regulations competencies

Regulations competencies	*Detail*
1 Knowledge of international maritime laws and conventions	1.1 IMO 1.2 SOLAS convention 1.3 MARPOL convention 1.4 COLREG convention 1.5 STCW convention 1.6 Maritime labour convention (MLC) 1.7 ISM code 1.8 ISPS code 1.9 EU ship recycling regulation
2 Know the laws for autonomous vessels and the ROC.	2.1 Should know the emergency responsibilities of ROC operators according to the law. 2.2 Able to report operational events according to the ROC legal standards format. 2.3 Know the legal risks of operating vessels through the ROC. 2.4 Ability to identify the legal liability of the ROC owner, operator and manager.

(*Continued*)

TABLE 7.6 (Continued)

Regulations competencies	*Detail*
	2.5 Ability to communicate with nearby vessels in accordance with international laws. 2.6 Familiar with emission regulations according to the operating region. 2.7 Familiar with safety regulations. 2.8 Knowledge of operation requirements in a restricted water area.
3 Familiarity with port operations and transporting cargo according to international laws.	3.1 Understand and maintain knowledge about the different port terminal requirements. 3.2 Familiar with laws related to cargo goods, including each port's requirements and international regulations.
4 Must know the international maritime traffic laws.	4.1 Know the regulations for operating areas such as inland waters, open sea, near the port area, narrow passage areas and so on.
5 Be familiar with the regulations governing the installation, use and repair of equipment.	5.1 Know the regulations and standards related to installed equipment.

TABLE 7.7 Training module competencies

Training module competencies	*Detail*
1 Foundation of autonomous systems	1.1 Familiar with the basic principles of autonomous systems.
2 MASS command, control and communications skills	2.1 Able to operate and control communications with the MASS system. 2.2 Understanding the security features (e.g. cyber) and possible system reactions when communication system failures occur.
3 Be trained to act together through technology between autonomous ships, ROC and traditional ships.	3.1 Must perform a considerable number of hours of training related to operational tasks. 3.2 Allow ROC operators to understand basic hydrodynamic effects firsthand.
4 Weather routing and passage planning	4.1 Proficiency in using weather-routing software. 4.2 Ability to plan routes avoiding rough seas, strong winds, land and shallow waters.

(Continued)

TABLE 7.7 (Continued)

Training module competencies		*Detail*	
5	Spend a sizable amount of hands-on experience managing remote operations in all possible circumstances.	5.1	Prepare operators to manage realistic operational scenarios.
		5.2	Know the task and primary responsibilities of the ROC operator.
		5.3	Must have experience performing multiple tasks related to the monitoring, guidance and support systems of ROCs and vessels.
		5.4	Must perform some exercises related to vessel handling through ROC in all sea conditions.
		5.5	Must have enough experience to gain situational awareness remotely in different weather conditions.
6	Must experience the human element factors in ROC control	6.1	Must understand the limitations of the available system onboard.
7	Experience the delay factor between the commands of ROC and the actual control of the ship	7.1	Perform different tasks to experience such system delay factors and limitations.
8	Understand the human-machine interface in an ROC environment	8.1	Must perform different tasks to understand human perception, attention, awareness and focus.
9	Must have experience in utilising AR and VR technology for operational monitoring and control through ROC	9.1	Experience utilising all available sensors and control functions in terms of hardware and software.
10	A refresher training course must be taken as recent technology is implemented in ROC and autonomous ships	10.1	As per the defined guidelines.
11	Learn project administration skills, such as completing a mission plan through the simulation-supported framework	11.1	The operator should be able to prepare plans and reports according to internationally recognised standards for inspection and so on.

(*Continued*)

TABLE 7.7 (Continued)

Training module competencies	*Detail*
12 Check the health status of all ship systems using the health monitoring system to identify any faults before the ship sails or leaves the port.	12.1 The operator must be familiar with all alarms and signal communications between the ship system and ROC. 12.2 Know the operation of all control equipment functions available in the ROC. 12.3 Perform all checks according to the checklist standard defined by the ROC authority.
13 Check the environmental conditions in place and forecast to plan a safe and efficient route for sailing.	13.1 The operator must know the available systems for information, both internal and external. 13.2 Know the terms and signals generated by the monitoring system well. 13.3 Must know the available functions that can be used for actions in response to weather conditions. 13.4 Must be familiar with the limitations of the installed weather-monitoring system. 13.5 Can manage crew absence onboard by using automatic monitoring sensors and the system.

[31] [41–48]. Currently, much R&D in the remote-controlled or autonomous ship domain is focused on technology and system development, with little effort being made to train ROC operators for future operations. New competence for ROC teaching and training is required to train these future operators, where the respective research activities should be conducted. A custom VR-based simulator training platform has been developed to train ROC operators and support R&D in this area, which is part of the OOC project [49]. The main objective of the OOC project is to create knowledge on how to train future navigators to control vessels from the ROC. A case study is designed and performed to identify the challenges in such remote ROC-based operations [50]. This study is part of the OOC project, as detailed in the acknowledgments. The content presented in the tables below focuses only on the ROC aspect, where remotely controlled ship technology and operator competence are required. Rather than focusing on traditional or existing required skills as per IMO training regulations, which are also required for ROC operators to learn, this is described in the section on proposed modifications to the existing teaching and research infrastructure.

Two significant parts of the maritime module must be updated according to the autonomous navigational and operational capabilities of future

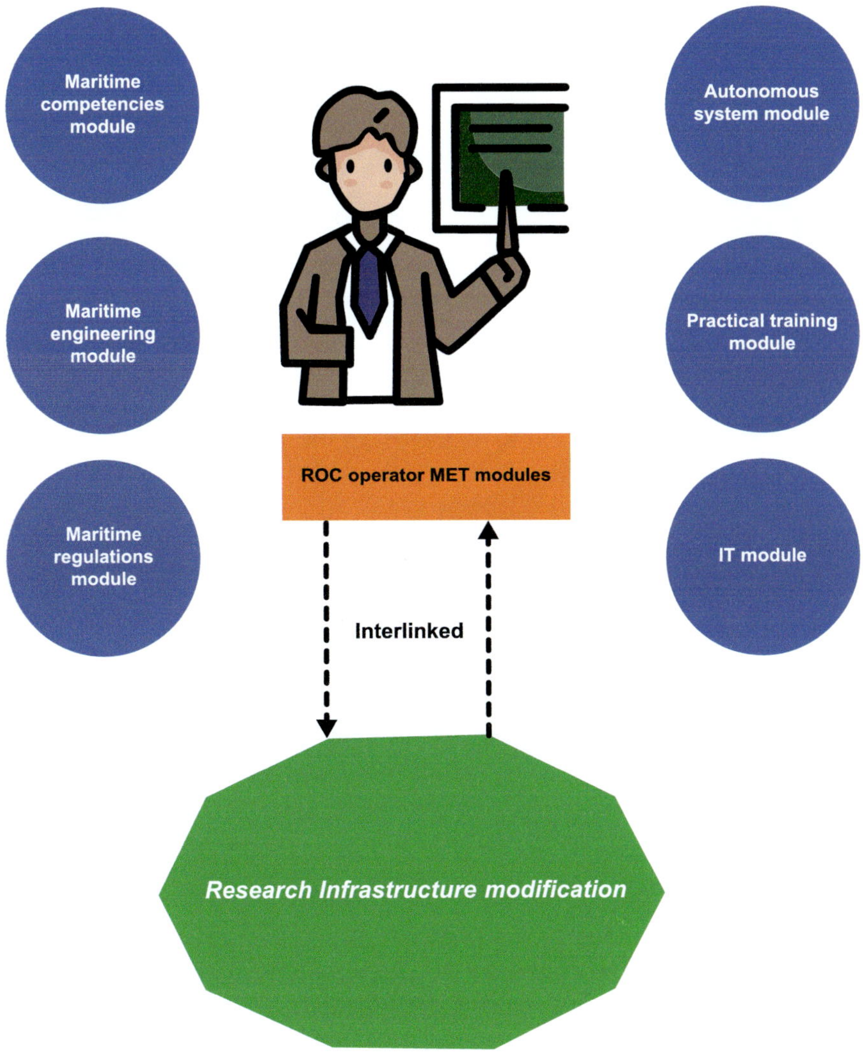

FIGURE 7.1 ROC operator MET modules

vessels. The ROC operator should learn and understand the ship's behaviour remotely, which can be helpful for controlling vessels from onshore. Tables 7.1–7.7 list the required MET modifications for ROC operators from a remote autonomous ship operation perspective. Subsequent tables cover the following modules: maritime competencies, engineering, IT, autonomous systems, regulations and practical training. Figure 7.1 shows that the ROC MET module is tightly coupled with the research infrastructure modification because the maritime training institute requires such infrastructure in order

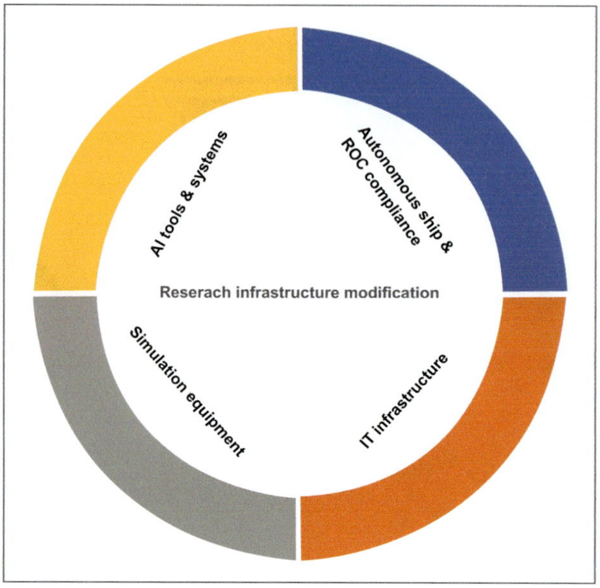

FIGURE 7.2 Research infrastructure modification

to provide robust training. The required research modifications are essential for training the ROC operator because such modifications can provide a training environment as close as possible to the real operational environment for future ship operations.

2.2 Proposed Research Infrastructure Modification

A significant modification of the research infrastructure is required to conduct research experiments related to autonomous shipping through the ROC. Some key areas that require modification are identified and listed below, including MET [48]. The changes demanded in different elements of the existing research infrastructure, such as facilities, resources and services used by the research community to conduct research for improvements in this domain, are shown in Figure 7.2.

2.2.1 IT Infrastructure

The latest sensors and systems will be utilised to improve the operational capabilities of autonomous ships and ROC. This may also include the items listed below.

1 High-performance computing infrastructure, such as high-performance server computers equipped with GPU clusters.

2 The latest sensing equipment can measure accurate temperature, wave energy, wind, sea current readings and so on.
3 Utilised high-throughput display technology and touch screens for easy monitoring and control.
4 Implement high-speed network technology, such as 5G and 6G, to minimise real-time delay in the communication and control system remotely [51].
5 Reliable database and cloud systems that store and fetch relevant navigational datasets online.
6 Strengthened IT security features of ROC systems. Besides the traditional security systems that protect against ransomware, spyware and viruses, the strengthened systems should also pay close attention to endpoint, cloud and security applications [52].

2.2.2 Simulation Equipment

Due to the high-risk involvement in maritime sector experiments, simulation-based research infrastructure is feasible for conducting research in all settings, including understanding high-risk operational procedures. Utilising advanced simulator technology will boost research and development in the maritime sector. Researchers can quickly analyse all risk factors and their development processes and suggest more feasible solutions in ship navigation. It can save time and cost when performing this kind of research compared to natural environments, where safety factors limit the testing range and scale. Due to the simulated environment, there is a low risk associated with human safety, which usually concerns all real-time testing cases. Some of the proposed modifications in the research infrastructure of the simulator environment are listed below.

1 Utilised AR and VR technology [53].
2 Utilised HCI techniques to gain a true sense of the process.
3 Build a dynamic simulator environment such as hydraulics and so on.
4 Utilised advanced AI-based systems for prediction and estimation [54].
5 Equipped with mirroring, meta-cognitive support and guidance.
6 A "feedback and improvement" mechanism in the simulator equipment that can help minimise the drawbacks in the system.
7 Multiple users can access the simulator, enabling research on the interactions and communication among remote operators.
8 Tools for simulating emergencies with a high degree of realism.
9 Build a hybrid simulation training environment to combine traditional and remote-controlled operations in training environments.
10 Scaled model training complex

   a. Develop a facility with scaled manned/unmanned ship models in a water basin.
   b. Integrate with full-mission bridge simulators for hybrid training.

2.2.3 AI Tools and Systems

Recent developments in AI make automation and control systems more intelligent and innovative. The research infrastructure should be equipped with these innovative AI tools and systems. These AI tools will create a new horizon for ROC capabilities for autonomous ship operations at all levels. The items listed below should be part of the research infrastructure for more optimised and advanced R&D.

1 Tools for advanced collision detection and avoidance systems [55].
2 Tools to generate all possible sea conditions to identify navigation risks.
3 Tools to check the robustness of autonomous systems.
4 Tools to identify the limitations of the ROC system.
5 Automatic system recovery modules.
6 Automatic control in case a communication failure occurs.
7 Advanced ship predictors that can estimate and predict the ship's relevant navigational status in the near or distant future (local/global scale).
8 An integrated and comprehensive navigational planning system based on big data and AI-supported technologies [56].
9 Real-time risk analysis based on big data and AI-supported technologies.

2.2.4 Autonomous Ship and ROC Regulatory Compliance

Due to the new concept of autonomous ships and ROCs, the research infrastructure needs to be updated in accordance with international laws and regulations related to autonomous shipping. Some possible modifications are listed below.

1 Update the research infrastructure as per IMO MASS standards.
2 Utilised only equipment that meets or passes international safety standards.
3 Update the research infrastructure to meet regulatory compliance.
4 Testing or trials at sea should be conducted according to MASS standards [57].
5 The designed system should be robust and flexible and able to accommodate new changes, such as technological changes and regulations for autonomous or remotely operated vessels, within a short period.
6 Should have comprehensive operational risk analysis tools for autonomous and remotely operated systems, so that the risk of failure of critical modules or sensors during navigation can be predicted [58].

3 Conclusion

This study investigates the required modifications related to MET and research infrastructure regarding remotely operated vessels through the ROCs. By inspecting the specific criteria and factors, perceptions of the technological, regulatory, training and human factors that shape the implementation of remotely operated ships were collected. This study also highlights the core areas that must be added to the training curriculum for the future workforce, especially for ROC operators. The requirement to establish a ROC training centre with an advanced training curriculum and tools, such as AR and VR simulators, AI and so on, for future maritime workforce training and development is highlighted. Based on operator feedback, the curriculum needs to be updated continuously according to the recently adopted technology in this sector. Conversely, upgrading the training simulator facility with advanced modules related to the ROC operator's training will be necessary, which is expected to differ from the training module for conventional seafarers. Furthermore, there is a need to improve the MET case study material concerning autonomous vessel technology for the rigorous training of ROC operators. Due to rapid technological changes, refresher courses and training will be made compulsory for these ROC operators to improve technology adoption and utilisation after a pre-defined period. This study specifies the required modifications in the existing teaching framework to train ROC operators for autonomous vessel operations remotely. It also highlights the critical competencies in each teaching module according to recently implemented technology in ROCs and autonomous vessels. The study's last section also highlights the required modifications in research infrastructure to conduct R&D experiments and which are also essential for ROC operator training, according to autonomous ship and ROC settings.

The current study has limitations in terms of practical demonstration and alignment with current training regulations due to limited work in this area such as IMO regulations. Due to a lack of R&D in this area, the standardisation and development of such a MET module are challenging for the IMO and ROC training institutes. Further R&D with practical demonstration is required to align the proposed changes with the upcoming IMO MASS training regulations for standardisation.

Acknowledgements

This work is supported by the Norwegian Ministry of Education and Research, Norway, under the MARKOM II project titled "Onshore Operation Center for Remotely Controlled Vessels (ROC)" (contract number PMK-2022\10014), a development project for maritime competence established by the Norwegian Ministry of Education and Research in cooperation with the Norwegian Ministry of Trade, Industry and Fisheries.

References

1. Kretschmann, Lutz, Hans-Christoph Burmeister, and Carlos Jahn. "Analyzing the economic benefit of unmanned autonomous ships: An exploratory

cost-comparison between an autonomous and a conventional bulk carrier." *Research in Transportation Business & Management* 25 (2017): 76–86.
2. Vasilijevic, Antonio, Jens Einar Bremnes, and Martin Ludvigsen. "Remote operation of marine robotic systems and next-generation multi-purpose control rooms." *Journal of Marine Science and Engineering* 11, no. 10 (2023): 1942.
3. Caccia, Massimo, Marco Bibuli, Riccardo Bono, and Gabriele Bruzzone. "Basic navigation, guidance and control of an unmanned surface vehicle." *Autonomous Robots* 25, no. 4 (2008): 349–365.
4. Cahoon, Stephen, and Hilary Haugstetter. "Shipping, shortages and generation Y." In *Proceedings of the Maritime Technology and Training Conference (MarTech)* (2008): 13–14.
5. Kooij, Carmen, and Robert Hekkenberg. "The effect of autonomous systems on the crew size of ships–a case study." *Maritime Policy & Management* 48, no. 6 (2021): 860–876.
6. Schubert, A. U., M. Kurowski, M. Gluch, O. Simanski, and T. Jeinsch. Manoeuvring automation towards autonomous shipping. *Zenodo (2018)* (2018).
7. Fukuto, Junji. "Automation levels of automated/autonomous ships." *NK Research* (2021).
8. Chan, Suzanna Razali, Norlida Abdul Hamid, and Kasypi Mokhtar. "A theoretical review of human error in maritime accidents." *Advanced Science Letters* 22, no. 9 (2016): 2109–2112.
9. Ramos, Marilia Abilio, Ingrid Bouwer Utne, and Ali Mosleh. "Collision avoidance on maritime autonomous surface ships: Operators' tasks and human failure events." *Safety Science* 116 (2019): 33–44.
10. Björk, Eric. "Social and economic impacts of maritime automated surface ships." Dissertation, Chalmers University, Sweden (2021). https://odr.chalmers.se/server/api/core/bitstreams/d7a25a3e 3cf6-4386-b6a4-03e2fbef8ab6/content
11. Hannaford, Elspeth, and Edwin Van Hassel. "Risks and benefits of crew reduction and/or removal with increased automation on the ship operator: A licensed deck officer's perspective." *Applied Sciences* 11, no. 8 (2021): 3569.
12. Streng, Martijn, and Bart Kuipers. "Economic, social, and environmental impacts of autonomous shipping strategies." In *Maritime Supply Chains* (2020): 135–145. Elsevier.
13. van den Broek, J. Hans, J. R. Jaco Griffioen, and M. Monique van der Drift. "Meaningful human control in autonomous shipping: An overview." In *IOP Conference Series: Materials Science and Engineering* 929, no. 1, (2020): 012008. IOP Publishing.
14. Wróbel, Krzysztof. "Searching for the origins of the myth: 80% human error impact on maritime safety." *Reliability Engineering & System Safety* 216 (2021): 107942.
15. Porathe, Thomas, Å. Hoem, Ø. Rødseth, K. Fjørtoft, and Stig Ole Johnsen. "At least as safe as manned shipping? Autonomous shipping, safety and "human error"." In *Safety and Reliability–Safe Societies in a Changing World* (2018): 417–425. CRC Press.
16. Ramos, Marilia A., I. B. Utne, and A. Mosleh. "On factors affecting autonomous ships operators performance in a shore control center." *Proceedings of the 14th Probabilistic Safety Assessment and Management, Los Angeles, CA, USA* (2018): 16–21.
17. Wahlström, Mikael, Jaakko Hakulinen, Hannu Karvonen, and Iiro Lindborg. "Human factors challenges in unmanned ship operations–insights from other domains." *Procedia Manufacturing* 3 (2015): 1038–1045.
18. Burmeister, Hans-Christoph, Wilko Bruhn, Ørnulf Jan Rødseth, and Thomas Porathe. "Autonomous unmanned merchant vessel and its contribution towards the e-Navigation implementation: The MUNIN perspective." *International Journal of e-Navigation and Maritime Economy* 1 (2014): 1–13.

19. Emad, Gholam Reza, Hossein Enshaei, and Samrat Ghosh. "Identifying seafarer training needs for operating future autonomous ships: A systematic literature review." *Australian Journal of Maritime & Ocean Affairs* 14, no. 2 (2022): 114–135.
20. Lazarowska, Agnieszka. "Research on algorithms for autonomous navigation of ships." *WMU Journal of Maritime Affairs* 18, no. 2 (2019): 341–358.
21. Öztürk, Ülkü, Melih Akdağ, and Tarık Ayabakan. "A review of path planning algorithms in maritime autonomous surface ships: Navigation safety perspective." *Ocean Engineering* 251 (2022): 111010.
22. Janssen, T., M. Baldauf, and G. Claresta. "From ship to shore–studies into potential practical consequences of autonomous shipping on VTS operation and training." *TransNav: International Journal on Marine Navigation and Safety of Sea Transportation* 17, no. 2 (2023): 383–390.
23. Ahvenjärvi, Sauli. "The human element and autonomous ships." *TransNav: International Journal on Marine Navigation and Safety of Sea Transportation* 10, no. 3 (2016): 517–521.
24. Toresano, Cristina Campos. "The next step on the maritime education and training in the era of autonomous shipping: A literature review." In *Maritime Transport Conference* no. 9 (2022).
25. Markopoulos, Evangelos, Jenny Lauronen, Mika Luimula, Pihla Lehto, and Sami Laukkanen. "Maritime safety education with VR technology (MarSEVR)." In *2019 10th IEEE International Conference on Cognitive Infocommunications (CogInfoCom)* (2019): 283–288. IEEE.
26. Patil, Mahesh, Rajoo Balaji, and Rachana Shikhare. "Smarter education methodologies for MET: An approach with augmented reality." In *OCEANS 2022-Chennai* (2022): 1–8. IEEE.
27. Mallam, Steven C., Salman Nazir, and Sathiya Kumar Renganayagalu. "Rethinking maritime education, training, and operations in the digital era: Applications for emerging immersive technologies." *Journal of Marine Science and Engineering* 7, no. 12 (2019): 428.
28. Convention on the International Regulations for Preventing Collisions at Sea, (COLREGs) IMO (1972). https://www.imo.org/en/About/Conventions/Pages/COLREG.aspx
29. International Convention on Standards of Training, Certification and Watchkeeping for Seafarers (STCW) IMO (1978). https://www.imo.org/en/About/Conventions/Pages/International-Convention-on-Standards-of-Training,-Certification-and-Watchkeeping-for-Seafarers-(STCW).aspx
30. Sharma, Amit, and Tae-eun Kim. "Exploring technical and non-technical competencies of navigators for autonomous shipping." *Maritime Policy & Management* 49, no. 6 (2022): 831–849.
31. Kim, Tae-eun, and Steven C. Mallam. "A delphi-AHP study on STCW leadership competence in the age of autonomous maritime operations." *WMU Journal of Maritime Affairs* 19, no. 2 (2020): 163–181.
32. Bogusławski, Krzysztof, Mateusz Gil, Jan Nasur, and Krzysztof Wróbel. "Implications of autonomous shipping for maritime education and training: The cadet's perspective." *Maritime Economics & Logistics* 24, no. 2 (2022): 327.
33. Lee, John D. "Review of a pivotal human factors article:"Humans and automation: Use, misuse, disuse, abuse"." *Human Factors* 50, no. 3 (2008): 404–410.
34. Parasuraman, Raja, Thomas B. Sheridan, and Christopher D. Wickens. "A model for types and levels of human interaction with automation." *IEEE Transactions on Systems, Man, and Cybernetics-Part A: Systems and Humans* 30, no. 3 (2000): 286–297.
35. Adnan, Muhammad, Lokukaluge Prasad Perera, Hasan Mahbub Tusher, and Salman Nazir. "Functional requirements for onshore operation centers to support remotely operated ships." In *ISOPE International Ocean and Polar Engineering Conference* (2024). ISOPE-I. ISOPE.

36. Adnan, Muhammad, and L. P. Perera. "Navigational support framework for maritime autonomous surface ships under onshore operation centers." In *Advances in Maritime Technology and Engineering* (2024): 373–383. CRC Press.
37. Adnan, Muhammad, and L. P. Perera. "Operational support framework for maritime autonomous surface ships under onshore operation centers." In *Advances in Maritime Technology and Engineering* (2024): 365–372. CRC Press.
38. Adnan, Muhammad, Yufei Wang, and Lokukaluge Prasad Perera. "Role of onshore operation centre and operator in remote controlled autonomous vessels operations." *Journal of Ocean Technology* 19, no. 3 (2024).
39. Kennard, Alice, Pengfei Zhang, and Sriram Rajagopal. "Technology and training: How will deck officers transition to operating autonomous and remote-controlled vessels?" *Marine Policy* 146 (2022): 105326.
40. Yoshida, Masanori, Etsuro Shimizu, Masashi Sugomori, and Ayako Umeda. "Regulatory requirements on the competence of remote operator in maritime autonomous surface ship: Situation awareness, ship sense and goal-based gap analysis." *Applied Sciences* 10, no. 23 (2020): 8751.
41. Saha, Rana. "Mapping competence requirements for future shore control center operators." *Maritime Policy & Management* 50, no. 4 (2023): 415–427.
42. Bachari-Lafteh, Mohammadreza, and Abbas Harati-Mokhtari. "Operator's skills and knowledge requirement in autonomous ships control centre." *Journal of International Maritime Safety, Environmental Affairs, and Shipping* 5, no. 2 (2021): 74–83.
43. IFE Report. "Operating autonomous ships remotely from land-based operation centers: The current state-of-the-art." https://ife.brage.unit.no/ife-xmlui/bitstream/handle/11250/2738266/IFE-E-2020–008.pdf?sequence=1 (access on: 30.08.2023).
44. PLATINA3 Report. "Report on competences needed to operate on board systems allowing for automation of inland navigation vessels D3.3." https://www.danubecommission.org/uploads/doc/Platina3/03_Jobs_and_skills/D3.1_standards-for-competence-zero-emission.pdf
45. Bureau Veritas eRules. "Guidelines for autonomous shipping2." https://erules.veristar.com/dy/data/bv/pdf/641-NI_2019–10.pdf
46. DNV-ST-0324. "Competence of remote-control center operators." https://standards.globalspec.com/std/14569937/dnv-st–0324
47. DNV-RP-0323. "Certification scheme for remote control center operators." https://standards.globalspec.com/std/14569937/dnv-st–0323
48. Skillsea Report. "Future skill and competence needs." https://ntnuopen.ntnu.no/ntnu-xmlui/bitstream/handle/11250/2648963/Oksavik.pdf?sequence=4
49. Onshore Operation Center for Remotely Controlled Vessels (OOC 2023) Project. https://app.cristin.no/projects/show.jsf?id=2574001
50. Adnan, Muhammad, and Lokukaluge Prasad Perera. "Virtual reality based simulator platform utilization for training remote vessel operators." In *International Congress of the International Maritime Association of the Mediterranean* (2025): 350–361. Cham: Springer Nature Switzerland.
51. Wang, Jun-Bo, Cheng Zeng, Changfeng Ding, Hua Zhang, Min Lin, and Jiangzhou Wang. "Unmanned surface vessel assisted maritime wireless communication toward 6G: Opportunities and challenges." *IEEE Wireless Communications* 29, no. 6 (2022): 72–79.
52. Tabish, Nimra, and Tsai Chaur-Luh. "Maritime autonomous surface ships: A review of cybersecurity challenges, countermeasures, and future perspectives." *IEEE Access* 12 (2024): 17114–17136.
53. Lager, Mårten, Elin A. Topp, and Jacek Malec. "Remote of unmanned surface vessel through virtual reality-a low cognitive load approach." In *Proceedings of*

the 1st International Workshop on Virtual, Augmented, and Mixed Reality for HRI (VAM-HRI) (2018).
54. Wang, Yufei, Lokukaluge Prasad Perera, and Bjørn-Morten Batalden. "Kinematic motion models based vessel state estimation to support advanced ship predictors." *Ocean Engineering* 286 (2023): 115503.
55. Zhang, Ke, Liwen Huang, Yixiong He, Bing Wang, Jiahao Chen, Yanfei Tian, and Xingya Zhao. "A real-time multi-ship collision avoidance decision-making system for autonomous ships considering ship motion uncertainty." *Ocean Engineering* 278 (2023): 114205.
56. Perera, Lokukaluge P., Paulo Oliveira, and C. Guedes Soares. "Maritime traffic monitoring based on vessel detection, tracking, state estimation, and trajectory prediction." *IEEE Transactions on Intelligent Transportation Systems* 13, no. 3 (2012): 1188–1200.
57. IMO. Working group report in 100th session of IMO maritime safety committee for the regulatory scoping exercise for the use of maritime autonomous surface ships (MASS). *Maritime Safety Committee 100th session, MSC 100/WP.8* (2018).
58. Li, Xue, Poong Oh, Yusheng Zhou, and Kum Fai Yuen. "Operational risk identification of maritime surface autonomous ship: A network analysis approach." *Transport Policy* 130 (2023): 1–14.

INDEX

Note: page numbers in **bold** indicate a table and page numbers in *italics* indicate a figure on the corresponding page.

For Product Safety Concerns and Information please contact our EU representative GPSR@taylorandfrancis.com Taylor & Francis Verlag GmbH, Kaufingerstraße 24, 80331 München, Germany